NEW SCIENCE LIBRAR

presents traditional topics from   u-
larly those associated with the l   , biology,
and medicine—and those of the human sciences—psychology,
sociology, and philosophy.

The aim of this series is the enrichment of both the scientific and
spiritual view of the world through their mutual dialogue and
exchange.

New Science Library is an imprint of Shambhala Publications.

*General editor/*Ken Wilber

Fisherman's Guide

A Systems Approach to Creativity and Organization

Robert Campbell

NEW SCIENCE LIBRARY
Shambhala
Boston & London
1985

NEW SCIENCE LIBRARY
An imprint of Shambhala Publications, Inc.
314 Dartmouth Street
Boston, Massachusetts 02116

NEW SCIENCE LIBRARY
An imprint of Shambhala Publications, Inc.
at Routledge & Kegan Paul
14 Leicester Square
London WC2H 7PH

First edition
Printed in the United States of America
Distributed in the United States by Random House
and in Canada by Random House of Canada Ltd.

Library of Congress Cataloging in Publication Data
Campbell, Robert, 1936-
   Fisherman's guide.
   1. Fishing—Miscellanea.   2. Knowledge, Theory of—
Miscellanea.   3. Creation (Literary, artistic, etc.)—
Miscellanea.   I. Title.
BF1999.C255   1984   191   83-20064
ISBN 0-87773-265-5 (pbk.)
ISBN 0-394-72334-1 (Random House: pbk.)

Design/Eje Wray
Typesetting/Graphic Composition/Athens GA in Linotron Palatino

The poem in Chapter 7 is from THE WAY OF LIFE by Lao Tzu as translated by
Raymond B. Blakney, © 1955, 1983 by Raymond B. Blakney. Reprinted by
arrangement with New American Library, New York, New York.

*Dedicated to you, the reader,
with the hope that you will
not readily accept the ideas
presented here, but ponder
over them with great care,
so that any new perspectives
derived may be to your
lasting benefit.*

Contents

Preface

This book is about a universal "system" of organization that underlies the whole of experience. The book is therefore about the whole of experience. It is about the creative process and the whole of creation.

In the main, man's scientific and spiritual pursuits have led to divergent perspectives of creation. The universal system that is introduced here indicates that these two pursuits are essential complements to one another in the search for an understanding of our natural heritage through an evolutionary record that reaches back billions of years. The deciphering of the system can help us to read the record, not only in the biosphere, the planets, the stars, and distant galaxies, but also in the structure of our bodies and in the workings of our nervous system. The system can help us to see our part and place in relation to the whole.

The book should be of interest to any reasonably informed reader that has ever seriously reflected on the meaning of life. It should be of special interest to any that follow the dialogue of science, even in a modest way. The book, however, is not confined to science. It includes a review of history, it touches on ancient systems of understanding, and it assesses the problems of organization in the business world. Most important, the book is also about the wilderness and fishing.

Overture

In the three centuries since Newton, science has skyrocketed like a fireworks display that in this century has exploded into nearly every area of human experience. The fragments of the spectacular display have not yet lost their brilliance, but still hang suspended as a great blossom of light, holding sway over man's mind as he marvels at the pageant he has created for himself. In the fascination with such a display one seldom pays much attention to the grandstand, even though the brilliance of the show may illuminate the whole environment. The fragments cool and lose their luster, then flutter back to earth in darkness as the audience stumbles homeward with only memories of a moment left behind.

It's been over two thousand years since the last fireworks display in the golden age of Greece, and it was a long period of darkness in between. Already there are signs that the energies of the current show are waning, and one wonders if we must soon fumble through another age of darkness. But the scale and magnitude of this extravaganza threaten planetary bankruptcy. Perhaps we will not be able to afford another show. Perhaps forevermore we will have to stumble on in darkness through the ashes, half animal, half man, not knowing who we are, but worse: knowing that we had a chance and lost it. Perhaps it is not too late to look around and, while the light is good, kindle some enduring flames.

Acknowledgments

I would like to acknowledge the very great help that I have received from Albert Low, a friend and former colleague. I have no hesitation in saying that without his encouragement and assistance this book could not have been written. He has both directly and indirectly influenced the development of many of the ideas expressed. In particular his theories on the "structure/process" of a business organization have been invaluable to me in giving expression to the universal system of organization presented. For a number of years we corresponded at length, and it is largely out of this correspondence that the central ideas in this book have evolved. I don't wish to convey the impression that Albert necessarily agrees with all aspects of the book, but wish only to emphasize my great indebtedness to him.

I am also grateful to my niece Wendy for her patient typing of early versions of the manuscript and to her husband, Paul, my sister Beverly, and her husband, Bill, for their friendship. I am indebted as well to Peter Swan for helpful criticisms and suggestions on the manuscript, to Dominique Leenutaphong for her proficient typing of this version, and of course to Shambhala Publications, especially to Emily Hilburn Sell, Ken Wilber, and Sam Bercholz. Thanks also to Chuck and memories of many fishing trips, to Dick and Ann for many favors, and to Adam and Agnes for letting me tell a few stories.

Part 1
The Road
to the System

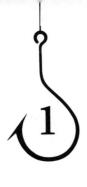

Night Fishing

The boat rocks gently to the rhythmic beat of waves against its hull. It is the kind of soft hypnotic roll that brings a certain harmony to a contemplative mood. The sharp-crested ripplets that have been stirred by a mild evening breeze are beginning to mellow at last. Soon they will be no more than glimmering shadows blinking a mottled dance on a slippery surface. At this time of year, the pattern seems the same each night. It is a ritual perfected through countless centuries of repetition, yet each occurrence preserves the freshness of a premiere performance. There is an insistence to the stillness that settles here each evening, as if the world were holding its breath in anticipation of the coming night. It penetrates the being, making all thoughts seem redundant and strangely out of place. It is a stillness that can almost be seen vibrating in the air. There is an immediacy to it that makes one feel that he can reach out and touch it. There is peace, but it is a peace that is vital, filled with energy, and alive. The crickets and frogs have started now to tantalize the stillness, which stands out the more. The sun has set, and the remnants of color are rapidly draining from the sky. A first few stars have penetrated the encroaching darkness.

The boat is anchored in nine or ten feet of water, about fifty feet from a pile of underwater rocks that extends about forty feet in diameter. Just at dusk the mosquitoes can get bad for a short while, but tonight there are only a few. The bass should be feeding on the surface now. The stillness is broken by a quiet reach for the fishing rod. On the surface, plunkers are as good as any, and tonight a hula-popper will get its chance. Darkness is coming quickly. The wooded shoreline looms like a ghost looking at itself in the water.

Smallmouth bass have a habit of surface feeding at night. Although not many are caught at one time, they are usually a nice size. The first cast is directly over the center of the rock pile. The rocks are covered by only a foot or two of water in most places, although well out from shore and surrounded by deeper water. In the fading light, the plug can be seen as it lands and generates a series of concentric ripples. The high arch of the line plummets to the surface, marring its perfection. The plug bobs to a standstill and sits there for a moment. The slack in the line is taken up, and the popper jiggled just a little. Another smaller series of circles grows, and another. Often bass have to be teased into biting by this gentle jiggling. Now the pole is jerked sharply to one side. There is a solid-sounding plunk, and the popper bobs back to the surface. Now a wait in anticipation, but no takers. More gentle jiggling and another more moderate plunk. There is a sharp-sounding snap, but from a small rock bass hitting short on the rubber skirt. Soon the plug is near the boat and reeled in to throw again. Several more casts attract only some small fry. Maybe there will be no action tonight.

Another cast tries for a run over one side of the rock pile. No sooner does the plug land than a very loud splash signals a strike. It must be a nice one, although it is too dark to see. The slack line is frantically reeled up. Sometimes, before one can get a taut line, they will swim straight for the boat, break water, and shake the hooks. The slack is caught up just in time. The fish feels heavy as it clears the water, shaking furiously. No sooner is it back in the water than it is out again. It breaks water several times in succession, then starts digging for the bottom, taking line. The tension adjustment is tightened up a little. The fish comes up again quickly to provide a glimpse. A nice one! Down again it goes, digging for the bottom and heading toward the anchor rope. An attempt to horse it a bit to keep it away is too late. Around the rope once, a little slack line, and the fish is gone.

Too bad, perhaps, but there is no point in feeling remorse at losing a fish. The anchor is lifted and the hula-popper retrieved from the anchor rope. Fortunately the line isn't broken. There is nothing to do now but settle back across the seat to let the stillness once more take command.

The night is clear. The air is moist and fresh. Gazing into the cosmos brings back amazement at the spectacle of grandeur unfolded before the eyes. The feeling is remembered from early boyhood, with wonder that it has not changed in so many years. Over a hundred thousand million suns in our galaxy alone. Even such numbers cannot register its true immensity. Only a few thousand can be seen with the naked eye. The rest merge as a milky expanse across the sky as we look into the edge of our own spiral galaxy we call the Milky Way. It is one of a number in our cluster. Andromeda, a misty blotch to a good pair of eyes on a clear night, is hardly distinguishable tonight. Another world of suns as immense as ours—yet, to intergalactic space, we are like two ants on an ocean. The instruments of modern astronomy reveal countless clusters, some of which contain hundreds of galaxies. They all appear to be moving away from one another in such a way that each appears to be at the center of a gigantic expansion. To each the most distant clusters seem to be moving away fastest, such that the perceptual limits to the universe appear to be determined by the speed of light. The mind boggles! Physical conceptualizations begin to dissolve into myth. Space and time lose meaning. These concepts have no absolute reality in themselves. They result from a more fundamental order that underlies the nature of things. The experience had vividly demonstrated this, but now is not the time to go into that.

Instead, the mind turns toward science, that huge body of formalized thought that has been laboriously constructed by thousands of brilliant minds, and which has pieced together large patches toward a landscape of understanding. It has provided man with many conveniences, in many ways expanding the possibilities of experience. It has provided a degree of mastery over disease, extended the average life expectancy, and alleviated untold suffering. To many people science has assumed the proportions of a religious dogma. They have an unquestioned faith that, whatever the problem, science will one day find a solution. Other people focus on the negative consequences of science: they see a runaway technology undermining human values and exhausting resources, only to threaten the environment. Some people, however, search beyond either of these simplistic views. They recognize that, although there has been an enormous growth of knowledge, this growth has been paralleled by a certain nagging deficiency. Although science has resolved many problems and afforded many new opportunities, it has also created new problems of severe proportions and bewildering complexity. Still, the deficiency is an elusive one, and even those who recognize it cannot quite put their finger on it. They cannot put it into words.

The attention drifts out again into the cosmic spectacle that embraces the origins of time and space. It does not take an expert to recognize that science is not yet a match for this. One doesn't have to scrutinize a theoretical framework in search of an error. The deficiency permeates the whole structure of science. It is necessary only to experience the immensity and precision of a clear night to sense the inadequacy of our words and signs and symbols in the face of such a scene.

We are such latecomers to the stage—just a flash, an instant in evolutionary time—yet we have the temerity or the need to seek and wonder, with curious searching thoughts, led on a leash of language. Language distinguishes us most from other earthbound creatures. Through language we evolve our cultures, our social structures, and our sciences. Language has altered the workings of our nervous system. It shapes our perceptions. We use it to see, to understand, but in the face of this vast mystery we are left with a flickering candle to illuminate a universe. Our vision captured by our proximity to a diffusing, undirected light, we catch only fleeting shadows through a veil. We sense the distance better with the flame snuffed out. Gazing skyward, waiting for the stillness, with words and thoughts extinguished, we feel that there is sense in wonder. Lost in time, absorbing subtle energies, the mind drifts deep in formless wonder, filled with a feeling of long ago.

A bat swoops near the boat to bring back the present moment. The boat has drifted. It is time to stretch out some kinks and paddle quietly back toward the rock pile. The moon has begun to rise in the east—maybe its light on the surface of the water will help the fishing some. Casting is resumed as before, but there is no action whatsoever. Even the rock bass have quit their occasional snapping. After a few casts it seems clear that the fish have lost all interest. It is about midnight and time to head back to camp.

The steady drone of the outboard motor is an unseemly intrusion in the night. Behind the boat the wake rises in a pile, spreading itself evenly into two trailing rows of waves clearly visible in the moonlight. The moon itself looks like an omniscient cyclops rising for a better view. It moves in unison with the boat, keeping an even pace over the horizon as the boat skims across the surface. There is no escape from its surveillance. Its motion is effortless and silent, with that aura of magic often regarded as just a romantic illusion of dreamers and foolish lovers.

Science deals with facts. Does this mean that reality can be reduced to facts, to something permanent, rigid and cold like a mummified corpse? Surely few scientists would agree. Some see beyond the facts to a transforming world of magical relationships, and they explore the mystery there. Facts are what we make of them. They must have relevance, of course, but it is in that relevance that magic is revealed.

The moon has a profound influence over life on earth that the language of science can do little to elucidate. It soars through space like a great pendulum regulating the rhythm of life on the planet. This influence is most obvious in relation to the tides, but there are parallel influences on the atmosphere and the force fields of gravity and magnetism, as well as other more subtle fields. All of these influences interact in a rhythmic, repetitious pattern, as they have done throughout the millennia of evolutionary history.

Although the energy for life comes from the sun, the pattern of its manifestation on the earth is modulated and blended by the rhythms of the moon. It is the moon that presents the dominant daily rhythm to life in such a perennially steadfast manner that all other influences must be reckoned by its pattern. Only the motions of the earth itself—its revolution around the sun and the seasons that result, and its rotation on its own axis to make a day—can alter the manifestation of the pattern. The massive rhythmic movements of the tides against the contours of the earth provide a modulation to the currents of the ocean and the distribution of energy from the sun. The winds and weather of the world are regulated in accord, the conditions and energies of life being constantly brought to harmonic balance. The moon thus effects a rhythmic variance to the distribution of intensities that provides a basis for a harmony to life on earth. Is harmonic balance not a measure of romance?

Life on earth has been indebted to the influence of the moon throughout the ages, yet the moon itself supports no life. Profound, unchanging clarity and stillness proclaim its nature. To really see the moon is to feel the reverberations of its rhythm recalling from the depths of our unconscious being the harmony of our ancestral past. The romantic significance of the moon is as real as the starkness of its mountain ranges or the power in the tides. Yet the magic and the mystery of the moon go deeper still. That same unchanging solitary face has cast its silly grin toward the earth through countless revolutions. What an extraordinary thing that for each revolution it should rotate precisely once on its own axis such that its face toward us never changes.

The outline of the dock is hardly visible in the moonlight as the boat is turned for shore. The motor is slowed to a troll, then shut off to let the boat glide smoothly in beside the dock. The path to the cottage is only sixty or seventy feet up a small rise. The fishing gear is set on the porch. The cottage is entered in darkness and a chair selected in front of the window facing the lake. The familiar array of tree trunks stands silhouetted against the silver-gray surface of the lake.

The crickets and frogs are still busy squeaking and croaking their monosyllables. Each tiny, intermittent contribution is absorbed into the eerie chorus of a choir of millions that undulates and fades into the distance. The haunting refrain proliferates in waves, in a vibrant, living web that is laced in an intricate pattern throughout the countryside. The persistence of the rhythm saturates the stillness to pace the procession of the night. This strange, enchanting language has a message that's implicit.

There is an underlying system to the natural order that is both implicit and communicative. It is intelligent. What we observe in natural processes are the explicit manifestations of this underlying system of order. This is the world of fact—the starting point for piecing together a scientific framework of understanding.

Science seeks to develop a framework that can be universally applied, but it falters through the deficiencies of its language. It observes that an object can be moved by applying a force against it, then explains the fact with a principle of objective causality. Events are said to occur in external action sequences of cause and effect within a space-time framework.

The Western idea of causality goes back to ancient Greece, but only three centuries ago Isaac Newton first formalized the notion of a continuum to time and space. These fundamental ideas fitted nicely together with basic laws of motion, permitting largely arbitrary but convenient definitions of physical concepts. With the development of more advanced mathematical language, the approach enjoyed a growing measure of success, stimulating an exploration of electricity, magnetism, chemistry, and thermodynamics. The approach has been very productive, but the best of efforts have been unable to produce a unified framework of understanding.

This principle of causal determinism which underlies the majority of science is seriously challenged only in the world of particle physics. Subatomic particles—electrons, protons, and many others—are found to display the characteristics of both waves and particles. This is something like saying that the water in a river may consist of both solid ice and a series of fluid ripples, in the *same* interval of time. In order to devise a framework to account in some measure for this unusual behavior, science has accepted a principle of indeterminacy in the realm of quantum wave mechanics. Energy is observed to be quantized or packaged in discrete amounts that portray a wave behavior that is also associated with a particle behavior. Wave-particle behavior is said to be governed by rules of chance, requiring a language of probability to predict events. If the water in the river is energy, then whether it behaves more like solid ice or more like fluid ripples depends on a roll of the dice. There is a range of possibilities, but some are more probable than others.

On the other hand, when we observe natural processes from an implicit perspective, a quite different underlying system of order emerges. It is neither a linear causal determinism nor an indeterminacy governed by chance. It is an order that is deterministic and cyclic.

Everywhere we look, things can be observed moving in cycles. The motion of the planets, the seasons, the patterns of growth and decay, the related processes of photosynthesis and metabolism, the migration of birds, the spawning patterns of fish, the recurring patterns of industrial production, even the routines of daily living— all have a cyclic character. Nothing is exempt. Each of these cyclic patterns has a degree of independence, yet all are related in a vast complexity of cycles within cycles within cycles. There are sometimes contingent disruptions where the cogs of interacting cycles don't mesh, but there is a preponderant determinism that pervades all.

The determinism is of such precision that it can maintain order in the galaxies for billions of years, preserve the integrity of species through millions of generations, and coordinate the myriad factors in a complex, thinking human being. The deterministic order is not restricted to events in space and time; rather, it determines them. There is a staged, evolving progression to it that is also cyclic and that can make allowances for intelligent adjustment at many levels. This cyclic, deterministic order is intelligent.

It is possible to gain an insight into this underlying system of order because there is an isomorphy to the structure of experience. In other words, there is a common underlying structure to all phenomena that recurs again and again, regardless of the scale of magnitude or the diversity of circumstance. Despite the complexity of structure, isomorphy renders it communicable.

There are many clues that point in this direction. For instance, as different as people are as individuals, we all share the same biological structure. With minor variations, we also share the same skeletal arrangement with the mammals and reptiles. At a more basic level, we share the same genetic language—neatly locked up in the DNA molecule—with all forms of cellular life on the planet. Further underlying the chemistry of our cells, our bodies share the same chemical elements with the universe. There is thus a unity of organization that underlies the diversity of experience. This system of organization can be called simply "the system," because there is no other system possible. It embraces all of the possibilities to experience. What are normally called systems are surface fragments of "the system."

The essentials of the system were revealed in an unusual personal experience. Over a period of years a way has been devised to make it communicable, but it should be emphasized that the system is not just a theoretical concoction of the human mind. The experience was profound beyond description, unbearably intense, and vividly explicit. Sanity and life were left hanging by the slimmest of threads, unable to disbelieve the depth and scope of its revelation, or to directly assimilate it. It has taken many years to make appropriate sense of the experience, to understand the system that was demonstrated, and to find ways of making it communicable.

There is a journey involved in learning to understand the system. It is a journey through a very changeable landscape, like an extended fishing trip with many good fishing spots along the way. There is an intuitive kind of fishing that must be done to understand the system.

We will be going on the fishing trip together; I will be along as an ordinary fishing guide hired for the price of this book. My job will be to make the trip interesting, to point out the fishing spots, and to draw on personal experience in an effort to communicate the essence of the system. The real guide, however, is the system itself, as it works silently through the intuition of each of us. Each of us is really on the fishing trip alone. Each of us must fish for ourself, yet there are areas where we can benefit to an extent from the experience of others.

We will make stops in many fishing holes, including history, business, evolution, chemistry and physics, biology, earth science, astrophysics, philosophy, religion, and psychology, and others, all of which will be mirrored in the constant traveling companion of nature. This kaleidoscope of experience is presented to illustrate the universality of the system through which all experience is integrated. It is more fundamental than language, and for that reason it is difficult to properly communicate. Insight into the system must be personal and direct. It depends on an appreciation of a basic creative dilemma that prescribes an implicit and explicit aspect to experience.

The dilemma of the moment, however, is the time of night and the need for rest. A cloud has masked the moon to dull the shimmer on the lake. It is time for bed.

2 Whitemen and Indians

There is a small bench under a cedar tree by the lake that is a good place to sit and let breakfast digest. The day has already become quite warm, though still fresh and comfortable. The morning dew has dissipated, and a quiet breeze is softly wafting through the cedar grove. A young robin is taking a solitary bath next to some reeds by the shore.

This part of the country is very beautiful. It consists mostly of thick forest cover over granite rock and muskeg swamps, interspersed with literally hundreds of thousands of lakes—part of a vast wilderness stretching for over two thousand miles, from the Labrador coast into northern Manitoba. Known as the Precambrian shield, it is one of the oldest geological areas on earth.

To the early settler the area was virtually impenetrable. Except for Indian resistance, there was ready access to the parklands of southern Ontario, and to the river basins of the Ottawa and St. Lawrence, but settlement halted at the fringe of the shield. There was simply no possibility of major movements through it. Transport was limited to the fur trader and canoe, as a new way of life evolved throughout the intricate system of waterways draining toward the St. Lawrence. The *coureur-de-bois* and *voyageur* tirelessly paddled and portaged their goods for hundreds of miles to the cities of Montreal and Quebec, the seaports to the world. With the formation of the Hudson's Bay Company the same process took place on the water systems flowing to the north and from the west, throughout the shield and beyond, all the way to the Rocky Mountains. It was the fur trader and early missionary who first established a continental identity for Canada. Permanent settlement and agricultural development to the west came much later, lagging behind that of the United States by a couple of generations.

The discovery and colonization of the Americas coincided with discoveries in many other areas. An exploratory quest was simultaneously ignited in the fields of art, literature, music, and science, with repercussions in religious, political, and economic reform. For the white man the Renaissance was an awakening from a creative slumber that had lasted for fifteen centuries, since the golden age of Greece. Suddenly the white man was asking questions, wondering about all manner of things, and following an intuition of discovery that brought with it a great variety of creative expression. It began in Italy, the homeland of the former Roman Empire that had transplanted the essentials of Greek thought alongside the Christian teaching. Soon the germ of inquiry infected the whole of Europe, while colonial empires spawned and spread, first exploring, then exploiting, sea routes throughout the world.

Donatello and his contemporaries pioneered a naturalist interpretation in sculpture and painting that was refined by Botticelli and da Vinci. Da Vinci combined his artistic talents with daring excursions into anatomy and science. Michelangelo perfected the depiction of the human form through a study of anatomy, then in later years turned his skills toward architecture. He never lived to see his enormous plans for St. Peter's Basilica completed, but Bernini followed through to provide some classic finishing touches. Subsequent masters like Rubens and Rembrandt inherited a wealth of artistic insight on which to draw.

Meanwhile paper was replacing parchment to give an impetus to literature, while Gutenberg's innovation of typeset printing made literary works much easier to reproduce. The writings of Rabelais, Montaigne, Cervantes, and Shakespeare were well received, their humanist views making a significant impact on prevailing opinions of the day. The value of the written word became widely recognized, stimulating intense interest in every field of human thought.

Musical innovations began within the church, where fundamental contributions to musical theory established a basis for the long series of majestic new forms of music to follow. The church, however, began to have its problems. While it was reconstructing the basilica in Rome, John Calvin and Martin Luther were taking issue with the dogma of the church, intent on reconstruction of another kind. Meanwhile King Henry VIII of England severed papal ties with Rome for passionate reasons of his own. The new enthusiasm for inquiry was to bring with it many confrontations along the way.

While colonial empires were rapidly being extended, men like Copernicus, Galileo, Kepler, and Descartes were pursuing new insights into science and mathematics. These found a synthesis with Isaac Newton, who firmly built the foundations of modern science. Scientific interest brought with it applications to machines. New and concentrated forms of industry emerged, followed by more and more complex machines. This development was matched by increased complexities in finance, trade, and economic organization generally. The white man's mind was seized by the relentless spirit of discovery that was in the air. It was a new and creative framework of understanding that was being explored, but not without some negative consequences.

The colonial history of North America was also the history of the decline and fall of a great civilization. The Indian culture had survived for thousands of years, evolving in a variety of related forms, all in a common spirit of harmony with nature. This was a framework of understanding that looked toward the implicit side of experience, toward the underlying spirit. The appearance of the white man on the continent brought a confrontation with a framework of understanding that looked toward the explicit side of experience, toward the application of technique.

These two aspects, one implicit and one explicit, reflect the two poles to a fundamental creative dilemma. The dilemma arises from the need to reconcile the internal or implicit aspects of experience with the external or explicit aspects. A creative reconciliation of these two poles must be communicative. It must embrace both polar aspects within a common framework of understanding. Unfortunately, the white man and Indian lived in very different cultures, neither having developed to the point where the nature of the dilemma could be perceived. The conflict that ensued between them was inevitable.

In Canada, an initial period of friendliness gave way to hostility, particularly with the Iroquois, who effectively controlled early colonization of their territory. As with the Indian nations further to the south, they had been obliged to fight as a matter of survival. To the south, the forests of the east were destroyed to make way for agriculture, while in the west, the buffalo was slaughtered wholesale, without regard for the Indian way of life.

Conflict with the Indian was averted in central Canada, but not through any effort on the part of the white man. It was the austerity of the Precambrian shield that subdued the whiteman, forcing him to come to terms on common ground. Through fur trading the Indian and white man reached a limited degree of mutual understanding.

There was, however, a more subtle threat eroding the foundations of the Indians' social sanity. They became more and more dependent on the way of the white man, gradually relinquishing many of their beliefs, traditions, and customs. They progressively lost touch with their own heritage and had little or nothing to replace it. The most hapless were left in a sort of limbo, to flounder in the white man's vices, reaping isolation and neglect as the only reward for their misfortune. The spirit of their traditions, their legends and folklore, were lost to the new generations.

Before the white man came, life was quite a different experience for the Indian. To the Indian everything had a spirit. Everything was alive. There were spirits in the wind, in the water, in the earth, and in the mountain. Each of the flowers, plants, and trees had a distinctive spirit of its own, some of which were recognized as healing spirits capable of counteracting the evil spirits of disease. The animals represented another level in the spirit world. As the Indian boy matured to manhood, he went alone into the forest to wait there for a sign, a dream, or a vision. The animal whose spirit was attuned to his nature was in this way revealed to him. It was to this guardian spirit that he usually prayed, and in which he found support through burdensome times. Animals—accorded the respect due spiritual brothers—were basic for food and shelter but never killed for sport. The spiritual life of the Indian was an integral part of his technology and the basis of his entire framework of understanding. Their folklore, ritual dances, and ceremonies were filled with spiritual significance. Their world was teeming full with spirits, great and small, strong and weak, good and evil. Presiding over all was the Great Spirit, to whom they made special petition on the most serious matters.

The Indian looked at a mountain and felt its presence. The white man looked and saw a pretty pile of rocks. The essence of the Indian's framework of understanding was integration with his environment. The essence of the white man's framework was separation from it. The white man strove to conquer nature; the Indian sought nature for an ally. It is easy enough to appreciate the Indian's approach. Despite our inability to reconcile it to the white man's culture, it strikes a responsive chord in the hearts of most men. It was not necessary for the Indian to segregate his religion and his science which, crude though it may be have been, was derived from his spiritual insight. Explanations of natural phenomena, predictions of weather, famine and plenty, the determinations of the curative power of plants—all had a spiritual basis.

In contrast, it is difficult to understand the reasons for the white man's divergent approach to science and religion. Many of the most important contributors to science have been profoundly religious men, yet the two fields of endeavor have been treated as mutually exclusive. Whatever the reason, white man's science has been founded on two very strange but complementary concepts. The first is the concept of causality, commonly understood as the belief that every effect has a cause and in turn can act as a cause for a subsequent effect: everything is a series of chain reactions like a succession of tail-end collisions on a freeway. This belief has become so firmly entrenched that many people cannot imagine the possibility of an alternative. The second concept is embodied in the white man's scientific method, which requires that all scientific observations be objective. All traces of subjective interpretation must be avoided in the firm belief that the only substantial reality exists between the external surfaces of things. In other words, there are no drivers inside the cars that collide on the freeway. Together the two concepts cannot lead to an impartial interpretation of experience, for they exclude the subjective pole.

A nice, tidy short circuit was thus introduced into the pattern of the white man's mentation. By the objective concept of the scientific method, certain structures could be observed in nature, then the concept of causality tried out to see if it explained events. This introduced other concepts such as force, mass, acceleration, and so on, and a scientific language based on objective causality proliferated.

The white man was particularly gratified by his degree of success, since he was so thorough in excluding his own psychological and emotional experience from the process. Since these subjective qualities had no substantial reality, there was no reason to believe that they should be conditioned according to his understanding or behavior. Having therefore mastered nature, he was free to do as he pleased.

To keep whims in check, the white man acknowledged a social morality based on religious doctrine that was totally divorced from science. In essence it was very simple—reward or punishment was to come in heaven or hell. Although no one knew where heaven and hell were, this was irrelevant from a scientific viewpoint, as it was not a substantial reality that went there anyway. Your body rotted in the ground.

The more sophisticated the white man's science became, the more it determined his social organization, and the less the religious component was required. Any real basis to religion was in fact discredited by the concepts of objective causality from the day of their inception. White man's science now shapes the worlds of industry, trade, and commerce—economic and social survival being inextricably dependent on it. At the same time, the deficiency of science is creating such a formidable complex of problems that it threatens economic and social survival. There doesn't appear to be anywhere to turn. How have we gotten into such a fix?

Nonetheless, objective causality has led to a journey of discovery that has lasted for over three centuries. The world of fact has been rooted out, to accumulate an enormous fund of knowledge. We owe a great deal to science, but it has not brought with it a parallel development of understanding. This requires an insight into the implicit side of experience.

The objective approach has required science to search for answers in two independent directions: toward the center of things, and toward the periphery of things. Although these correspond to the two poles of the ever-present creative dilemma, the objective language of science has been obliged to treat them independently. They stand apart, like the white man and Indian, to present the many contradictions in our situation.

In penetrating toward the center of things, science has learned that pure substances are molecular combinations of ninety-two naturally occurring elements. Underlying atomic structure, an elaborate array of particles and antiparticles has been found to display remarkable symmetries, transformations, and also wave properties that present an enigma to the objective language of science.* How can matter be both hard little lumps and, at the same time, a smeared-out wave propagation? Unable to determine the precise nature of events at the center of things, science has been forced to adopt a principle of indeterminacy.

In the other direction, science looks out toward the periphery of things, toward the external limitations to events. On the assumption that time and space are like an infinite vessel in which physical events occur, science devised laws of motion, ascribing them to nature. Then it was discovered that light does not obey these laws, that it travels at the same velocity in relation to all objects, irrespective of how fast they may be moving in relation to each other. Rela-

---

*Several books that describe particle physics for the general reader: Banesh Hoffman, *The Strange Story of the Quantum* (New York: Dover Publications, 1958); Fritjof Capra, *The Tao of Physics* (Boulder: Shambhala, 1975); Michael Chester, *Particles* (New York: Mentor, 1980); Gary Zukav, *The Dancing Wu Li Masters* (New York: Bantam Books, 1980).

tivity theory was devised to compensate for the constancy of the speed of light: objects moving at great speed relative to an observer appear shorter in the direction of travel; their mass tends to approach infinity; and their time frame gets drawn out to a relative standstill.* For instance, if we could see an astronaut inside a rocket ship approaching the speed of light as it passed the earth, he would appear his normal height but would look thinner, even though his mass had increased, and his wristwatch would run slower. Since science sees us to be part of an expanding universe in which the farthest galaxies recede from us at speeds approaching that of light, the perceptual limits to the universe lose meaningful significance to our space-time frame of reference. Questions about a periphery to experience become as indeterminate as those about a center.

The deficiency of science is most apparent at its extremities: its language is unable to reconcile the center-periphery polarity within a common framework of understanding. Thus the two poles of the creative dilemma are linguistically opposed, just as they were culturally opposed in the white man and Indian. The same deficiency simply generates a different set of problems in a different situation.

The many sides to the center-periphery dilemma are manifest in every area of experience, but there are a few features that always present themselves irrespective of the circumstances. Of prime importance is that neither the center nor the periphery can be known to the exclusion of the other. The one owes its existence to its relationship with the other. This relationship implies an interface—a structural element across which a process occurs from a center to a periphery. But an interface does not isolate a center from a periphery. Interfaces have two basic properties that often go unnoticed because they are so common: they are active, and they are unbounded.

Everything that we know we owe to the active properties of interfaces. Interface processes define the complexity of experience, including the perception and integration of our senses. We see, hear, feel, taste, smell, and think by means of interface processes. They constitute the subject matter of all scientific study.

Interfaces must be unbounded in order to relate a center to a periphery, but they may be closed or open. All physical surfaces are closed interfaces that are unbounded within themselves. For in-

---

*Several books that describe relativity for the general reader: James A. Coleman, *Relativity for the Layman* (New York: Pelican Books, 1969); Bertrand Russell, *ABC of Relativity* (Edison, N.J.: Allen Unwin, 1969); Nigel Calder, *Einstein's Universe* (New York: Viking Press, 1979).

stance, since we cannot find an edge to the surface of a billiard ball, we can say that it has a surface that is continuous or unbounded. But it is also closed, since any continuity of direction on the surface goes around the ball to intersect itself. The same is true of any physical surface, regardless of irregularities of shape. A sheet of paper, for example, is really a rectangular cube of pressed wood pulp that is very thin: it has no open edge that exposes a center to a periphery. The surface has corners, but it is unbounded within itself and closed.

Open interfaces are unbounded in the sense that they are indeterminately extended, detectable more by their physical *effects* than by physical *form*. They are not hard surfaces—they can penetrate and be penetrated to varying degrees. Wave propagations are examples of open interfaces interacting with closed interfaces, but the interaction lends them a degree of closure and also some of the characteristics of their propagation. Radio waves, for instance, radiate outward from a transmitting source in a series of expanding spherical wave fronts. The spherical pattern represents a degree of closure, but it rapidly expands to indeterminate limits, and the waves can penetrate obstacles such as building walls to reach radio receivers.

Communicative interfaces associated with language and culture also have an open and unbounded component. These concern the conscious ordering of communicative energies into a patterned energy interface that sustains an ongoing balance between a subjective center and an objective periphery. Unfortunately, the deficiencies of language usually constrain this polar balance within narrow limits established by cultural bias. Communication across cultural interfaces frequently runs into stormy weather, especially when cultures are so widely divergent as those of the white man and the Indian.

At this point, it is not possible to elaborate further on the many properties of active interfaces or how they come to be ordered as they are, but it is important to know that they are very fundamental to the system. As our journey progresses their properties will gradually become apparent, especially when we get to the elaboration of the system itself.

The position of the sun indicates that the morning has slipped by. The wind has picked up just a little. Sitting by the lake and soaking in the scene that is so old, yet always fresh and new, one feels as if the hand of time is halted and held prisoner in the present. The greenery still exudes the same persistent vitality with which it bursts forth in early spring. Now as the plant world coasts with the season into summer, the vital tempo assumes an air of confidence that projects the certainty of completing a magic mission for another season.

The lazy ripple of the water laps listlessly at the shore. In the sand beside the dock, and at the edge of the water, there is a small frog, hardly finished changing from a tadpole. It is sitting half in, half out of the water as if unable to decide between two worlds. It too is soaking in the scene and reflecting on it, but without need to reconstruct the process. During the day it sits and suns itself, or feeds on bugs, or seeks shelter in the shade. At night it too marvels at the mystery of life from its station by the shore, in its own direct, uniquely wondrous way. It looks out across the surface of the water or upward to the secret messages of a starry semaphore, adding its raucous croak to the chorus of the night.

The oldness of the scene is a tribute to its newness, its newness likewise a tribute to its oldness. What is time except a notion to explain away uncertainty? Yet it is a notion that turns on us, condemning us to the certainty of a death march down a blind corridor of our own construction. Here in this scene, there is no such thing as time. There is only life going on, a complex living process complete with all the polar attributes of birth and death, joy and suffering. Time and its partner, space, are only dialogue in the play, not the players.

There is just enough wind to do some drift fishing for pickerel. After a short swim and some lunch, the fishing gear is collected and taken to the boat. The minnows in a styrofoam bucket in the shade are gathered as well. With enough gasoline in the tank everything is set. The wind is from the southwest—just about right for drifting along the edge of the big shoal. Sometimes in the afternoon the pickerel come in there to feed. With one pull of the rope the motor starts and the boat heads up the lake.

Circles and Squares

The threat of a late-afternoon thunderstorm has forced an exodus from the water, none too soon. The rain is coming down hard now. A glance out the window catches a ragged flash of lightning followed quickly by a shivering crash of thunder. The phone burps a few unsteady rings. Close! Before heading in, good fortune had provided a couple of pickerel for supper, just big enough for a good feed. Bass, trout, and northerns are fun to catch, but when it comes to eating fish, pickerel are the best.

The thunder has become an almost continuous rumble with occasional sharp cracks nearby. There is a good-sized hill behind the cottage which offers protection from a direct hit by lightning, but sometimes a minor charge will follow the telephone or hydro wires in. These systems are not nearly so well grounded as they are in the city.

The two pickerel are filleted on a board that is kept for the purpose. They are not very large, about fifteen inches, but enough for a good meal. Pickerel is a fish from which every bone can be removed without destroying the fillet. All fish have fine bones protruding from the rib cage into the flesh—these have to be severed when removing the fillet. In pickerel, however, they form a single row that can be removed in a neat sliver of flesh with little additional waste.

Usually fishing serves as an effective technique of clearing the mind of debris. One has to adopt a special kind of concentration in order to fish. The fish world is very different from the world of our experience, but one has to establish a contact with it to catch a fish. There is, of course, the obvious physical contact through the fishing line, but it seems that another contact is called for, a psychic or communicative contact. Fish live in a world of water, we live in a world of air. The two are separated by a surface through which perception is very limited in either direction. There are as many worlds of fish as there are lakes, each requiring a framework of understanding distinctive to the fish within it. Although different species of fish have distinctive habits, it is also necessary to learn how those habits are displayed in each specific lake.

Generally speaking, fish tend to be very selective in their choice of feeding ground. In some lakes this might be restricted to only a few spots; in the case of pickerel or bass some of these spots might be only a few yards across. There are also lakes where it is difficult to distinguish any special spot. The size of lake is also a factor, although not necessarily a predominant one. For example, there are small lakes that are teeming full of northern pike, but you rarely catch a large one. There are also small lakes that seem to contain very few northerns, but you rarely catch a small one. The characteristics of the lake can therefore be as distinctive as the characteristics of the species. One has to have an understanding of them both, but this understanding is still far from complete.

The fish of a given species within a given lake tend to behave as an individual. To a lesser degree this is also true within a district of lakes. When one feeds, they all feed, and when they aren't biting, it is often hard to catch any. Feast or famine seems the order of the fish world, especially where man has not yet seriously disrupted its natural order. Where the incessant roar of speedboats has chewed up the weed beds and turned an underwater wonderland into a hi-fidelity resonator, it is a wonder that fish can survive at all, let alone demonstrate distinctive habits. Weather seems to have an effect on the collective response of fish to feed, but it is by no means a consistent effect. While fair weather from the prevailing direction seems best for fishing, minor storm centers don't seem to hurt any. On many occasions, there is excellent fishing both in the midst of thunderstorms and in steady drizzle. Sometimes there are long periods of poor fishing in good weather. There are always exceptions, and that helps make fishing what it is. It has to be experienced to be appreciated.

Whatever the conditions of fishing, the essential experience is always the same. It is a formless search beneath the surface of the water in a strange world where perception is very limited. It is a quiet, almost meditative endeavor to establish contact with a living member from that world through the material aid of a fishing line and bait. This, of course doesn't include the hook dunkers. There are fishermen and there are hook dunkers—very often you cannot tell them apart by their technique. Sometimes hook dunkers have the very best of equipment and know everything there is to know about fishing. Some have traveled to inaccessible places and can boast of unexcelled catches, but every fish they catch amounts to no more than a fortuitous accident. Hook dunkers are consciously engaged only in mechanically dunking a hook in the water, using a variety of methods. A fisherman is engaged in a communicative experience. The fisherman isn't concerned with trophies or record catches, nor does he get perturbed if he catches nothing. To catch nothing is as much a part of the communicative experience as to catch a boatful. Fishing in this sense is more than a contact with the world of fish. In its purest form, it is a contact with our own beginnings, a groping for an ancestor from our evolutionary past. It is a search beneath the surface of our thought into the formless depths of being, as clear and refreshing as a drink of spring water.

One must be an intuitive fisherman to understand the system. It is beneath the surface that one recognizes the universality of the system, a sort of master template to experience. Because the system underlies all experience it can offer unlimited potential. It can provide a new and better perspective on problems of every kind, but one must be careful not to undertake an understanding of the system just to solve the problems of the world.

The problems of the world may be collective, but they are collective because they are individual. Nobody has the solutions because everybody has them. The problems of the world are signposts to an individual search for understanding. Each of us is presented with a set of problems according to our circumstance; each of us is obliged to cope according to our understanding.

Understanding implies perceptual insight within a framework in which things are seen to fit into place. Complete understanding implies a universal framework—a requirement for common understanding. It is therefore a requirement for genuine communication. This implies not an explicit foreknowledge of all things, but an implicit relationship between all things. Our responses to circumstances in this way fit into a universal framework. Whatever the caliber of our understanding, each of us contributes through the responses we perceive to be suited to our situation.

The thunderstorm is not letting up any. It is a hard, driving rain. Water is running in makeshift rivulets down the slope in front of the cottage. It should make the farmers happy, but the timing also seems right for other reasons. There is something about a thunderstorm that clears the air.

The pickerel is delicious—more than enough to eat. Things are cleaned up before once more sitting down to listen to the erratic rumble of thunder and the staccato pattern of rain on the roof. The food has improved the mood—maybe the rain has too. Atmosphere and mood are related somehow. Moods tend to affect our perspective and the content of our thought, but they are often initiated by external influences. They are associated with activities covering a wide and varied spectrum, from very passive to very dynamic. They set the tone of the body, tuning the mentation process in a certain way that is suited to the activity concerned. Moods are an implicit component to spirits, although we do not always recognize spirits as such, calling them by various names. The explicit component is the pattern of animation associated with the activity concerned. Spirits emote a pattern to activity through our emotional apparatus, the autonomic nervous system. We adapt a spirit to activities of every kind, from sports and work to music and war.

Spirits are patterned energies that become organized on many levels through experience. These energies are refluxed via the autonomic system into the mentation process in a reciprocating, ongoing way that modifies and refines them in a manner deemed appropriate to the needs of circumstance. They are tailored through mentation by overriding frameworks of understanding.

Attachment to the patterns or routines of activities tends to produce closed belief systems that become self-perpetuating and sufficient unto themselves. In a changing world, they eventually lose relevance; the energies concerned become dissipated. In contrast, a universal framework of understanding has the capacity to maintain an evolving relevance to changing circumstance. A universal framework doesn't change: it prescribes the pattern for change in any circumstance.

The system places experience in a communicative context that is neither static nor rigid, although it never changes. All possible varieties of experience are expressions of the system. Although the system is very flexible and adaptable, it does nothing in itself to resolve problems as we see them. It is insistent that personal problems are personal. In this respect it is without compromise. If this were not so, we would be denied the opportunity of learning to cope in a pertinent, responsible manner. Problems teach us—they make us take notice, observe, wonder, and search for a better basis of understanding. The system reveals itself through search and wonder; thus problems bring us to the system.

There have been other expressions of the system in the distant past, products of other ages and other civilizations. Today only fragmentary remnants of such systems remain, often regarded by the language deficiency of science as products of primitive and superstitious civilizations. There is, nevertheless, a large body of evidence to the contrary that points to a highly developed understanding of the creative dilemma and of its cosmic significance.

Strangely enough, the last of these ancient systems of understanding began to lose its influence at the beginning of the Christian era, which coincided with the dawn of the Piscean age. The early symbol of Christianity had in fact been the sign of the fish, derived from a figure called the *vesica pisces*. (See Figure 1.) The *vesica pisces* is that figure bounded between two overlapping circles of equal radius such that the center of each is on the periphery of the other. It is therefore a representation of the center-periphery dilemma. One circle is taken to represent the world of spiritual essences that permeates the world of material phenomena represented by the other circle.

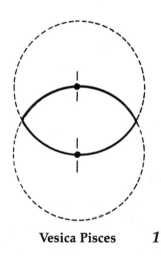

Vesica Pisces   *1*

John Michell in his book *City of Revelation** has explored some of the significances of the vesica pisces. He shows that St. John's description of the holy city in the Book of Revelation conforms to the principles of a system of sacred geometry that is extremely old and is demonstrated in the structure of the pyramids, in the temple at Stonehenge, in the ground plan of Glastonbury Abbey, and in the

---

*John Michell, *City of Revelation* (New York: Ballantine Books, 1977).

English system of measurements. The problem most fundamental to the sacred geometry was that of cubing the sphere or squaring the circle, which involves drawing the square whose circumference is identical with that of a circle. To the ancients, the square and the circle represented two contrasting geometric principles that must find reconciliation within a common framework. The ruler and compass were the only tools permitted.

This problem amounts to a slightly modified presentation of the center-periphery dilemma. The square was representative of the static, materialistic regularities of earthly considerations, the circle, of the dynamic, spiritualistic regularities of the heavens. The squaring of the circle represented a reconciliation of these contrasting principles within a common framework. It is given expression in the plan of the holy city, as it is in the structure of the universe, and as it is in man.

The ground plan of Stonehenge, constructed some two thousand years before St. John's revelation, also corresponds to the geometric proportions of the holy city. The temple, consisting of two concentric stone circles and two U-shaped structures, stands within a circular moat and bank. The outer circle was originally made up of thirty pillars of sarsen stone, the inner circle of some sixty bluestones. Within the limits of error possible in the reconstruction of the ground plan, the temple represents, among other things, a circular presentation of the problem of squaring the circle. If the sarsen circle is rearranged to form a square of equal perimeter, it will exactly contain the bluestone circle.

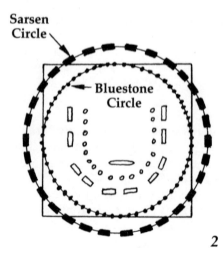

Sarsen Circle

Bluestone Circle

2

Michell also points out the structure of the Great Pyramid as another monument to the squaring of the circle. The height of the pyramid corresponds to the radius of a circle, the circumference of which is exactly equal in length to the perimeter of the base of the pyramid. Students of the pyramids still cannot reconstruct a believable plan for their erection. The Great Pyramid is aligned with its four corners toward the four points of the compass with a deviation of only a fraction of a degree. It has none of the usual attributes of a tomb, no sculpture or artistry to the interior, no hieroglyphics—just the stark accuracy of its geometric design. To add to the mystery, there has never been a mummy discovered inside a pyramid. The stone coffin or sarcophagus inside has always been found empty.

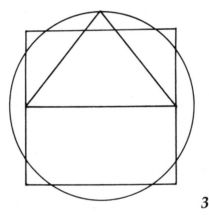

3

The most impressive example of squaring the circle is given in the relative dimensions of the earth and the moon. When they are drawn to scale tangent to one another and each is enclosed in a square, then the circle scribed concentric with the earth through the moon's center will have a circumference equal in length to the perimeter of the square containing the earth. This arrangement is similar to the circles at Stonehenge, and the relevance of the pyramid can also be seen. In addition, if the corner of the square containing the moon is joined to the corner of the square containing the earth, then the enclosed right-angled triangle has sides in the proportion 3, 4, and 5. This is a triangle of special geometric significance, and it is demonstrated here as related to the problem of squaring the circle. It is remarkable that the relative dimensions of the moon and earth should provide a geometric representation of the moon's significance to the harmony of life on earth.

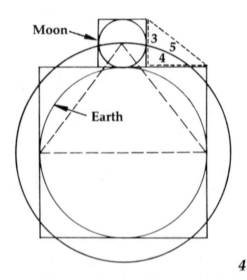

4

Why have there been no successful attempts to piece together an understanding of the ancient systems of knowledge? At least part of the answer should be apparent. It isn't possible to do within the context of an objective determinism, since it cannot encompass both poles of the creative dilemma. It gives expression to the explicit pole at the expense of the implicit pole.

The language of Western science is dichotomous. It engenders an either/or type of logical approach that tends to prove or justify one thing at the expense of another. Either this or that is the cause. It chooses one alternative to the exclusion of another, which tends to fragment experience rather than to integrate it. Choice is seen as an expression of dominance that is often pursued to extremes. Aggressive competition, organized anarchy, open warfare are the extremes of choice when confined to an objective determinism. The ancient systems were polar, insisting on a unified perspective that exhibited great integrative power. With a single stroke they grasped the essence of the universe in all its diversity of form. Ancient systems were expressions of the system couched in a language that was appropriate to their age.

There is a special technique for delineating the system that is not dependent on language, yet it can be used to develop language that is pertinent to science or to other forms of social and economic organization. It can be difficult to understand, not so much because of its complexity, but because it is so fundamental. It requires that old frameworks be refluxed and reassimilated. This can sometimes be painful psychologically, emotionally, and even physically. It can also invite reactions of many kinds. One should be on guard for these reactions and cautious of overzealous efforts to understand the system. It takes time to understand, time to fish, time to wonder at the stars, or just to listen to the rain and let things settle into place.

There are many sides to it all, just as there are to fishing. One can understand the habits of the species, but this in itself is not enough. It is necessary also to know the lake. There are many worlds within the world and there is not time to fish in them all, but neither is this necessary to become a master fisherman. First it is necessary to become more than just a hook dunker seeking a quick catch. One must learn to search beneath the surface.

The thunder has let up some but the rain continues in a steady downpour. It is already dark. There will be no bass fishing tonight. Another day has passed with little progress toward the system. However, this preliminary ground must be covered well. The mind has absorbed enough for one day. Although it is still early, it feels time for bed. The patter of the rain brings an easy sleep.

Clouds

The sun is rising over the horizon, peering with a large red eye through a flimsy curtain of cloud and struggling to clear its vision. The rain has passed to leave the promise of a nice day, but everything is sodden, a little hung over from the storm. Although it is early, sleep has run its course. A little exercise is good to get the vital juices flowing; a thirty-minute run is followed by a swim.

After breakfast the hill behind the cottage is climbed, and a comfortable-looking rock is chosen for a seat. The morning air is beginning to warm up, and the grass exposed to the sun is already dry.

The attention gravitates to the spectacle of life, abounding with variety, singing a common song. A few birds are trying out the freedom of the air. Trees and plants are politely bowing in the breeze, whispering silent messages too intimate to hear. Everything is thrilling to the casual excitement of a part perfected through the ages, performed with ease and grace. A monarch butterfly comes fluttering by in typical erratic fashion. It comes to within a few feet to check things out. It flutters a few figure eights while conducting its examination, then flutters off, only to return in a couple of moments to double-check. It seems that everything is in its place except for man. A newcomer to the choir, we have yet to learn to read the music.

An insight into the system first came quite a number of years ago as a result of a prolonged, intensive effort to understand the nature of a business organization. This effort had been imposed by the special circumstances in a company of about five hundred employees that was being taken over by a larger company of about two thousand employees. The nature of the takeover introduced a power struggle that brought many problems, imposing an intensive personal search that lasted for two or three years. Many people are exposed to unreasonable pressures in business organizations, and since these are often the result of faulty structure, it is worth reviewing the events in a general way. They also led directly to the experience that revealed the system.

It was a gas distribution company that had earlier experienced a period of exceptionally rapid growth, brought on by the conversion from manufactured gas to natural gas in a community that was also growing rapidly. Although there had been many problems, the employees were young and energetic. Gradually, a responsive and effective organization had emerged. During this period, my personal responsibilities evolved until they included a major sector of the company's operations.

It happened about this time that the takeover bid of a neighboring company was finally brought to completion. The process of integration was gradual at first. Specialists began to arrive from head office with many questions, particularly about paperwork and methods. It soon became clear that the parent company had a very different set of problems and was not nearly as well organized as its acquisition. It was essentially a sprawling rural company made up mostly of many small centers, whereas the smaller company was concentrated in a rapidly expanding urban area.

About then a large, new head office building was constructed, soon filled to capacity with experts who were constantly involved in meetings. Now, instead of a trickle of specialists, there were study teams. Standardization became the theme. Everyone knew, or thought he knew, the benefits of standardization; everyone jumped on the bandwagon. What a marvelous way to integrate the operations of the two companies. No one seemed to notice that there are oceans of difference between standardizing nuts and bolts, and standardizing a communications system. Having obtained a large new computer, everyone thought that with the standardization of forms and methods, everything could be done more efficiently at one central location. The operation of the organization was surely a minor issue that could be adjusted locally. However, the question could not be brushed aside so lightly. Too many nights of burning the midnight oil had gone into piecing together a workable system of order in a period of chaotic growth.

A system of forms is an integrated matrix that provides very necessary communicative links between the various working parts of an organization. The more effective a system of forms, the more independently the various working parts can function, and the more responsive an organization can be. The urban company was necessarily more complex than any of the operational centers within the parent company. It involved more working parts—its communicative needs were very different.

The parent company also had a peculiar structure: what is called a "line-staff" organization. The decentralized line organization was responsible for getting results, while the centralized staff organization was arranged into departments of specialists, according to specific functions, to advise and assist the line organization.

Theoretically, the staff organization had no authority over the line organization, but there was a monkey wrench in the works—things called procedures. Being closely related to forms, they could be legislated into existence upon recommendations from the staff organization. Procedural matters involved the behavior of the entire company. Those who decided procedure had authority, those who did not had none. Line people were thus responsible for getting results, but not for deciding how to get them. Staff people decided on procedures in committee, but were responsible for neither the success nor the failure of their decisions. For conscientious, intelligent people, such an organizational structure is a battleground.

When talk of standardization persisted, it became necessary to dig in our heels. How could anyone voluntarily agree to scrap a smooth-running communications system that had taken years to evolve—and that worked—in exchange for a system that could not work at all? If the new system were imposed, it would be necessary to implement a third system to compensate for it. How could anyone willingly agree to impose on themselves and their colleagues the frustrations of such a change for no other reason than to satisfy grandiose delusions about the universal benefits of standardization? The committees were far removed from the reality of daily problems. The integrity of the existing system had to be defended against the onslaughts of a head-office organization whose numbers by this time had reached three hundred.

The more persistent these onslaughts became, the more desperate became efforts to explain the very real needs of the organization and to point out the benefits of existing methods. The head office simply had no improvements to offer. They seemed to listen, but they weren't absorbing anything. Why couldn't they understand?

As they intensified their efforts, it was necessary to intensify responses. Invariably their proposals failed to take into account difficulties that had been mentioned time and again. Reports, outlining the problems once more, were submitted to line management, who in turn forwarded them to the head-office top management, who in turn referred them to the specialists. As the procession around the vicious circle gained momentum, tempers began to fray. The whole organization began to feel the strain. Why should anyone have to fight for the right to do his job?

As the circle of controversy continued, a stream of questions began to flood back. Why can't you do this? Explain why this won't work? Why do you do this? Why? Why? Why? Why indeed! Why anything? Any reasonable person should have quietly left for greener fields, but it seemed there was too much at stake to quit. Inching its way ever closer into the midst of the fray was the matter of standardizing all forms and procedures. It was decided to make a final stand. Line management of the urban company supported the effort. Since the president of the parent company was an accountant, the convincing argument must be a financial one; thus the present system of operation must be demonstrated to be the more economical of the two. (Anyone close to it would know that it was, but to demonstrate it was another matter.)

A complete analysis of the entire communications system in the company was undertaken with emphasis on the operations department. It required the concerted effort of a half dozen people for seven months. The distinctive working units within the organization structure were identified. The distinctive tasks of the organization were identified, and the formal communications required between working units were assessed for each task. In this manner, the communications matrix was progressively exposed for examination. The study then resolved itself into two parts. The first part was an analysis of the communications required between working units; the second, an analysis of the communicative work required within each working unit. In assessing the second part, a series of unit operations was defined, and a time study of the processing of nearly every piece of paper in the company was conducted. The total number of pieces of paper flowing, and the filing references required, were assessed. The same thing was done for the proposed system of standardized forms by trying to mentally adapt it to the organization with the aid of a supplementary system of forms and by making hypothetical organizational changes. Aside from the fact that the standardized system would leave the organization in a state of frustrated confusion, it was established that it would cost several hundred thousand dollars more to administer annually. This did not take into account the thousands of pieces of paper that would flow into the marble halls of the head office. All of this information was

condensed into a lengthy report and submitted for the spe
consideration. Let them refute it if they could.

Throughout this period of analysis and assessment, tl
to which any organization is a communications system came to be
appreciated. The first level of work in an organization may be physical, but all work in internal levels is essentially communicative.
There are communications between working units, communications
with the past through record systems, communications with the
future through plans, generalized communications with experience
through the compilation of data, and communicative interpretations
of experience through computing and assessing data.

It became clear that a communications system is an intelligent
system. The word *intelligence* itself implies a telling within. In a
company it is people, of course, who do the telling, but they must
also be organized to function intelligently. There is also a tension in
bringing to balance the internal and external aspects of the communicative task. Work is an intensional process that must meet structured communicative needs in the organization.

The company dispute represented not a polar communicative
task, but rather a dichotomy. The tension was oppressive. At times
it was stultifying. Thought processes became like huge, heavy
wheels churning through a morass of uncertainty, digging deeper
and deeper for answers. Why? Why? Why? Sometimes perceptions
were distorted, almost surrealistic.

During this period of intensive search and struggle, another
concept cropped up that was quite simple, but very fundamental. It
was later to play a very important part in giving the system expression. It involved the recognition that activities do not consist of
causal sequences, but instead are triadic cyclic processes that inter-
mesh in a complex variety of ways. The basic components of the
triad can always be expressed in the same manner: *means*, *goal*, and
consequence. This is a universal pattern to activity, related to memory
or recall, and is thus applicable to accounting or keeping track of
things. The universal triadic pattern of activity will be called the
"primary activity"; this initial insight was an important contributory
factor to the experience that revealed the system.

There was no response to the report. There was no acknowledgment, there were no questions, there was no indication it had
even been read. On the basis of the evidence the report could not be
discredited—maybe the specialists could not decide which department should handle it. Whatever the case, it did not really matter

anymore. Everything had been done that could be done. As time passed the atmosphere remained strained, but a certain edge was gone. They had not backed off altogether, but maybe there would be a temporary reprieve.

It was during this time that contact was first made with Albert Low's ideas on organization structure. Albert was a psychologist in the personnel department at the head office, an unusual kind of psychologist. His ideas, presented in an article entitled "The Systematics of a Business Organization," were extremely well thought out and far-reaching in their implications.

The article made extensive reference to the work of a man named J. G. Bennett, who had apparently developed a geometry of six dimensions, including the three dimensions of space, together with time, eternity, and hyparxis. What kind of strange marriages were these? Was physics related to religion? Were both relevant to the structure of a business organization? Were such insights really possible? Something clicked. Something dovetailed with the tumult of the past couple of years—with the interpretation of a communications system and with the concept of a universal form to activity. But how? There must be an answer. The mind was pregnant with possibilities, ready to search in any direction. The chance to pursue the ideas further didn't come just then. The experience intervened . . .

It began during a short rest on the couch after coming home from work very tired one night. It was not a nap, just a rest to let the daily tensions fall away. The attention fell to the rhythmic rise and fall of the breathing. The mind seemed to empty of all rubble. It wasn't very long before an odd phenomenon occurred. Inside the head, toward the back lower-right-hand corner, there was suddenly a tiny instantaneous spark, little bigger than a pinprick. From it a single shower of little lights trickled across the mind like a miniature fireworks. It wasn't startling, it was just observed. Then the attention returned to the rhythmic rise and fall of the breathing. In a few minutes a very strange but wondrous thing began to occur. It started ever so gently. There came a special awareness of the form of the body while lying there observing the regularity of the breathing. There was no attempt to control the rhythm or to ignore it. It followed a natural pace that was simply observed without purpose. The mind was empty.

Next there came an awareness of a form to the form, with the breathing assuming a vibrant harmony between the two. It was like being an impartial witness to a vibrant phenomenon of breathing.

Gradually the harmony enveloped the whole body with a swelling feeling that filled every fiber of the being. As it did, the area of the chest seemed to open and become alive. A vibrant golden light began to glow, blossoming forth to fill the mind and engulf the body. Then in a most ordinary fashion there appeared before the eyes, although the lids were closed, a self-image, like looking into a mirror of living gold. It was a momentary vision of the self looking impartially, intently, at the self. It quietly appeared, then faded in a moment, leaving the formless ecstasy of living gold.

It was some time before slowly sitting up. As the eyes were opened it was like having been asleep from birth, acting out some vague distorted dream, and now, for the very first time, waking up. The root of all anxiety was gone. Everything was vibrantly alive, bathed in light. There was a spontaneous awareness of every muscle, nerve, and cell in the body. For several days it lasted with a sense of unity and equanimity, imbuing every waking moment with a joyous rapture. At night sleep would come in blissful thankfulness; each morning the new day was greeted in the same way.

The energy transformations of living processes were illuminated and could be seen visually. The living essence of a bird singing could be not only seen, but implicitly felt, in a way that brought a unity of appreciation to what it is. The vital energies of plants growing could be seen and appreciated in a similar way. The emotional problems and attachments of total strangers could be seen visibly as they passed on the street. The sorrow of it was apparent, but not in a way that disrupted the equanimity of the experience.

It was late one night, after a few days, that the major experience began, during a period of sitting and wondering what should be done. It began with a direct and unmistakable telepathic message: twelve words, one sentence. It was severe and startling. After a mental response there appeared a face a few feet in front of the eyes, but with a presence that extended infinitely in two dimensions, like an unbounded interface of ordered energy. It was the face, the head, the shoulders of an aging smallish man, but it was ghostlike in appearance. It had no color. The face implicitly embraced the whole of humanity, from the genesis of human history up to the present. Its depth was written in human suffering—incredible suffering. It was scarred—almost mutilated—by tragic events that reached back thousands and thousands of years. There was one particularly bad gash in the neck, several inches long, that was still not healed over, having occurred in relatively recent times. There were many similar events that were written in the depth of suffering and recorded in the face, reaching back to the origins of history.

In spite of this, the face embodied a will of absolute impartiality that carried with it the social burden of mankind from its inception. The frightful part came with an intuitive recognition of the future that it knew it faced. The problems that are impending are overwhelming, cataclysmic, yet it must not falter in its impartiality. It seemed an impossible dilemma that imposed an extreme severity to the presence of the being, yet it was consciously sustained with gargantuan strength and depth.

The message was rejected in fear, with a hasty retreat into another room, but the feet were stopped in their tracks. Suddenly all organic feedback from the body to the mentation process was suspended. It was as if the slate had been wiped clean. There was a clarity of perception into the indeterminate, formless distance that could be seen right through the walls of the room. A series of realizations intuitively occurred in an orderly sequence, as if they were being intentionally fed to the mind. First there was a perception, into the formless distance, of unlimited possibilities: a recognition that possibilities need not be restrained in any way. Anything is possible. This was followed by a few examples. One of them, a little frightening in its implications, was the real possibility of unlimited life span. This brought anxieties: how to relate to an indefinite life span when our thoughts are so conditioned to a lifetime of striving, ending in death?

Another step or two was taken, when the most disconcerting thing happened. Everything vanished! The room, the city, the planet, the universe, even the body, all just vanished! There was no loss of identity, but it was an identity in emptiness experienced with wonder. There was a perceptual balance in a field of wonder. It was like a moonlit night without the moon or stars, a void with a certain quality of indeterminate depth. In a moment everything returned, but just for a moment. Then it was gone again. This happened several times in succession, as if someone was switching the universe on and off, to demonstrate something.

Next, that *someone* appeared in the room about eight feet away and directly in front, but it was not part of the world of material form, so that distance or magnitude had no real relevance. It was just suddenly there, all at once, an indescribable, intelligent being. It was round, six feet or more in diameter, both with form and without, both with color and without, constantly transforming within itself, yet staying the same. It was just hovering there in the room, a being of intelligent energies, immaculately ordered and harmonized unto itself, seeing and knowing all, yet balanced and impartial.

It could change its texture at will and communicate through emanations of energy. After its initial balanced appearance, it began to radiate friendliness, just like meeting a new and genuine friend, only more so. It changed its texture again, this time to mercy. Unrestrained mercy came pouring from it in a shower, from every part of its being. It changed again to unlimited compassion, and again to love. A deluge of infinite love came raining from it in a way that no words can describe.

While the gaze was fixed in amazement on this being, it became balanced again, just hovering, as if it were considering something. Then it began to spin its wheels in meaningless activity that induced a minor similar activity in the area of the chest—like a kind of assessment. It paused again for a moment, then increased the intensity of its living texture, became slightly smaller, and moved up and away a little bit. It became pure creative energy, a dynamo of every manner of creativity. Then it changed to an absolute independence of everything, an unthinkable freedom beyond all conceptions.

It paused once more as if considering something. Then, in its very center, there was a tiny blip of light. From it came a transmission, like a speeding bullet of energy that brought a momentary self-awareness, followed immediately by a sweep out into the void. The world faded from view. It was as if a magic wand of energy had been waved across the void. There before the eyes was a universe of stars, cast in a great spiral galaxy. It was seen with awe and amazement from the extremities of space, from an angular perspective complete with the feeling of being suspended in emptiness thousands of light-years out into space, gasping at the profusion of stars in a great spiral swirl.

The room came back, only to fade again as two titanic power masses became suspended in the void. They were facing one another, one on top with an interface that curved upward, like part of a huge sphere, and one on the bottom with an identical interface that curved downward. Both interfaces were extended in an indefinite way, being open in opposite directions, as if an enormous sphere of energy had been ripped in two, with the top half placed underneath the bottom half. On the inside of both interfaces were dark, dangerous-looking, seething energies of raw power, concentrated against the inside of each interface such that they were under great strain to contain themselves.

Separation and balance were maintained between the monstrous power masses by an exceedingly fine single thread of light, just a glistening hair stretched between their closest points. It soon became apparent that order in and to the entire universe was dependent on the maintenance of this incredibly intricate balance of energies. It represented a polar dilemma of cosmic proportions. These enormous energies that are both open and closed must be independently contained, yet mutually balanced to the most minute degree.

No sooner was this recognized when the huge masses began to tremble on the verge of horrendous instability. Terror-stricken at the unthinkable consequences that this instability implied, the desperate thought came that there could be some personal responsibility for maintaining the balance. But the energies appeared infinitely beyond the capacity of a human mind to control. Gripped helplessly with horror, there was an eruption in the body that began in the lower part of the abdomen. Irregular, uncontrollable energies came cascading up through the body into the head, where they were transformed into an extreme transverse tension. It was nothing at all similar to a headache confined to the head. It was as if the conscious mind were being ripped apart, torn limb from limb, on a cosmic torture rack.

The being, which had been hovering and watching on, increased again in intensity and moved up a little more, becoming unlimited universal power—conscious power that could be constrained by no obstacle whatever, exceeding all the forces of nature in the universe combined. Then it began to increase its power continuously, becoming smaller and much brighter as it moved up and away on a steep incline a little to the right. Size, distance, and magnitude lost relevance to the world of form.

As its intensity and power reached extreme proportions, it began to consume the void. The void in the vicinity all around the being began flying into it to be devoured in the intensity of its dynamism. As the void around the being was consumed, a pitch-black emptiness was exposed beyond. The being became an absolute center of very bright, intensely active energy in an absolute periphery of pitch-black emptiness, but more and more of the void was being consumed. It became apparent that this active center of being, and nonactive periphery, were the void in some way, but also much more than the void. There was no time to think. It became obvious that the void embraced everything, not only the universe and everything in it, but everything that has ever been. The void is an eternal, empty side to the world of form and to the totality of experience. Now this Absolute Being, Almighty God, was bringing everything to consummation, to a final end, to completion, before a witness that faced the same annihilation.

The eyes were glued to the terrifying spectacle of great tongues of the void flying into the Almighty Being. The transverse tension in the mind became unbearably immense. The awe of the spectacle brought a tunnellike opening in the void, from the perception in the head down through the body and beyond. Turning away from the being in an act of utter desperation to stave off the destruction of the universe, there was an energy transmission through the back of the head, like another speeding bullet projected from the being. This time a tunnellike hole opened in front of the perception down into the void, and there was a very rapid zigzag streak of light projected down inside the tunnel to inscribe what appeared to be an irregular, six-pointed figure that vanished as quickly as it was formed. Almost simultaneously, there was a wheel of energy a few feet to the right, stationary, but churning over and over with the momentum of a speeding train. Inside the wheel were faces and fragments of human bodies being mangled by the emotional energies they embodied through cycles of birth and death. Horrors devouring horrors with indulgent delight.

A couple of more desperate steps were taken. The feet stopped again. From a point in one side of the back, a dark abstraction of energy began to rise like a vapor through the body, into the head. There was an internal perception of the event, as if an invisible finger had touched a tiny spot to release the energy from the void. As it flowed up through the neck into the center of the head, it became very bright and intense, then went streaming out through the eyes as they watched in sheer disbelief. It projected out about twelve or fifteen feet into a structured pattern of transforming energies a couple of feet in diameter. It was a visible idea, complete with images in brilliant color. There were interfaces with transformations going on as the energies worked themselves out to demonstrate the idea. Then they vanished in the void. Another dark abstraction of energy began to rise from another point in the body up into the head in the same manner, then intensely out through the eyes to project a different idea. No sooner would one vanish than another would begin, a number of times in succession. The ideas were recognized from memory—in fact they were themselves memories—but they had no particular significance other than to demonstrate a principle and a pattern that can't be properly described. All vanished into the void. The room was like a transparent veil that faded out depending on the intensity of events.

Suddenly there appeared in the void a city of light in brilliant color. It was suspended in the void in such a way that the underside of the city along the nearest edge was at first visible, and there were dark tendrils of energy reaching down into the void like roots from which it drew its sustenance. The perspective rose to provide a clear vision across the city and down into the streets on the nearest side. It was a beautiful city, immaculately clean, with cobblestone streets and mostly masonry-type buildings in a variety of pastel shades, none of which were over a few stories high. There were both peaked and flat roofs, domed structures, and varied-shaped buildings, extending over quite an area, but it was not modern or as large as many cities are today. It was like a new Jerusalem, brilliantly illuminated, with no people or vehicles apparent.*

While looking incredulously at the splendor of the view, dark abstractions of energy began to rise through the body as before. This time they originated from the void beneath, slightly behind the transparency of the body, the energies being stronger than before. As they rose up into the head to be projected out through the eyes, the intensity was severe; each time there was an inversion of emotional energy in the body that is hard to describe. It was like a minor death. The ideas went streaming out from the eyes with extreme tension in the mind, only this time they went flying down into the city. They couldn't be specifically recognized, but they were being used in the completion of the city. As soon as one was finished another and another would begin to rise up through the body. Then other ideas began flying into the city from different points in the void, as if they were being fired from invisible canons. It was a gathering of creative energies from diverse points, all being integrated from experience into the completion of the city. There was terror, amazement, tension, awe, and wonder all at once, but there was no time to reflect or think. The timing of everything was regular and ordered, with nothing wasted in between.

The city gave way to a magnificent landscape; the perspective rose as to the top of a mountain. Like the city, it too was brilliantly illuminated in vivid color, extending out to a distant horizon as far as the eye could see. Its contrasts were splendid—with wooded hills in the distance, a river flowing along the base of a high precipice, ravines and areas of semidesert to one side toward the foreground. The ideas stopped streaming from the eyes as the body

---

*The city bore no specific resemblance to Jerusalem. No churches, temples, or mosques were noticed.

went unnoticed, but they started flying from various points in the void from above, down into the landscape, completing it and filling it out. A world of light was being gathered through the timeless void.

The room returned, with time for another couple of desperate steps, but there was no escape. The transverse tension in the mind was severe, with a heart full of terror at the prospects of what was going on. A series of thoughts on various subjects began to come. The energies were not dark abstractions as before, but were refined, hardly noticeable, from diffuse areas of the void around the body. The thoughts just infused the body, but as they became conscious, the perception thrust through into a burst of white light in which absolutely everything relevant to each thought was spontaneously known. As thought succeeded thought, burst of light succeeded burst of light, and everything was known. There was no thought or question to which all aspects couldn't be spontaneously known. It was total omniscience, but this turned into the greatest horror of them all. How could anyone live with knowing everything? As it ended, a jungle of quandary came crashing in through the usual thought processes, along with the belief that total and irrevocable madness must have seized the mind. But if that was true how could everything make so much sense? Even belief in madness was insane. Nothing made sense. Everything was and it wasn't, it was both and it was neither. This was the only thread of sanity that could be found, and for the next few hours it was very important. Uncontrollable energies were coursing through the body with unbearable tension in the mind. Again and again the tension would build to extremes too impossible to hold, then break, with the whole of phenomenal existence slipping away in a vortex. Waves of nausea were succeeded by a clutching to any flimsy semblance of stability. Everything was hanging in the balance.

It was three months before reluctantly deciding to return to work. There are no words to really describe the experience or the effect it had. Only a distorted glimpse can be given, and the wisdom of giving it is questionable.

The workings of the mind and of the universe had been revealed, but in a way that brought everything that is normally accepted into question. It resolved nothing, yet offered unlimited promise. It begged to be given expression, yet language was hopelessly inadequate. Fortunately, Albert provided the intelligent assurance that was so badly needed, seeming to understand something of what had happened. Study and reading on many subjects began to occupy much of the time, and a quest with a different flavor began to take form. There had to be a way of communicating the system.

Before the year was out, the company was quietly left behind. There had been a great deal of work put into those ten years. Many good friends had been made. It was like leaving behind a lifetime; a lot had been learned. The specialists would start their games again. They had to. It was their job.

It is time to get up from the perch on the hill to stretch the legs. The stomach says it must be lunchtime. The wind has become quite strong. It feels good. The sky is filled with fleecy white clouds, as if they were trapped in an irregular blue net. What makes them hang together in bunches like that in such a wind? The eye fixes on a particular gossamer fragment and watches it for awhile. In a few minutes it dissolves into the blue. If the clouds are dissolving at their edges near the top, they must be forming in their center from the bottom, for they show no sign of disappearing altogether. They are like billowy thoughts in a gigantic mind, in a constant state of formation and dissolution, changing form and substance to suit the winds of time. It is just a dreamy version of the system, for the process by which they change is left untouched by change.

This afternoon would be a good time to go to North Bay. There is some shopping to do, and it is time to go to the laundromat.

5 Laundering Experience

The road to North Bay goes through hilly, wooded countryside, except where occasional rolling valleys and flatlands make farming possible. Most farms in the area are only marginally successful, many still being worked by the descendants of the original settlers. Occasionally there are vestiges of abandoned farms, their dilapidated buildings overgrown with brush. There is not the same commitment to the land that there used to be.

Driving is conducive to thought, especially to the kind of mental journey involved in approaching the system. Maybe it is the constantly changing stream of landscape that helps to induce the developing flux of ideation. Whatever it is, the two seem to go together with little difficulty, and the train of thought is taken up again.

While the power-struggle dispute was going on, Albert had been developing ideas on what he calls the "structure/process" of a company, trying desperately, but with very little success, to communicate them. Although still not an accepted idea, Albert's "structure/process" is an accurate evaluation of a business organization as a communications system. It applies equally well to any company. After the experience, it had proven to be an essential focal point in piecing together the system. It is, in fact, a simplified representation of the system adapted to a business organization. The system itself, however, is universal. It may be applied to anything and everything.

Albert recognized that there are certain regions of activity that always apply to any business organization, and that these regions are not just arbitrary divisions of work. Each is a distinctly independent region of activity, although they are all relevant to the operation of a company as a whole.

All companies are involved in selling a product or a service of some kind. All companies are involved in a production activity associated with their product. All companies are involved with financing their activity. All companies are involved with structuring and staffing their organizations. All companies are involved with assessing market needs and opportunities. All companies are involved with developing product ideas. The words and descriptions may change slightly, but these same six regions always apply to any company.

There are only six regions and there are always six regions, although the extent of delegation depends on the size of the company. In a one-man business, all six regions exist within one man. Delegation does not occur in all six regions until a four-level organization is reached. At that point, two or three thousand employees may be involved.

Three of the six regions may be called structural dimensions, since they each interface with a different structured environment. The other three regions may be termed process dimensions, since they each prescribe a process relating to one of the structural dimensions. The three structural dimensions are:

1 *Marketing*, which relates to the customer in the structured environment of commerce and the market.
2 *Treasury*, which relates to the stockholder in the structured environment of finance.
3 *Organization and manning*, which relates to the employee in the structured environment of crafts and professions.

The center of gravity of each of these regions is environmental to the company. The customer seeks the greatest quality for the least price; the stockholder seeks the greatest return for the least risk; the employee seeks the greatest remuneration for the best conditions. Each of these regions is of equal importance to the company; none can exist without the others. They also represent conflicting interests that exert a centrifugal influence on the company, tending to pull it apart.

The three process dimensions are:

1 *Sales*, which takes place within the context of the customer's needs as they are assessed by marketing. Marketing is not itself concerned with selling.
2 *Product development*, which takes place within the context of the resource capacity of the company as it is determined by treasury.
3 *Product processing*, which takes place within the context of the orga-

nization structure as it is determined and staffed by organization and manning. This latter region is most often referred to as the personnel function, but it goes beyond usual personnel policies.

The three process dimensions all have a direct common concern with product activity—with developing, making, and selling a product. This exerts a centripetal influence on the company and tends to pull it together.

It can be seen that the three process dimensions function within the context of the three structural dimensions. In other words, the structural dimensions provide the behavioral space for the process dimensions.

Together, the six regions generate a state of tension in the field of the company. The managing director is responsible for maintaining the balance in the field. Albert illustrated this tension and balance with two overlapping triangles as shown in Figure 5.*

A company can also be illustrated as three polar relationships of center to periphery, as shown in Figure 6. The six regions are related in pairs. Each pair represents a center-periphery polarity that provides for structural insight into the relevant process of the company. In each case, the process dimension is central to the peripheral structural dimension. Insight is possible only through these polarities. The point can be emphasized a little more as follows:

1 Sales must be geared to meet market demands. Marketing is concerned with the assessment of the customer's needs as they are expressed in the marketplace and therefore with determining market potential and trends. This assessment may disclose a need for more and better products, for a change in emphasis as between quality and price, or for a change in emphasis on product lines as the demand for some products falls away in favor of others. The sales-marketing polarity thus presents an insight into the effectiveness of sales as it relates to market potential. The sales effort may be inadequate, excessive, or misplaced. Or it may be that product changes are called for from product development and product processing.

2 Product development must evolve within the context of the resource capacity of the company, as reflected by the treasury. There is an evolving product theme to a company that is expressed by its exper-

* A. W. Low, *Zen and Creative Management* (Garden City, N.Y.: Doubleday Anchor Books, 1976).

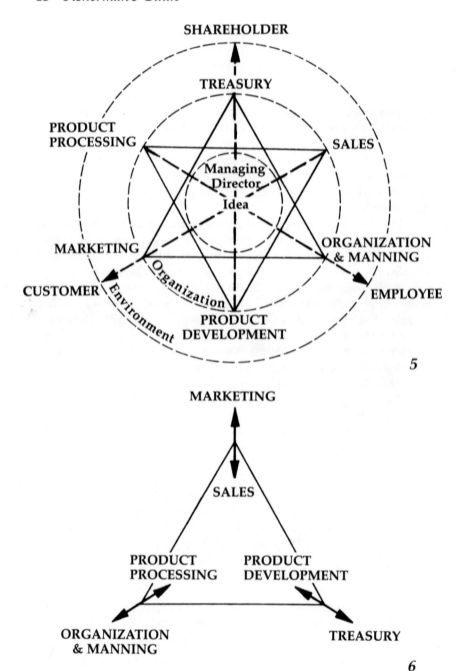

tise in certain product lines. This is reflected in the productive resources of the company: in its assets, operating budget, and balance sheet. The evolution of the product theme must be reasonably consistent with the company's history of success as indicated by these resources. For instance, it is out of the question for a private machine shop to undertake the development of a new automobile, but it may be practical for it to develop certain automobile parts. Available resources must not be strained to the breaking point, yet advantage should be taken of available resource potential. This is seen through the polar relationship between product development and treasury.

3   Product processing is the production of the goods or services associated with the product idea. The effectiveness of this region is always seen in polar contrast to organization and manning. When things are not running smoothly or effectively, the reason must be sought in the organization structure. There may be a problem with the structure itself, with the personnel performance within the structure, or with both. An important point here is that the whole organizational structure is involved. An organization is a communications system that will function or malfunction according to the way it is structured, even if it is staffed with the most competent people available. The impact is always felt by product processing, which must carry the burden of productive efficiency for the whole company.

These three polarities introduce a very basic structural constraint into the organization of any company. The delegation of authority by the managing director should *always* be undertaken *separately* in each of the six regions. This may be called the "first structural constraint."

Each of the six regions must be independently organized in order to maintain the three polarities that provide for insight into the structural dynamics of the company. In a one-man company, this is done in one man's mind. As authority is delegated, the managing director must still maintain the balance of tensions in the field. To do this, he must continue to see each of the six regions as being structurally distinct. If two regions are delegated to one person, the managing director loses direct experience of the communicative relationship between those two regions. Instead, he or she must depend on secondhand information that is colored by someone in a specially privileged position. The resulting imbalance will also prejudice feedback from the other regions. The distorted communicative tensions in the company will preclude a balanced perspective for everyone involved.

The three polarities are the headlights of the company; they illuminate the road through a fluctuating landscape of circumstance. They permit adjustments to be made in speed and direction to safely navigate the turns and avoid the hazards, but there must also be only one driver at the master controls. If his sight is impaired, the frantic shouts of the crew will do little to ensure a safe journey.

The road stretches out through a corridor of tall maples along a high ridge, then breaks over a crest. For a moment the horizon recedes to the bulging ridges on the far side of North Bay, more than twenty miles in the distance. Then the road sinks down a long winding hill into some sharp turns and dips that settle out into a wooded flat. The dark amber waters of a creek ignore the traffic as they snake lazily under a bridge, then the road turns past a small cemetery that belongs to a little village coming up. There are only half a dozen houses and a store, then the road crosses another bridge into some sweeping turns and more gently rolling terrain.

So far the road to the system has been pretty good—a few sharp corners and ravines, but generally clear going. Up ahead there are some hills—not many—but there are some steep valleys in between where visibility is not too good. These will be explored another time. For now, it will be enough to peruse the view from the tops.

Albert's ideas on organizational structure were influenced considerably by the works of J. G. Bennett and G. I. Gurdjieff. Bennett, a student of Gurdjieff, contributed many ideas toward a universal framework of understanding, broadly outlined in four volumes entitled *The Dramatic Universe*.* Gurdjieff, a Russo-Armenian, spent many years searching through the Middle East and central Asia assimilating a teaching. There are many groups and individuals around the world that still make intensive studies of his ideas.

One of the central themes of Gurdjieff's teaching is the significance of the enneagram. Considered to be a universal symbol of perpetual motion, it is used to demonstrate harmonic relationships of cosmological significance. A geometric illustration of the enneagram, involving nine terms, is shown in Figure 7.

---

*J. G. Bennett, *The Dramatic Universe* (London: Hodder & Stoughton, 1956 [Vol. 1], 1961 [Vol. 2], 1966 [Vols. 3, 4]).

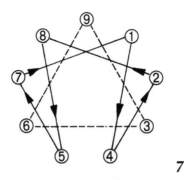

7

Gurdjieff regarded the symbol as a reconciliation of what he called the laws of three and seven, corresponding respectively to the dotted triangle 9, 3, 6, and the irregular six-pointed figure. The triangle is a direct representation of the triad, while the six-pointed figure represents an inversion of the number seven. Seven divided into one gives the dynamic sequence of the six-pointed figure 0.142857142857, with the six digit sequence repeating to infinity, hence the significance of the symbol as a depiction of perpetual motion. While the origin of the symbol is unknown, it is very old.*

Although it was not known at the time, certain aspects of the experience conformed to the pattern of the enneagram. The zigzag pattern of the six-pointed figure had been seen as a fleeting streak of light, but it was the pattern of energy transformations through the body and out into the visual field that most strongly seared the pattern into the memory.

The "primary activity" is related to the enneagram as well, while the center-periphery dilemma is most basic of all. Over a long period of time all these things began to piece themselves together. Albert's understanding of the nature of the dilemma and his ideas on organizational structure provided an invaluable focal point.

The general form of the primary activity can be simply illustrated as a triad as shown in Figure 8. (We shall return later to explore how the system determines the primary activity through the various relationships of three centers to a common periphery.) The "means" term defines a perceptual interface or axis between an objective "goal" term and a subjective "consequence" term, maintaining a dynamic balance between the two. The goal term, in fact, transforms into the consequence term, then back into the goal term,

---

*Gurdjieff learned of it from an obscure Sufi brotherhood.

and so on around the perceptual axis of the means term.* For now it is enough to know that the primary activity establishes a subjective and objective aspect to all experience. Later we shall see that this concerns a dynamic identity between form and emptiness respectively.

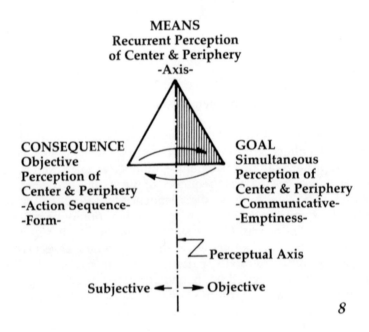

MEANS
Recurrent Perception
of Center & Periphery
-Axis-

CONSEQUENCE
Objective
Perception of
Center & Periphery
-Action Sequence-
-Form-

GOAL
Simultaneous
Perception of
Center & Periphery
-Communicative-
-Emptiness-

Perceptual Axis

Subjective ◄— ┊ —► Objective

8

The goal is communicative. It is effected through the void, as was so vividly demonstrated in the experience. All experience is integrated through the void, which goes unnoticed, partly because it is masked by form, just as the projection of a movie masks the blank screen. The world of physical form is an extremely rapid succession of three-dimensional space frames that are selected from the void to lend a continuity to events.

The enneagram consists of a matrix of activities in the pattern of means, goal, and consequence, but they are not primary activities. The primary activity subsumes the whole enneagram. In other words, the enneagram is an elaboration of the primary activity.

*There are two modes to the means term that induce the goal-to-consequence transformations. An explanation of how it works will be given when we get to the system.

The matrix of activities can be illustrated as shown in Figure 9. The six-pointed figure resolves itself into two reciprocating activities, one objective and one subjective, represented as symmetrical to the central axis of the mediating activity, represented by the large triangle. For the present, all that is important is a familiarity with the overall pattern.

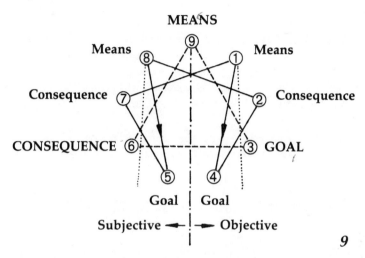

9

Each of the nine terms of the enneagram has a universal significance that applies in any context. Although words are used to describe this significance in Figure 10, the nine terms are generated by the various relationships of four centers in a common periphery, as

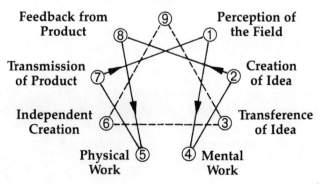

10

they transform from one into another through the matrix of activities. It is a structural insight into the process of each term that defines the significance of the words. The words are only the most appropriate that can be found to designate the significance of each term. The enneagram elaborates on the primary activity in a way similar to that in which the story plot of a movie elaborates on the technique of movie projection. A drama to the creative process begins to unfold.

Albert made extensive use of the enneagram, relating the six company regions to the terms of the six-pointed figure as shown in Figure 11. When the terms of this figure are matched with the universal significance of each term as shown in Figure 10, the relevance of the region to the activity matrix is indicated:

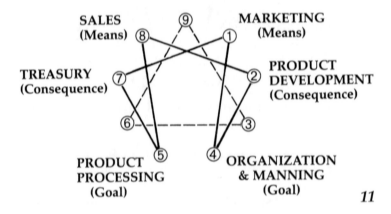

11

1   Marketing is concerned with perception of the field.
2   Product development is concerned with creation of idea.
4   Organization and manning is concerned with mental work.
5   Product processing is concerned with physical work.
7   Treasury is concerned with transmission of product.
8   Sales is concerned with feedback from product.

Each of these primary concerns of the whole company likewise has six regions that elaborate on the nature of each concern.

The mediating triangle is related to the three polarities of the six-pointed figure that cross the medial axis as illustrated in Figure 12. Taking the polarities one at a time from the top, they can be interpreted as follows:

12

1 The sales/marketing polarity provides for a *renewed perception of the field* through recurrent cycles of performance. The value inherent in the productive effort of the company is perceived in the marketplace through product acceptance. The resultant feedback not only sustains the company, but also gives it direction in subsequent cycles, to promote a continuing perceptual renewal. The polarity corresponds to the means term of the mediating activity, which acts as a perceptual axis for a company.

2 The product-development/treasury polarity provides for the *transference of idea* through resource commitment to product development. Money defies definition in physical terms, but it is more than paper and numbers. It simulates a communicative void that links a company to a wider economic environment, allocating a freedom to act that has been earned through recurrent cycles of experience. In this context it reflects a capacity to perform. Although this capacity is manifest as form in the extent of facilities and trained personnel, the treasury, by its fiscal policy, mirrors the collective idea of these resources. Fiscal policy does not generate wealth; it makes possible the development of ideas into viable products that can find acceptance in the marketplace. This polarity is communicative, concerned with the transference of idea. It corresponds to the goal term of the mediating activity, representing an identity in emptiness.

3 The product-processing/organization-and-manning polarity represents the corporate body of the company in action. This in itself
   is an *independent creation* of the company that evolves through recurrent cycles of production, embodying the creative capacity of the
   company. It is the physical form of the company, the land, buildings,
   equipment, and people, assembled together in a structured, creative
   undertaking. This polarity corresponds to the consequence term of
   the mediating activity, representing an identity in form.

   From this assessment of the three polarities, it is clear that they
bear a direct correspondence not only to the terms of the mediating
activity (Figure 10), but also to the terms of the primary activity
(Figure 8), which subsumes the whole enneagram.

The turnoff to North Bay is coming up. Traffic is fairly heavy, and a
minute or so passes before making the turn onto Lakeshore Drive.
There is a shopping center this way with a convenient laundromat.
   North Bay is built on the shores of Lake Nipissing, a beautiful
lake about sixty miles long, with many beaches. Most of the lake
is shallow with a sandy bottom, making it treacherous in high
winds. For such an accessible lake, the fishing is reasonably good,
particularly in the mouth of the French River, the outlet from the
lake.
   The car is parked near the laundromat. The clothes hamper is
taken from the back seat. A couple of washers near the front are
started, and the clothes are dumped in. The place is fairly busy,
probably because of vacationers in the area. There is a lunch counter
in a department store nearby; a cold drink might taste good and
pass some time.
   A table, facing out into the main shopping area of the store, is
selected. People are milling around in the store, some sauntering
slowly, some rushing, some smiling, some staring, some frowning.
Each is embroiled in a world of individual concerns. For the most
part, people make little effort to observe their experience closely,
except in terms of a stream of wants that constantly flow into the
mind. This doesn't mean that people are greedy with conscious
intent. Some are, of course, but most people are concerned only
with getting along in a world with others. The trouble is that we are
regularly encouraged to chase after this endless stream of wants,
even though we are constantly forced to curtail them in light of our
resources. Carried to the extreme it becomes a mentality of want
that attracts more wants, requiring more and more sacrifice and

compensations to accommodate the endless accumulation of more. For those intent on possessions for their own sake that far exceed any reasonable needs or appropriate standards, the fulfillment of a balanced perspective can never be found. Why do intelligent people so often get caught up on this treadmill as if their lives depended on it?

The mentality is a close relative of a popular myth that is fervently perpetrated in business circles: the goal of a company is to make a profit. It is usually justified by adding that without a profit a company cannot stay in business. No reasonable person will argue that profit is not essential to the survival of a company, but how does that make it a goal? The intent of a goal is to provide an integrating purpose or intelligent direction to some kind of activity. In the case of a company this means bringing together large numbers of people with diverse interests and skills to participate in concert to realize the goal. The idea implicit in the goal is what must integrate the diversity of their numbers.

One must then ask, what is the idea implicit in profit? If we are to make it, we must know what it is. We can make a chair, build a house, manufacture a car, fix a television set, because there is a clear idea implicit in these things. How do you make a profit? How are people to relate to the idea of profit in such a way that it will bring about the concerted activity of a company? Does anyone seriously believe that one man will willingly work for another man's wealth at the expense of his own? How are people to think or understand their place in order to make a contribution to such a goal? What is the idea implicit in profit?

There is no integrating idea implicit in profit, because profit is not a goal. The goal of a company is given in the idea of its product; this integrates the structured activity of a company. The goal is communicative; it must fulfill a market need.

Profit is earned as a *consequence* of making a contribution of value to the market. Through the recommitment of profit in recurrent cycles, a company evolves both its products and its capacity to produce them. Profit thus becomes vested in the corporate body of a company, sustaining it in a state of renewal that is tailored to current creative needs. Profit is the freedom and capacity of a company to create; it says little about how this freedom should be exercised. It is a mute potential to act. The survival of a company is ensured not through the accumulation of wealth, but by giving expression to its potential through a responsive commitment to the market.

The drink finished, the bill is paid. A couple of items are purchased in the store, then some window-shopping is done on the way back to the laundromat. The timing is about right—the wash is finished. The clothes are transferred to the dryers, and with another wait in store, a walk will pass some time.

Albert also illustrated the six regions of a company in a way that defines a product as an *idea* in a *form* with a *demand*, as shown in Figure 13. Each of the three polarities indicated in capitals gives significance to one of the words *idea*, *form*, and *demand*, respectively. Thus the goal implicit in the product is also implicitly defined by the six regions of activity that constitute the whole company. Value is therefore *always* perceived through polar balances that by their nature preclude a place for profit maximization.

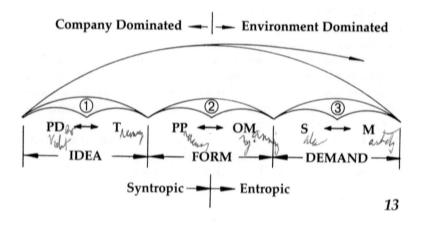

13

It is safe to say that nothing contributes more to lower profits and higher costs than campaigns for profit maximization and its companion, cost reduction. Both of these ideals, like so many ideals, introduce disruptive imbalances and a futile chase after a will-o'-the-wisp. Nevertheless, many people extol the merits of profit as a motive. Some even attempt to equate profit incentive with free enterprise, or inflate it into a basis for human values.

Unfortunately, it doesn't end with a harmless myth. The enshrinement of the profit motive invites an army of social and political reactions and counteridealisms. The energies that are so fervently projected in the futile chase must find an equally futile reactionary balance. This is demanded by the nature of the dilemma, the ultimate toll being exacted in human suffering.

There is neither virtue nor evil in profit. It simply provides a certain freedom to act in an economic and social context. How that freedom is exercised is the crux of human values. This is an individual dilemma, a function of the perceptual capacity of people and the sense of responsibility that goes with it. It is not something that can be easily acquired by the ready adoption of a set of principles of thought or behavior. Rather, it is earned through an effort of search and careful self-observation. It comes from profit of another kind.

Yet the profit mentality persists. The reason lies in objective frameworks of understanding and the deficient language that ensues. A clear perception of the polarities involved is lost. The implicit pole of the dilemma is masked; in its place, an emotional need is experienced to endlessly compensate in direct experience. Around and around the vicious circle goes.

The walk has taken a circle through a tidy residential district of modern homes. Not far from the laundromat on the return, one of life's dramas presents itself. A boy, two or three years old, is standing in the yard in front of a house. He has obviously gotten outside without his mother's notice. He is standing there naked, trying to decide in which direction to explore first, when his mother comes screaming from the house. He makes a run for it, but she catches him on the bound. Rushing him back to the house, she gives him the details of her framework of understanding in no uncertain terms.

The little boy is having his experience laundered. It happens to us all throughout our lives, first with the help of our parents, then by schools and religions, and eventually by the frameworks of understanding that we come to adopt or evolve along the way. Emotional energies are refluxed into cerebral awareness to be consciously cleaned up and suited to the needs of circumstance. Each of us contributes through refining energies and bringing them to an appropriate balance.

Back at the laundry, the wash is dry. After it is folded, everything is collected and returned to the car. There is still some shopping to do; maybe later there will be time to take in a movie. There is a good comedy playing in town, and a little diversion might help the perspective some.

6

More Laundering

It is already mid-morning. A couple of hours of unsuccessful trolling has brought the boat into a long, sheltered bay that is especially peaceful, squeezed as it is between two bulky hills that are both heavily wooded. There is an abundance of life here, much more than can be seen. Most impressive is the preponderance of plant life. The air is steeped in its vitality. Everywhere majestic limbs reach out to cloak the earth and embrace the sun, transforming energies into a storehouse of life. Plants dress the stage, and generate the atmosphere, to sustain all the other players in evolution's drama. From tiny origins their numbers exploded in the sea, then on the land, to dominate the early acts of the play, assisted by lower life forms working behind the scenes. Even now, plant life remains in many ways aloof unto itself, with only certain treasured concessions to such intimate friends as pollinating insects. But what a lavish gift it makes for every higher form of life. A miracle of transformation has turned a naked landscape and pungent atmosphere into a setting fit for a festival of animation.

Plants stock the shelves to overflowing in a large section of nature's marketplace, for all the rest of us to shop. They offer the nutrition and shelter of their form, but in the process something more is done. They assimilate and exact a balance to energies that provide a vital basis for all higher forms of sensitivity. Stalks strain skyward, from roots searching blindly into earth, to bring together—from darkness and from light—energies from soil and sun. Heaven and earth stand reconciled in plants through the eternal patterns of vitality they project. Each species lends its flavor to a polar balance until all varieties have been explored and need for more has been exhausted. The graceful pine, the hardy spruce, the gentle fern, each has a vital character, a spirit of its own. From mushrooms

and moss to mountain flowers, the dilemma of creation is continually resolved in plants with vital spirits.

These early acts in the drama began as gloomy affairs, but gradually a vast fund of vital energies enveloped the globe and saturated
the seas. As the bank balance accumulated, and when the timing
was right, this fund of profit from experience was drawn upon to
make new investments into certain lines of diversification. New
creatures came on the scene, confined to the sea at first, with specialized yet simple organs for digestion and respiration. The early
versions were mostly slow-moving, sluggish things with plantlike
traits, but as their variety increased, so did their complexity. Vital
energies became ingested and transformed into new levels of sensitivity, with a capacity for response. Worms and jellyfish came, then
shellfish, and great varieties of arthropods, with insects infesting
and exploring to the limits of experience. All manner of invertebrates
explored techniques of metamorphosis, metabolism, reproduction,
locomotion, and sensitive response. Nature's marketplace was thriving, but in this classic drama the trading is in the energies of life.
Another vast fund of patterned energies accumulates, this one much
more complex in its organization. These spirits are of sensitive,
responsive creatures that have learned both pain and pleasure. The
profit in the fund is boiling over.

The next major excursion into diversification of the product line
introduces the vertebrates to the drama, with backbones and skeletons immersed in flesh. These models come with a unique innovation, very crude at first. The fragmentary beginnings of an
autonomic nervous system are detectable in the primitive eels and
fishes. In the reptiles, it is accompanied by a companion development of the head brain, where a bulge of nerve cells bursts outward
into cerebral hemispheres. Now an emotional apparatus is distin-
guished from a mental capacity to reflect emotive experience. These
creatures don't just sense and respond; they are aware of sensitive
response. Both vital and sensitive energies begin to be transformed
and refined into conscious patterns of behavior. In the reptiles, these
simple patterns are quite fixed, but a groundwork is established.

With the introduction of the lower mammals to the showroom
come many refinements to style and structure. New hides with hair,
new tails, and new hoofs and claws and teeth are all displayed with
many little added extras, like protruding ears and eyelashes. The
wealth of patterned sensitivity worked out with the invertebrates is
blended with the experience gained from the reptiles to find renewed expression in the mammals. This requires a further develop-

ment of the autonomic system, accompanied by a second major bulge in the cerebral hemispheres. The second bulge takes preeminence over the first bulge, but both are present and closely associated. Now much-enhanced patterns of mobility are possible, along with a greater capacity to modulate the content. The horse is much more spirited than the crocodile. It can display a moderate repertoire of moods and sensitivity that is unknown to the reptiles.

The entrance of the higher mammals upon the stage signals a dramatic expansion of a third bulge in the cerebral hemispheres that displays an independence from the first two. (All three are present, even in the reptile, but two of them are undeveloped.) The third bulge is called the neocortex, or new brain. It can sustain a much greater range of mood and sensitivity, along with an embellished capacity to think and make intelligent responses. The dog and chimpanzee develop distinctive personalities, learn to assess their situations, and can select a variety of behavioral patterns. The chimpanzee can mimic behavior, dogs tend to adopt personality traits of their masters—even some birds can reproduce a range of sounds and actions. The independence of the new brain from the two older brains adds another tier to the refinement of patterned energies. The players are given a new tool to perfect their parts through the further reflux of spiritual essences.

The marketplace is now bubbling with activity. With each new development, there are cascading benefits down through the sequence all the way to plants and germs, then back up again, until a new equilibrium is reached. Nature's energy refinery is becoming very sophisticated, with each tier in the evolution of the drama acting like a tray in a fractionating column, distilling spiritual vapors from the trays below, yet spilling over to enrich them in return.

The entrance of man into the celestial theater is marked by a further explosive burst of the third bulge in the cerebral hemispheres, such that this new brain totally enshrouds the first two bulges. In man, the brain of the reptile and of the lower mammal is enfolded inward to surround the brain stem at the top end of the spinal column. These two primitive brains remain closely associated with the now highly developed autonomic nervous system; together they continue to reflect emotional responses and emotive behavior.

This functionally integrated apparatus is called the limbic system: it independently perceives a polar balance between emotive behavior and the market environment. This constitutes the sales/marketing polarity of the individual enterprise. The limbic system perceives the suitability of behavior to the environment in accordance with established needs. In doing this, emotional energies are both fed back and refluxed into the mentation process, to be dealt with by the new brain.

The neocortex consists of some tens of billions of neurons that furnish an immense potential intellectual capability to develop and process new behavioral products. Patterned emotional energies can be broken up, dispersed, refined, modified, or reconstructed, then projected anew to spill through the body in new patterns of behavior and experience. New spirits are born from the energies of old ones, their suitability assessed once more through the limbic polarity.

The evolutionary drama of biological life has unfolded over a time scale of hundreds of millions of years. Yet man as we know him made his entrance as recently as forty thousand years ago, the assets of previous prototypes being liquidated and reinvested. Of all the players in the drama, man comes into the world most helpless. Although we have the greatest intellectual potential, we are born knowing the least. The dumbest of animals, we must learn everything, and we do not learn quickly.

Essential to the learning process in man is language; some form has likely been with us from the beginning. The development of language introduced a drastic revision in the function of the hemispheres of the new brain. One complete side of the neocortex is generally devoted to techniques of performance associated with language*—sciences of all kinds, applied mathematics, analytical abilities, all learned techniques of explicit performance. The other half is devoted to intuitive perceptions, esthetic appreciation, visual-spatial assessments, and the formation of related concepts. It can understand language but it has no capacity for explicit expression.

This transverse or bilateral polarization of the new brain is associated with the remaining two polarities of the individual enterprise. The language side is the product-processing/organization-and-manning polarity, concerned with specific expression in a context of social organization. It processes behavior in a structured social environment. The intuitive side is the product-development/treasury polarity, concerned with the development of ideas through a treasury of wonder. Wonder describes our access to the communicative void of balanced energies from experience: these energies fund the development of idea.

---

*The most direct evidence is given by the researches of R. W. Sperry and associates on split-brain patients. R. W. Sperry, "Hemisphere Deconnection and Unity in Conscious Awareness," *American Psychologist* (1969).

The neurons of both hemispheres are arranged nonuniformly in six layers that constitute an outer thick skin, or cortex as it is called, that covers the convolutions of the hemispheres. The overall polarity of each hemisphere exists across this cortex, outwardly relating to the overall structural dimension, inwardly relating to the overall process dimension, while at the same time subsuming mentation processes within the cortex itself. Energies are exchanged outwardly with the environment through the cortex as if it were a highly complex antenna system. Inwardly, energies are processed through neuronal connections within the brain and throughout the body. The limbic cortex of the two primitive brains is directed inward around the brain stem, exchanging energies with the evolutionary heritage through the autonomic nervous system and its terminations.

The bilateral polarization of the two hemispheres does not occur to a major extent in other animals, with the possible exception of the porpoises and whales. In man, however, there is a frontal development to the hemispheres associated with purposive activity that our comrades in the sea do not possess, although their brains in other respects are more developed. Man has a unique capacity to evolve himself within the framework of his relatively fixed biological structure. The whole of our evolutionary heritage is structured into our bodies, from the molecular constituents that we share with the universe to the intricacies of our nervous system. Our skeletal structure, visceral organs, flesh and blood, the food we eat, the air we breathe, are all contributions from our ancestors, representatives of them all remaining to project the energies that keep us running and sustain us.

The whole of nature's energy refinery is recreated in man, a microcosm of the universe and a multitiered fractionating column of every stage of life on earth. We are the privileged proprietors of a very sophisticated piece of equipment, yet we haven't begun to understand the nature of its processes, its regulation and control, or how to bring it to a proper balance. The energies that we refine and project are substandard, often to the point of being unfit for consumption even when generated for our mutual needs, while the evolutionary market environment has been disrupted into a shambles. Every day we incur more and more debt to the future, with little hope of reversing the tide of events. The drama is rapidly gathering overtones of tragedy.

The greatest of gifts, language, is both our blessing and our curse. What has given release to our creative potential erodes our own foundations. A clear perception of the creative dilemma lies buried in meaningless words, the polar development of the intellect being coerced into the service of the emotional cravings of the croco- dile and horse structured into the limbic polarity. The most evolved of creatures, we get caught on a treadmill that gives amplified expression to the basest of beasts.* We disinherit ourselves from the wealth of our experience through an exclusively objective formalism; then, approaching the theater from the outside, we read a few no- tices, pretending that we understand the plot and enjoy the play.

The boat has drifted a long distance from the end of the bay, moving parallel with one shore about sixty or seventy feet away. The shore- line is slightly scalloped, with little points jutting out every few hundred feet. The beach is covered with an assortment of stones and boulders, patches of wildflowers and reeds sprouting up be- tween them. A few water lilies inhabit the shallows close in to shore. The bottom falls off quite steeply into deeper water here.

Up ahead there is an animal standing by the water's edge. It looks like a small dog, yet the nearest house is a couple of miles away. The boat is paddled slowly into shore as it drifts toward the animal, which still doesn't make a move to leave. It is a young fox about two months old, captivated by this strange-looking apparition floating on the water. It has no fear, just large inquisitive eyes with the innocence of youth. It has the same sense of wonder as a human child. After several minutes, it has seen enough, and turning on spindly legs, steps nimbly over the stones to disappear into the bush. The mother is nowhere to be seen.

The boat is pushed off again to continue the drift, but is turned around to alter the direction a little.

All mammals go through a learning process. With the higher mammals a degree of parental guidance is involved. They must learn to cope with many contingencies in an environment that is often hostile toward them. Animals establish a routine and a terri- tory, associated with their framework of understanding.

The situation for man is not all that different, except that lan- guage and the complexity of our activities require us to live in struc- tured societies. In organized undertakings we achieve a mutual benefit from independent efforts. Everyone recognizes the need to

---

*An interesting account of man's social dilemma in terms of his biological develop- ment and the split in his brain is given by Arthur Koestler, *The Ghost in the Machine* (London: Pan Books, 1970).

structure our activities, but few appreciate the fundame[ntal impor]
tance of doing it properly, or the serious consequences [of]
relatively simple mistakes. This can best be illustrated b[y a]
story about a hypothetical company.

In reading the story, keep in mind that the "first structural
constraint" requires the separate delegation of authority in each of
the six regions. There is also a "second structural constraint" that is
associated with the number of levels in a company, and that is required by the system. We will get to this later. For now the idea of
half-rank positions will suffice to illustrate the second constraint.
Half-rank positions result when there are more than the required
number of levels in the hierarchy of a company.*

The story illustrates that in a sense an organization is a communications machine which, like any other machine, functions according to the manner in which it is structured. When it is properly
structured, everyone can see his place and is encouraged to respond
according to his capabilities. When it is improperly structured, this
perception is lost: the participants in the organization become the
unwitting pawns of the communicative forces implicit in the structure. For many this means a lifetime of frustration, while for some it
means a free pass to an empty success. For everyone, it means the
substitution of illusion for the simple knowledge of one's worth and
commitment. When either or both of the structural constraints are
violated, the result is always the same. The organization will develop lopsided aspects. Some people are placed in positions of dominance unwarranted by their jobs, while others are placed in
positions of disadvantage in relation to the needs of their jobs. The
struggle for power replaces the struggle for reasoned solutions to
practical problems through a meaningful role within an organizational context.

The story is that of a small, growing construction company. A certain
construction foreman decides to go into business for himself. He
begins from his backyard with a crew he runs himself and secondhand equipment he repairs himself. His business prospers. He
secures a loan, rents or buys equipment, and starts one more crew.
Now he supervises the crews, and he has a mechanic and part-time
accountant. His wife answers the phone, and he estimates projects,

---

*Albert Low's work is also indebted to that of two psychologists who first developed
the idea of half-rank: Wilfred Brown, and Elliott Jacques, *Glacier Project Papers: Some
Essays on Organization and Management from the Glacier Project Research* (Carbondale, Ill.:
Southern Illinois University Press, 1965).

calls on clients, and sometimes pitches in to help the mechanic. Before the loan is paid off, he is able to begin another crew, but his organization is starting to show signs of strain. He now has an apprentice with the mechanic, a woman in the office, and the accountant works full-time. He has very little money ahead of him, his premises are inadequate, and more than half of his equipment is in poor condition or in need of replacement.

Another opportunity in the market presents itself. He secures another loan, moves to rented premises, replaces some of his equipment, and outfits two more crews. He now has two clerks working for the accountant in the office and a foreman in charge of his shop, together with two mechanics and one apprentice. Five crews are running in the field, and an estimator helps him to price projects and keep work ahead. He is quite a busy man, but his organization seems to be stable, his people are responsible, and the financial position of the company is steadily improving.

After some time, the pressure begins to tell on him. His doctor advises him to take it easy. He decides to appoint one of his foremen as a "construction superintendent." Now he is confronted with a dilemma of a different sort: should he, or should he not, include the shop duties related to the maintenance of equipment under the jurisdiction of the new superintendent? With the most warranted trust in his new superintendent, he decides to include them. The superintendent is overjoyed at the appointment. The other foremen also seem to take it quite well, except the shop foreman, who for some reason has reservations about the whole affair. The accountant and estimator don't see how the decision should affect them, hardly noticing that they are a little miffed as well. The damage has been done, and no one is likely to see the real cause of the conflicts that are certain to arise.

Now the accountant and estimator, who used to communicate freely with the shop foreman, keep getting "unnecessarily" involved with the superintendent. It doesn't happen with the field foremen since they now deal with the superintendent "instead of" the owner-manager. Through no fault of the superintendent, he begins to assume a "special" position in the company, which is not relevant to the work involved. Not to be outdone, the accountant and estimator begin to proclaim their equally "special" positions. The effect on the shop foreman becomes progressively more crushing. He has always dealt regularly with the accountant, who can no longer accord him equal status on the matters that they must mutually resolve. This foments strong reactions from the shop foreman. Since the superintendent is in no position to resolve the dispute, he is put in the position of having to take sides. Only the superintendent or accountant can take the dispute to the owner-manager, so that the shop foreman is denied the right to state his own case. In addition the owner-manager, although he has officially delegated the shop management to the superintendent, unofficially considers that he should have the right of direct access to matters pertaining to his capital investment. The shop foreman thus becomes further confounded by having to work for two bosses, while the superintendent is put out by the boss's meddling.

There is a construction boom. Four more crews are added. The shop foreman has three more apprentices; there is another woman in the office. The superintendent is now under pressure, running a little too hard for his own good. He requests an assistant. The owner-manager approves, not for a moment reflecting on the outcome or the relative merits of appointing another superintendent on the same level.

Until now the foremen in the field have been almost free of the effects of half-rank positions, but those days are gone. They are now afflicted by the same irritability they had noticed earlier in the shop foreman. They had enjoyed a good working relationship with the superintendent, but the new man in the middle doesn't seem to know what he's doing. He can't know what he's doing because he must constantly try to anticipate what's on the superintendent's mind. He is condemned from the beginning to fail, there being no way that he can make an independent commitment to his role.

Unfortunately the superintendent begins to meditate on his unusual success, while the accountant makes sanctimonious efforts to maintain the communicability of his position. The rift between the accountant and the shop foreman widens.

The owner-manager has inadvertently overdone his doctor's advice, partially abdicating his position as manager. Although puzzled by the shop foreman's disposition, as well as by the accountant's negative attitude, he is unable to diagnose the problem. He gives much of his attention to the superintendent, who seems most pleasantly disposed toward him. Missing the intensity of interest he experienced during the difficult years, he often talks about the good old days. More and more he must find ways to justify his own position. Talking makes him feel better, and he turns to an increasing number of private theories about business and its politics.

Encouraged by theoretical discussions with his boss, the superintendent begins to consider himself as one-half of a management duet. He can easily justify replacing the accountant who has become nearly impossible to communicate with. If he can also establish his superiority over the estimator, he will have totally eclipsed the owner-manager's position. The owner-manager will be that in name only, having been effectively eliminated from the day-to-day operation altogether.

Although the superintendent may consider himself a regular whiz, he has been on a free ride, carried along by the communicative forces inherent in the distorted structure of the company. His rise to the top was predestined from the day he was delegated two regions of the owner-manager's job instead of one. On the one hand he was pulled there by the attraction with the manager; on the other hand, he was pushed there by the repulsion between the accountant and his own subordinate. Only two options can resolve the communicative tension that has amplified the superintendent's ambitions: he can either abandon his role, or achieve the job of manager. He can either make a new start, or bring about the failure of his friend. As is the case with everyone else, he has been denied the possibility of fulfillment through meaningful expression in his role.

From the time of the owner-manager's eclipse onward, the attraction between him and the superintendent will change to repulsion, while the repulsion between the accountant and the shop foreman will tend to normalize. The owner-manager will have been automatically ousted. He may announce his retirement; his physical or mental health may fail him; or he may fire the superintendent and start the same cycle all over again.

From the day of the faulty appointment, the events could not have turned out differently. With that single act the entire plot was written. It was left to the actors only to enrich their individual roles. The sad thing is, the most competent, conscientious people turn into the strongest protagonists. Friends become enemies and enemies become friends, depending on where they are plugged into the plot. The only solutions are to leave the plot, or to change it.

The faulty structuring of the construction company automatically self-corrects to the point where the error was made. If the owner-manager retires, the structure becomes technically correct, with the superintendent becoming the new manager, and the man in the middle becoming an overworked superintendent. The problem is that the corrective tension has no regard for the individuals concerned. It functions as blindly as the error that initiated it. The tension conflicts with the intentions of the participants, with no benefit to anyone except to make them wonder what is wrong. It does provide an incentive to search, provided a person is so inclined.

The boat has drifted out of the shelter of the bay into a moderately strong wind that is moving it across the lake. A good-sized creek comes into the lake on the other side—sometimes a good place to hook a nice pike. It's worth a try for a short while before heading back to camp, so the motor is started up. There is a large sandbar that extends out several hundred feet in a sickle shape from one side of the creek. By anchoring in the center of the area the semicircle along the edge of the sandbar can be reached by casting. The boat is steered into a position about forty feet upwind from the best spot, and the anchor lowered from the bow with lots of slack in the rope. The boat drifts back, the anchor catches, just about right. The lure is changed. Casting begins.

As a small company such as the construction company begins to grow, the delegation of work becomes progressively more important, taking place both in levels (or vertical tiers) and in different horizontal groupings within each level.

The first level of delegation is always functional in nature. Occurring first in the product-processing region, it is concerned with the specifics of performing essentially physical tasks, such as pouring concrete for a highway, or assembling parts in a manufacturing plant. The man in charge is often called a foreman. Although he may have group leaders or subforemen reporting to him, this sublevel of organization relates not to the company structure as a whole, but to the complexity of the work at the first level of delegation.

The next level of delegation, identified as the supervisory level, requires recognition of the six independent regions of activity, not only as they relate to the whole company, but also as they exist within each region. Usually by this time there will be a product-development activity in progress, but only as it relates internally to product processing. Nevertheless, it is premature to combine product development and product processing at the supervisory level. This was the first mistake made with the construction company— equipment maintenance is product development as it relates to the daily routine of construction, and it was included under the superintendent's responsibilities. Not only does this introduce the political problems that were encountered, but it also seriously and unnecessarily restricts the growth of the company. The superintendent will soon become overworked, but it will not be possible to appoint another on the same level without establishing a second maintenance shop. To avoid the expense of such a step, one or more assistants will be appointed for the superintendent. Half rank is thus further introduced, with more communications problems.

The next stage of delegation will be called the administrative level. If we had followed the growth of the construction company further, we might have seen one or more construction managers appointed. At this level all six regions within the product-processing region should be independently integrated under each construction manager, although they will not all be delegated by him. Each such manager will be responsible for a different division or geographical area. By this time delegation has proceeded in the other regions as well, but is not likely to have reached the administrative level.

Delegation will not likely occur on a continuous basis in the marketing and product-development regions until an administrative level exists in product processing. The role of product development for the whole company is different from its role within product processing. In a large construction company, it will consist of an engineering group to give specialized technical guidance on difficult aspects of major projects. The emphasis should be on the development of construction technique subject to trial, and not on imposing standards or methods out of a belief that this will reduce cost or improve control.

From the preceding description, it can be seen that each level of delegation involves a distinctly different kind of work with a different set of interpersonal interfaces. Each higher level of delegation requires thought at a more basic level of abstraction, so that broader horizons may be encompassed. These levels of abstraction reflect a hierarchy that is implicit in the nature of structure itself: they always recur in a similar pattern, just as the six regions do. The four basic levels may be described, beginning with the highest or most central, as follows:

1 *Managerial work* gives *form to idea* and direction to the company as a whole. Only the chief executive does managerial work.
2 *Administrative work* gives *form to knowledge* and direction to routine within the constraints of the company idea. It does this through specifying technique.
3 *Supervisory work* gives specific *form to routine* through organizing and committing the basic resources of labor, equipment, and material.

Together with the specification of objectives, supervisory work gives specific direction to others.

4   *Functional work* gives ultimate *form to resources* through applied technique. It produces the final product associated with each region.

These four levels of abstraction, working on four structural levels in the company, provide for a succession of active interfaces through which the company idea becomes translated in stages into a distributed product or service.

The "first structural constraint" concerns independent delegation in each of the six regions of a company. The closely related "second structural constraint" concerns the four stages of delegation. Together, these two organizational constraints define the limits of flexibility in structuring any company.

In one sense, these constraints are rigid, since they should not be violated. However, in another sense, the constraints are very flexible: they allow for different circumstances, they relate to any company, and they provide for the maximum degree of creative expression for all participants within the structure. The checks and balances are implicit in the polar relationships that provide for structural insight into the creative activity. Everyone can see what is going on. Everyone can see his place in the performance of the whole company.

These basics of organization do not lead to the overformalization of an artificial superstructure to which people try in vain to relate. On the contrary, they provide for only the appropriate degree of formalization necessary to define the working relationships between people. The resulting structure will not compensate for incompetence, but will tend to expose it. More important, those who are capable and committed to doing a proper job will not be thwarted. The end result will hopefully be welcomed by everyone: a clarification of the objectives, control of the resources needed to meet those objectives, and clearly defined interfaces with working colleagues. With these things understood and accepted, the work can proceed in a normal way.

If there is a big pike in the mouth of the creek today, it isn't hungry. The only action has been a strike close to the boat by a small one. It must be well past lunchtime. Although the day beckons to stay out on the lake, there are things to do back at camp. Soon it will be time to venture into some wilderness fishing on a lake farther to the north—there are many preparations to make. The system requires a venture into the wilderness also, a wilderness of thought where there are no organized ideas. The fishing up north will provide a helpful setting. The anchor is pulled in and the boat headed out around the sandbar, then back up the lake toward the cottage. The wind has quite a sweep from the end of the long bay. The splash of the waves against the hull sends spray flying over the side, but it feels refreshing.

The evolution of a business organization is analogous in many ways to the evolution of life on the planet, although the latter, having been in progress for a very long time, is much more complex than any man-made organization. Nevertheless the same system applies, the degree of complexity being related to the number of tiers. The system unfolds in phases associated with the number of tiers in the hierarchy of delegation, but these phases do not represent a progression in time. Each phase is subsumed within all of the phases that precede it, just as the enneagram, while elaborating on the content of the cosmic movie, is nevertheless subsumed within the technique of projection prescribed by the primary activity.

Within each phase, the levels of delegation may be called a discretionary hierarchy. There is a transference of patterned energies through the discretionary hierarchy from top to bottom—or from inside to outside—and there is also a feedback of patterned energies in the opposite direction. In a company these communicative energies are projected in a variety of ways in speech, gesture, behavior, writing, and in silence. They are not necessarily associated with formal communications channels, but are interpersonal within the structured context, intuitively perceived through the nature of the polar balances they effect. The point is that the discretionary levels of a company act as tiers in a fractionating column for the reflux and refinement of energies, just as do the levels of biological life on the planet, and the corresponding levels of organization in man. The process seeks a dynamic equilibrium through the regulation of reflux.

The system has another peculiarity: there is a recurring pattern to the manner in which the system unfolds. This makes it possible to gain an overall understanding of a system with a large number of levels, in terms of a system with a small number of levels in the discretionary hierarchy. The higher number of levels becomes subsumed in tiers within each tier of the lower number of levels.

This can be exemplified by looking more closely at nature's energy refinery illustrated in Figure 14. Biological life has evolved in

Hierarchies in Nature's Energy Refinery

MANAGERIAL CREATIVE MAN	Organized energies of cosmic origin give direction to independent insight.	MANAGERIAL
	Independent insight integrates spiritual & technical development with biospheric needs.	ADMINISTRATIVE
	Independent spiritual and technical development, each stresses individual responsibility in its own way.	SUPERVISORY
	Social organization is worked out at the cultural level through language along with spiritual guidance.	FUNCTIONAL
ADMINISTRATIVE CONSCIOUS VERTEBRATES	Higher mammals with more refined body structures and a third stage of conscious reflux develop the ability to think.	INTELLIGENT REFLUX
	Lower mammals explore refined body structures with second stage of conscious reflux in cerebral awareness.	CONSCIOUS REFLUX
	Amphibians & reptiles explore a dedicated limb structure in conjunction with beginnings of conscious awareness.	CONSCIOUS AWARENESS
	Primitive fish work out the basic format of vertebrate structure with a crude autonomic system.	ANIMATED BEHAVIOR
SUPERVISORY SENSITIVE INVERTEBRATES	Intelligence: molluscs-sea; arthropods-land. Giant squid & octopus have well-developed brains; social insects have collective intelligence (bees, ants).	INTELLIGENT ORGANIZATION
	Molluscs, insects, crabs, spiders, etc., explore independent bodies, forms of locomotion, & reproductive functions.	INTEGRATED ORGANIZATION
	Colonies such as sponge and coral work out collectively organized activity, some with specialization of parts.	COLLECTIVE ORGANIZATION
	Protozoa such as amoebae & parasites work out details of animal processes at the cellular level.	ANIMATE FUNCTION
FUNCTIONAL VITAL PLANTS	Higher seed-bearing plants have further refinement of independent structures in many forms.	REFINED ORGANIZATION
	Ferns, horsetails, & club mosses explore vascular systems with independent root trunk top structures.	INTEGRATED ORGANIZATION
	Lichens & larger fungi such as mushrooms work out collectively organized cell activity with root, trunk, top structure.	COLLECTIVE ORGANIZATION
	Algaes & simple fungi work out details of plant processes at the cellular level.	PLANT FUNCTION

14

four major levels, each of which subsumes a hierarchy within itself. From the bottom up, the vital energies of plants sustain the sensitive energies of the invertebrates, which sustain the conscious energies of the vertebrates, which sustain the creative energies of man. Although sixteen levels are shown, we can nevertheless deal with the hierarchy in the much simpler language of System 4.

This overall survey of nature's energy refinery indicates that the many tiers of biological evolution are subsumed into four major levels of development. These levels correspond to four stages of delegation in a planetary company that involves the whole of biological life on earth. From the top down, they correspond to the managerial, administrative, supervisory, and functional levels of work in an ordinary company. They may be summarized as follows:

1 *Creative energies* give *form to idea* and direction to knowledge.
2 *Conscious energies* give *form to knowledge* and direction to routine.
3 *Sensitive energies* give *form to routine* and direction to body movement.
4 *Vital energies* give *form to body form* and direction to molecular structure.

There is only one species of man. From this assessment of the evolutionary hierarchy, it appears that he is destined for a managerial position. The problem is that there is a four-level company to be managed, while as yet man is able to relate only to the functional cultural level, and supervisory technological level, in the managerial hierarchy. The administrative level requires a universal framework of understanding through which creative energies of cosmic origin can find appropriate expression.

The boat is turned sharply to head in straight along the upwind side of the dock. The water is shallow, so the motor is shut off and tilted to let the boat coast the last few feet to the dock. The stake at the end of the dock is caught from the rear of the boat to stop forward progress. Then the boat is swung around to the other side of the dock and tied up with the point facing out. This way the waves won't splash over the stern and fill the boat with water.

There is something about being near water that aids reflection on the many aspects of the system. Water is a fluid body that yields in compliance to the forces that enclose it. Its moods of change are expressed in the condition of its surface; accordingly, its surface reflects the conditions that contain it. Today, the wind has stirred its surface to angular, choppy waves following in unending procession to the shore. The colors of the sky, the scattered clouds, and the surrounding hills are all mixing by themselves as on a living palette left behind as a curiosity by some mysterious master artist long ago. In the middle of it all, the sun is reflecting in a million pieces, as if a colossal crystal chandelier has smashed to smithereens and is strewn across the surface. Each piece reflects with a knowing wink, then disappears to be replaced by another piece, as if the chandelier is still smashing even while the mess is being cleaned up. The polar aspects of the absolute are reflected in the animated mirror of creation. That's what it's all about.

There are a couple days of work needed to get everything together and checked out for the trip north. The tents must be erected and inspected before they are packed. Rainwear, winter clothing, camping equipment, tools, and various articles must be collected, not to mention food supplies and fuel. It is time to get started.

Three Mergansers

It is a hot sunny day—the last chance to get some fishing in before heading north. The boat is drifting slowly in a large shallow bay that extends from one side of the creek that was fished the other day. The water is only five or six feet deep. The bay provides ideal feeding ground for pike and also lends itself to casting, for the weeds are not plentiful enough to create much problem. The boat is paddled a couple of hundred feet, then allowed to drift while the circle around the boat is cast, then paddled some more, and so on. The lure, a red and white spoon about three inches long, is usually retrieved in spurts, with a rhythmic motion of the pole. This enhances the lure's action, also breaking its tendency to spin in one direction and twist the line.

Pike are loners who often range lazily in shallow water on sunny afternoons. A cast is placed beyond a patch of underwater ferns so that the lure will pass along one side. It is beginning to look like another dry run when a good-sized one comes out of nowhere, hitting only twenty feet from the boat. It strikes viciously, running about fifty feet before coming to a stop, then it takes off again. It is headed toward the open lake. The direction of drift is fortunate, for this one will take some time to land. Now it is dragging in heavily, angling to one side, and coming to the surface. Its tail breaks water in a flutter, sending spray flying, as it snakes out of sight like a rocket. Another good run, and it coasts to a stop. Again it begins to drag in heavily.

The pattern is always the same with big northerns. A sight to behold when they take off on a run, they soon tire, dragging back while they conserve strength for another run. It is a process of gradually wearing them down. With light tackle, it is wise not to bring them close to the boat until their strength is spent, but it is essential to keep the pole bent and the line taut at all times. The idea is to

play the fish at a moderate distance, working it closer as it tires.
Once or twice it tries to hug the bottom and pull away steadily, then
it reverts to the pattern of run and drag.

Gradually it can be felt weakening. A few more runs and it begins to turn belly-up. It makes another short spurt closer to the
boat, but now it is done. Brought in from the left, it is scooped into
the net, which is large, two feet across the mouth, but none too
large for this fish. It is a very nice northern, a shade over three feet
and well built, maybe fourteen pounds. It has taken twenty-five
or thirty minutes to land it.

It is beginning to kick around in the net. The fingers and thumb
are worked under the gill covers on each side at the top and
squeezed together hard. The fish becomes quite still. It was well
hooked, but not damaged. It is held up for one last look. It returns
an icy stare and cranks its body once. Placed gently over the side of
the boat, it first turns belly-up. A tug backward through the water
helps to oxygenate the gills, and the fish regains its equilibrium. At
first it glides slowly away from the boat, then it gives its tail a kick
and is gone.

That is enough of northern pike for one day. Across the lake
there is a point where flat rock angles into the water—a good place
to go for a swim. The boat is headed over, pulled up on the rock,
and tied to a bush. After a long, refreshing swim in a large circle out
into the lake, a comfortable spot is selected where the rock slopes
toward the sun.

The heat of the rock is pleasantly moderated by the moisture
from the swim. The sun feels like liquid life being poured over the
body. The song of a bird nearby echoes like an animated noise in
a world without form. The eyes are inadvertently opened for a second to look directly at the sun, then closed again quickly. The blind-
ing image of the sun persists inside the lids, gradually transforming
to a negative image of darkness against a vermilion background.
After awhile, this image also fades. It is strange that a positive image
should spontaneously transform into a negative image. There is a
polar dynamism involved that brings to mind the Taoist principles
of yin and yang.

Yin is the passive principle of darkness, while yang is the active
principle of light. This is another ancient expression of the center-
periphery dilemma. The two principles are mutually reconciled in a
dynamic, communicative equilibrium that defines the nature of
activity. The symbol in Figure 15 graphically illustrates this point. It

15

is as if the one principle were chasing the other in a circle, each one being interpenetrated by the other at its center.

Yin represents the female principle in the universe, exhibiting receptiveness, negation, cold, weakness, pliability, and so on. Yang represents the corresponding male principles of activeness, affirmation, heat, strength, and firmness. According to this teaching, everything in the universe derives from the harmonious blending of these two principles; all actions are properly undertaken in accordance with the seasons they define. Suns clustered in galaxies provide the passiveness of sky dimension. Light from suns interpenetrates the darkness to bring to light planets, which further exemplify the principles in their rotations, alternately exposing their surfaces to warm days and cool nights so that a rhythm to life is established in wakefulness and sleep. Weather develops according to concentrations of heat and cold, land and water. Growth and activity become regulated accordingly; thus the fundamental principles proliferate throughout existence.

It is a common error to regard light as something and darkness as nothing. Darkness too is something—something more than the absence of light. As the passive principle in the polar relationship, it is just as authentic as the active principle. Light and darkness are complementary aspects of the same totality. They are mutually defined through their mutual relationship.

The language deficiency of modern technology has entrenched its position by developing a form of binary logic that first acknowledges a polar aspect to all being, but then denies validity to the passive pole. Boolean algebra, the root language of the digital computer, depends essentially upon the ability to express all activity in variations of the copulative verb "to be." All activity is acknowledged as a form of being; all being is acknowledged as a form of activity. Being is a verb. Because it is, it also has an ambiguous quality associated with the interplay of a specific and a nonspecific aspect, the active and passive principles of yang and yin.

In the application of the digital computer, this polar nature of being is not recognized by the digital computer. Instead there is a constant presentation of a choice between *being* or *not being*. Being is treated as a concrete, material fact lacking any ambiguous quality, and not being is treated as the extinction of all trace of being quality. A language of division has been contrived that can only endlessly recite the already overworked lines of Hamlet's soliloquy. "To be or not to be" is the only question the computer can deal with. Nothing can be reconciled in its essence to anything else. A dichotomous language doesn't contribute to communicative understanding.

In contrast, the twin principles of yin and yang portray a harmonious marriage. The dualism transcends itself in the mutual interaction of the principles to give birth to a living interpretation of creation. The polarity provides for a language of life.

Taoism is very old. Legend has it that about twenty-five hundred years ago a venerable sage named Lao Tzu, disheartened by the uncomely behavior of his contemporaries, was leaving his village to live out his remaining time in solitude. At the China frontier, an official, wishing to preserve some remnants of the sage's wisdom, prevailed upon him to set down the basis of his teaching in writing. This he did in a book of eighty-one poems called the *Tao Te Ching*.* Regarded as central to Taoism, these poems are understood to portray the way of life. A prevalent theme throughout is the dynamic interdependence of the active and passive principles of yin and yang. Poem 11 is a good example:

> *Thirty spokes will converge*
> *In the hub of a wheel;*
> *But the use of the cart*
> *Will depend on the part*
> *Of the hub that is void.*
>
> *With a wall all around*
> *A clay bowl is molded;*
> *But the use of the bowl*
> *Will depend on the part*
> *Of the bowl that is void*
>
> *Cut out windows and doors*
> *In the house as you build;*
> *But the use of the house*

*R. B. Blakney, trans., *The Way of Life* (New York: Mentor Books, 1955).

Will depend on the space
In the walls that is void.

So advantage is had
From whatever is there;
But usefulness rises
From whatever is not.

About the time that Lao Tzu was writing his poems in China, a prince in India renounced his royal privileges, leaving his family to pursue an ascetic search for enlightenment. Subsequent to his quest, Siddhartha Gautama proceeded to teach of an enlightened mind, called a Bodhi mind, to which one may become awakened through proper discipline. As this Buddhist teaching grew in popularity, its message spread through Tibet, Southeast Asia, and China.

Buddhist teaching has followed two streams. The mainstream, called Mahayana Buddhism, has spread through Tibet, China, and eastward into Japan, while Hinayana Buddhism preserves a more conservative approach in the south. Zen Buddhism, of the former stream, has been influenced in its movement through China to Japan by an exchange with Taoist thought. The two are essentially in accord, since Buddhism also recognizes the polar character of experience. Of particular importance in this regard is the void, and the realization of a dynamic identity between form and emptiness. This is not just a matter of conjecture based on a few isolated insights in the distant past, but a current central part of the Zen experience that has been transmitted from teacher to student for centuries.

Buddhism preserves many of the ideas of its Hindu origins, essentially the main, underlying theme, but with the large assortment of divinities, semidivinities, and historical figures stripped away. The Hindu tradition is one of the very oldest in human society. The historical and archeological evidence indicates it is the issue of a marriage between an ancient Aryan people of unknown origin in central Asia and a culture in the Indus valley that was already well established four thousand years ago.

Hindu thought is thoroughly permeated by the idea of spiritual evolution. In its own way, it recognizes man's place as the last tier in nature's energy refinery. Evolution is seen as a progressive integration of spiritual awareness through successive cycles of reincarnation upward through the tiers of animate life forms to man, where the possibility exists of an awakening to the universal significance of creation. Also recognized is an involutionary counterstream, cascading down through the tiers toward fragmentation and decay.

The Hindu and Buddhist concept of karma concerns the influence of ordered energies from the past, including those from past lives, that tend to determine the destiny of the individual. These influences may be both involutionary and evolutionary. Both teachings strive to develop the evolutionary potential of the individual through their disciplines, which encourage the involutionary trend to fall away. A quest for certain powers, or unique qualities of experience, is not the main intent. Buddhism in particular recognizes a practical discipline of living as an essential basis for a proper spiritual development; sometimes special emphasis is placed upon it, as in the controlled environment of the monastery. In both teachings, basic elements of the system are recognized and communicated through a discipline of thought and behavior that can eventually lead to independent insights.

Throughout the East, for centuries, the emphasis has been on the development of the implicit spiritual side of experience, through an intuitive quest. The concern is not with a future objective salvation, but with an immediate realization, a more fundamental insight into one's own nature. Although such insights must be assimilated into everyday experience, it is the intuitive hemisphere of the brain that receives the primary focus of attention.

Through every kind of terrain, the signposts to the system are there along the roadside. Sometimes they point out the hazards, other times the general direction, the turns or forks in the road. Through the hill country of the Eastern philosophies, many of the basic signposts have been maintained in a good state of repair, standing out clearly against the landscape. It is in the congested valleys of the industrialized West that they are often obscured along detours or diversions cluttered with neon lights and billboard advertising. The system signposts are still there, but they have to be carefully sought out.

The mainstream of cultural development in the West has proceeded via the Judeo-Christian tradition, which also has origins reaching back four thousand years or so. Early Christianity had an esoteric side that was associated with insights into the system. There were definite links to the mysteries of ancient Egypt, preoccupied with questions of eternal life and resurrection. The pyramids are also related, particularly the great pyramids of the Old Kingdom at Giza.

A few centuries prior to Christianity, the Greek thinkers, notably the Pythagoreans and Plato, also had links with esoteric systems of understanding. Others, such as Plato's pupil Aristotle, rejected this as so much mystical nonsense. It was popular with the Greeks and Romans in those days to characterize ideal spiritual types in a variety of gods that rendered experience more easily manageable and served to regiment thought into definite channels. The gods, who were often invested with human failings, served as behavioral archetypes. It was the definiteness of ideas like Aristotle's laws of identity and causality that appealed to the regimented Roman mind. The esoteric side of both Greek thought and religion was brushed aside by the Romans—the empire served to accommodate the seeds of causal determinism, side-by-side with the explicit aspects of the Christian message.

The bones of the rest of the story have already been exposed. Events in the West have focused on the explicit, material side of experience. The language hemisphere of the brain, concerned with explicit techniques of performance, has received the bulk of attention. A complex technology has evolved that now implicates the whole of human society, yet it has matured independently of man's spiritual development. We shall come back to the reasons for this later.

The stream of thought is broken by the sound of ducks nearby, in a small cove beside the point. There are three young mergansers, commonly known as fish ducks, in the shallow water close to shore. It is unusual to see only three together—generally there are a dozen or so in a brood, and they usually stick together until migration. Over half grown, these are fending for themselves. They swim together back and forth along the shoreline, quacking occasionally to one another. Every once in a while they make a dive, one after the other, always emerging close together. Soon one of the ducks pops up with a minnow about four inches long held crossways in its beak. Before it can turn the minnow to swallow it, the two companions make a noisy rush for it. The duck with the minnow swims with the inspiration that the promise of a full belly provides, downing the minnow in a flash. All three of them then go back to their pattern of swimming along the shoreline.

One creature is often sacrificed to sustain another, but numbers are always sufficient to maintain a balance of species. In fact, this kind of sacrifice is often essential to maintaining a balance in the biosphere. Frequently, species that are higher on the evolutionary ladder have a defensive or predatory advantage.

The biosphere is the name given to the skin of biological life that encloses the surface of the planet. It consists of all of the inter-related complexity of living systems in the atmosphere, the oceans, and the top few meters of earth. The biosphere is a unified field, a closed, unbounded, active interface to all life on the planet. Therein, each form of life seeks a dynamic equilibrium with the whole.

As for mergansers, they are born fishermen. When just young balls of fluff, they can follow the erratic darting motions of a fright-ened minnow in flight, dunking their heads to pluck it from the water with unerring accuracy. They also have a wide variety of expe-rience. Their early life is spent almost exclusively on the surface of the water between two worlds, but as they mature, they learn a degree of mastery over both the world above and the world below. They learn to dive and swim considerable distances underwater, and of course, they are migratory birds as well. They are most at home, however, on the surface of the water where the great majority of their time is spent.

There is a sense in which this parallels human experience, but for us the surface is between the worlds of implicit insight and ex-plicit technique. We are at the surface where the two worlds meet, where spiritual insight is reconciled with material technique. There are many ways in which this reconciliation can produce a surface—we should be careful how we choose our rest. There is a different surface for every framework of understanding—like myriad worlds of individual lakes. Some are stagnant little ponds, some may be extensive water systems, even seas or oceans, but in relation to the biosphere there is a system through which all these independent surfaces are sustained alike.

All frameworks of understanding order our mental processes in a certain way, making it necessary to see the subject matter through special eyeglasses that focus on those aspects deemed important. Different subject matter requires a different set of glasses, but with the system we can avoid the necessity of changing glasses every time we change our focus.

This is where a special difficulty associated with understanding the system comes in. It is necessary to rework already formed iso-lated worlds of abstraction into a unified framework—to relearn what is already thought to be understood. The result is not some-thing different understood; it is something understood differently. This means bringing the two hemispheres of the brain into a mu-tually complementary function that also finds a suitable balance with the limbic polarity. The language of science and the language of spiritual insight, though each with independent concerns, must find a common framework that is consistent with our evolutionary heritage.

The three mergansers have worked their way along the shoreline, out of the little cove and around the point. Until now their view has been obstructed by the point of rock, but they are suddenly startled by a human presence. They all turn tail at once and scoot back along the shoreline, frantically flapping their wings to increase their speed in the water. When they reach what they feel is a safe distance they skid to a stop, returning to their normal routine.

It is only mid-afternoon, but time to head back to camp. There are still a few final preparations to make for the trip north. There is some high scattered cloud appearing, but with any luck the weather will hold good for the trip. There is no wind. The lake is like a mirror. Another short swim is taken to cool off, then the boat is pushed out and headed for camp.

8

Sky Walk

There is an ideal spot about a quarter of a mile from the cottage where the boat trailer can be backed onto a sandy beach to the edge of the lake. There the boat is cranked up onto the trailer, firmly secured, then driven back to camp to finish the chore of loading. One of the main problems is going to be gasoline. It will have to be used sparingly. Fortunately a ten-horsepower motor on a fifteen-foot open fishing boat is conservative on fuel consumption, since it will not be practical to take more than about fifty gallons along. The lake in question is quite large, about twenty miles long, so that an outboard motor is a necessity for getting around. The canoe will serve for fishing close to camp, permitting the use of the motor to be restricted to only a few hours a week.

Although there is no proper access to the lake except by aircraft on floats, there is an obscure logging trail that goes right to the water's edge. With care, this logging trail is passable by car. Apart from an unusual Indian couple, the lake is deserted and many miles from civilization. There are thousands like it, but this lake is especially familiar, and there will be a chance to visit with a couple of old friends.

Everything is loaded now—just needs a final check down the list. The tools check out okay; the extra rope is in; a couple of small pieces of plywood; a small roll of plastic sheeting; all the fishing and camping gear; heavy clothing; pots, pans, and dishes; enough groceries for three months—it makes quite a collection. How did the Indians ever get along?

After the evening meal a walk seems in order. There is a grove of trees nestled between the hill behind the cottage and the lake, extending for a long distance in both directions from the cottage. Toward the west it becomes almost exclusively cedars. The village graveyard is also in this direction, but on top of the hill that extends parallel behind the grove.

The thick fortress of cedar trunks supports a mass of matted verdure that blots out the sky. The ground is void of any growth, overlain with a spongy carpet of decaying foliage. The air is deathly still. The steeples of the treetops protrude in solemn silence above the unpretentious sanctity of a country church. Here and there along the way the dignity of the setting is shattered by a squirrel or chipmunk, chattering provokedly at the intrusion.

Nature's theater is a planetary extravaganza, an exotic tapestry of variegated stages, spontaneously transmuting in lighting, atmosphere, and mood. Abounding in phantasmagorical display, a multitude of scenes is synchronized into a symphonic orchestration, each performance reaching balance in blending with the whole. The drama is tastefully arranged across the master stage, in a broad, mellifluous band around its planetary girth. Even in the frigid wastelands of polar settings, fascinating epics unfold through months' long days and nights, with fluctuating twilights in between. Each of the continental stages is graced with a prodigious assortment of prairies, jungles, deserts, peaks, with many ingenious added touches to the sets. Sometimes the stages run independent scenes, others share the same cast of characters, while the performance in the oceans has a topology of its own, regulated by tides and major currents. This colossus of a theater is called the Biosphere, the totality of planetary life, and the name of nature's energy refinery.

Given the complex structure of a theater that has gone through so many renovations since the beginning of the show, the performers belong to an equally complex theatrical guild, many of them displaying temperamental preferences as to where they will perform. Most categories of invertebrates prefer a script written for the sea, the great exception being a million species of insects that infest the land. The mammals and reptiles are predisposed to play parts on land, yet the largest creatures ever, the whales, share their dominion of the seas with a supporting cast of cousins, the porpoises and dolphins. Few other mammals like the ocean setting—the only reptiles that have been persuaded to take extended parts are the turtle and the snake. Birds are the most versatile performers. Some migrate from one polar region to the other, supporting themselves by playing bit parts in local scenes along the way. Other birds, who can't be bothered with the exertion of such active roles, have given up on flight—the Oscar for the most bizarre going to the penguin.

Although many birds can swim and dive, this one does little else, choosing the most inhospitable stage on earth. As for man, he started out humbly enough, but now, with his machines, no stage is free of him. He dominates the drama, even changes the sets and tries to rewrite the script, without knowing what the plot is all about.

Just a brief theatrical tour impresses any visitor with the variety of the performance from one location to the next. There is such a range from the lavish mob scenes in the teeming jungles of Brazil, to the shoestring-budget productions in the desolation of the Sahara. The feedstock to the energy refinery fluctuates drastically in its constituents. The tiers are populated to the brim in places, while other barren sets are abandoned to a few derelict performers.

Whatever the constituents, the refinement of energies seeks harmonic balance up and down the levels of the hierarchy. Reflux becomes regulated through experience. The players on each level of the hierarchy belong to different instrumental sections in the orchestration of the whole, only certain notes being sounded by certain instruments within each section. Percussion, brass, strings, and woodwinds may all be richly represented in grand symphonic movements, while across the way, a few faltering notes from flute and cello strive to sustain a single resonating chord. All these renditions meld into a resonating topology to the refinement of energies in the biosphere, modulated by the pace of celestial movements from night to day and from season to season. The closed, unbounded, active interface resonates in patterns that seek a biospheric balance.

The daily and seasonal regularity to the modulation of the music has a tendency to induce both complementary patterns and compensating balances in opposite hemispheres of the biosphere. This is implicit in the polar nature of the energies involved, the closed, unbounded character of the biosphere, and the modulated regularity to the resonating whole. Thus we find many examples of converging evolution in different parts of the world from very different ancestral stock, together with the complementary divergence that this implies. The South American rhea, the cassowary and emu of Australasia, and the African ostrich all are very similar yet come from different parentage. The fennec fox of the Sahara is smaller than the kit fox of America but with essentially identical traits, yet the two are unrelated. The sea cow of the tropical coast in America is thought to share a common ancestry with the elephant, yet the sea cow has adopted the characteristics of the unrelated sea lion,

seal, and walrus. Another relative of the elephant, the rock hyrax of
Africa and the Near East, has all the characteristics of a rodent, living in burrows and rock crevices. The evolutionary marketplace is
full of such examples of copying wherever biospheric resonance requires. It is one way in which the music gets filled out to achieve a
better balance.

Sometimes these complementary patterns are coupled with
geographic isolation that prevents interference from parallel evolving streams. For instance, a number of species of the hoofed ungulates evolved independently in South America before becoming
extinct when the isthmus of Panama appeared about a million years
ago. These had a strong tendency to resemble ungulates in other
parts of the world. There are a few modern descendants; the llama
and alpaca, for example, are counterparts of the camel.

The continent of Australia has been isolated for many millions
of years, providing a haven for the independent evolution of the
marsupials. In these mammals, the young fetus is not nourished inside the mother with the aid of a placenta. Instead the tiny, undeveloped fetus is required to crawl from the vagina into its mother's
external pouch, where it attaches itself to a nipple for the remainder
of its development. The marsupials have evolved from an ancestral
branch independent of that of the placental mammals, yet a distinguishing feature has been the evolution of species that correspond
closely to placental species. There are pouched marsupial counterparts to the dog, cat, mouse, mole, badger, anteater, and others. Of
further interest, the marsupials do not have the benefit of a corpus
callosum, the main nerve bundle that in the placentals connects the
two hemispheres of the new brain. A basis of comparison is thus
provided in similar species between two modes of cerebral function.
This is of special interest because of its relationship to language and
the bilateral polarization of brain function in man.

Progress through the cedar grove is obstructed at the eastern edge
of the cemetery by a fence that runs from near the lake, in a north-
erly direction up over the hill. A few moments' pause brings back
fond memories of childhood days—these cedars used to be a favorite playground. The presence of the cemetery had always gone unnoticed during the day; then, as darkness began to fall, every shape
and shadow assumed a sinister appearance. Sometimes a few of us
would huddle together next to the graveyard fence, telling spook
stories. Then, when least expected, one of us would let out a blood-
curdling scream. We would run out of there terrified. There isn't

any sign that children play here anymore. There are no forts or tree houses. None of the trees has that climbed-in look.

Leaving the seclusion of the cedars for the shore of the lake reveals the magnificence of the evening sunset. The sky is streaked with feathered clouds, fanning out from the western horizon like huge ostrich plumes. The sun is sinking low behind them, flirting with them, casting shafts of light between them, like a fan dancer casting suggestive winks through the feathers of a fan. Near the sun the plumage is a brilliant molten gold, fringes ignited with pure light. The gold streams outward into a deeper luster, consumed by crimson as it flares across the sky. Great chariots of color wane to muted mauve, then blend toward the east with a retiring violet, dissolving into darkness.

The surface of the lake is as still as it can be. It gives no hint of being there. It is hiding in its stillness like a seeker after an exacting perception of reality, apprehensive that disruption might mutilate its vision, transform an integrated picture into its own confusion. It does not betray its presence, reflecting without a flaw, a symmetry to the surrounding hills. It mirrors the spectacle in the sky to absolute perfection. The far shore arches like a fantastic land bridge across a hole right through the earth. The colored clouds come down beneath the feet, poised on the edge of a horrendous cliff: there is only endless sky below.

The mind is a hall of mirrors that reflect a sky within us. We see not the mirrors, but reflections of experience in reflux across perceptual axes of the creative process, as it evolves along. Biospheric resonance is the theme song of the drama, providing an operating field for the creative intelligence implicit in the global undertaking.

Every culture has its creation myths, from the garden of Eden to grandfather fire, the embellishments of primitive cultures being no less credible than those of objective causality. The spectacles of science have been focused to overlook the evidence. Since Darwin, evolutionary theory has fixated on the natural selection of accidental mutants—survival of the fittest—as the sole determinant of linear evolving streams. A minor fragment of the picture has been overblown into the most elaborate creation myth of all. While it's true that the branches of the evolutionary tree have been meticulously sorted out, compulsory worship at the altar of accidental cause is sustained on very flimsy ground. The branches of the tree are also roots that converge again and again into a common trunk, which culminates in man.

The plants have minimal capacity for sensitive response. This drama is given to invertebrates to explore. Conscious reflux, the vertebrate domain, has been deprived the liberties of multiple limbs and eyes. The cornerstone of vertebrate evolution has been a fixed limb structure, refluxing energies through the autonomic nervous system into cerebral awareness.

The autonomic nervous system has two major divisions: the sympathetic system, concerned with fueling the energies to the organs and muscles of the body in an emotive pattern to sustain activity, and the parasympathetic system, concerned with the maintenance and long-term interests of the organism. The two divisions, which come together in the limbic system, function in mutual polar restraint. Explicit performance is weighed off against implicit capabilities.

Vertebrate evolution is the embodiment of spiritual evolution, facilitated by the conscious reflux of energies that are patterned through the experience of the drama. The two autonomic divisions mirror a correspondence to the bilateral polarities of the two cerebral hemispheres. The explicit sympathetic system corresponds to the product-processing/organizing-and-manning polarity of the language hemisphere. The implicit parasympathetic system corresponds to the product-development/treasury polarity of the intuitive hemisphere.

The mutual mirroring occurs across the sales/marketing limbic polarity which has functioned as the evolving stem. Cerebral mentation is thus the market for autonomic energies, while animating autonomic energies are the market for patterns of mentation. An emotive balance becomes effected between them through the lessons of experience. This general arrangement is illustrated in Figure 16, the polarities being designated by capital letters.

An outstanding feature of vertebrate cerebral organization is the topological representation of the body in mirror symmetries between left and right hemispheres, and between front and back in both hemispheres. Sensory data from each side of the body is represented in the opposite hemisphere, there being both a major and a minor area on each side of the brain to the rear of the central fissure across the cortex. Mirrored to the front of this central fissure are major and minor motor areas in each hemisphere, associated with formulating behavior for the opposite side of the body. The body is thus represented symmetrically by the neurons of the brain in a total of eight areas, four of them sensory, four of them motor. These function in motor/sensory polar pairs that act as focal points for

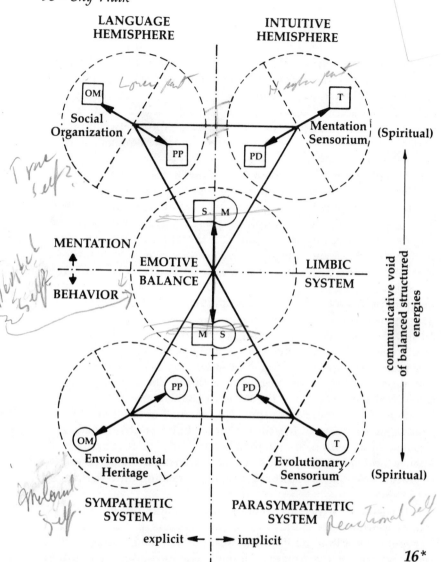

LANGUAGE HEMISPHERE

INTUITIVE HEMISPHERE

OM

Social Organization

PP

T

Mentation Sensorium (Spiritual)

PD

S M

MENTATION

EMOTIVE BALANCE

LIMBIC SYSTEM

BEHAVIOR

M S

PP

PD

OM

Environmental Heritage

T

Evolutionary Sensorium (Spiritual)

SYMPATHETIC SYSTEM

PARASYMPATHETIC SYSTEM

explicit ← | → implicit

communicative void of balanced structured energies

16*

*Emotive patterns do not necessarily bear a direct relationship to sympathetic function, but rather autonomic function is involved in recalling, monitoring, and tailoring them into a more appropriate pattern. The effect of removing the sympathetic system from animals is thus difficult to assess, whereas the parasympathetic system is essential to vertebrate life. Work in progress indicates that the sympathetic and somatic motor/sensory systems, working in parallel, are both tensionally linked to a common parasympathetic polarity that has two modes to it, as delineated in System 5. Ongoing sensory experience is thus tensionally coupled with parasympathetic recall of associated emotive patterns that may be refluxed into mentation for further tailoring and more suitable implementation.

two of the three polarities of creative activity, the third polarity being provided by the limbic system. Since only two polar pairs are sufficient to generate implicit ideation relative to explicit behavior, the two hemispheres of the brain can function independently, although they are both linked to a common emotional apparatus via the limbic polarity. This accounts for the adaptive flexibility of mentation, as well as for varying degrees of bilateral polarization between the two hemispheres, associated with the development of language and culture. At the same time both hemispheres of the brain are presented with a symmetrical data base to work from—the intuition and language can deal with the same set of circumstances.

Although language has given release to man's creative potential, it has also exposed him to amplified primal urgings from ancestral origins. Man's spiritual development is therefore a necessary companion to technological development, yet we have seen that these two aspects have developed independently. Not only are they concerned with different hemispheres of the brain, they have received independent emphasis in the hemispheres of the biosphere.

We have only touched on the host of evidence to indicate that biospheric resonance—the theme song of the drama—has been creatively exploited by converging species of the evolutionary tree. A similar creative exploitation is likewise evidenced in man's social evolution, reaching back to prehistoric times. The fossil record indicates an absence of man in the Western Hemisphere until about fifteen to twenty thousand years ago. One-half of modern man's brief presence on earth has thus been confined to Africa, Asia, and Europe, along with primitive man before him. The features, languages, and spiritual traditions of the American Indian all point to a migration from Asia, spiritual traditions persisting until the white man came.

It was during the latter half of modern man's presence that more sophisticated cultures evolved across parts of Asia, Africa, and Europe, the spiritual traditions indigenous to Asia being preserved securely apart by the American Indian. The roots of these traditions are still in evidence, in the spiritual beliefs and customs fostered across most of Asia today. They have survived these thousands of years without benefit of formal organization, undisturbed by the emergence of Taoism and Buddhism, there being no serious dissonance between them.

Early cultural development was confined to a functional level of delegation, involving manual techniques. The cultivation of human skills brought better tools, architecture, and art; then with the written word man acquired the ability to record his own development. Historic progress of the past couple of thousand years, though it has overlain these early events, has also interacted with them. The technological advance moving westward with Christianity conflicted sharply with Indian culture. In contrast, the complementary spiritual advance moving eastward with Buddhism was gained peacefully on its own merit. Any tendency to convergence between the two streams was forestalled by the expansion of the Islamic empire between them.

The resonant stepping-stones continued to be in evidence. The explosion of discoveries born in the Renaissance was accompanied also by explosive events in the East. In the years just prior to the Renaissance, Temujin, known to the world as Genghis Khan, was establishing a power base in Mongolia, committed to preserving a shamanist, nomadic tradition. The Mongolian hordes swept across China, thence into Turkestan, Persia, India, and Russia, to eventually establish an empire from the Pacific Ocean across the breadth of Asia into eastern Europe. A spirit culture reigned supreme for more than two centuries across half the world. Though it crushed the power of Islam, the ruthless conquest was marked by tolerance of all spiritual traditions. The Mongols had no organized tradition to impose, spirituality being acknowledged as an individual concern. Nevertheless, a spirit culture conquest in the East was complemented by the defeat of one in the West.

Since the Renaissance, technological growth has been linked to the evolution of machines, with a shift in emphasis from manual to intellectual involvement. Man's functional role has become secondary to his supervisory role, now expressed through a complex international economy that implicitly involves the organization and commitment of resources on a planetary scale. But this technological growth, linked as it is to a deficient understanding, has also not been without resonant implications. The dichotomous ideologies of East and West stand poised in readiness for mutual destruction, together with the obliteration of four billion years of evolution. Unfortunately, kind words alone are not enough to bridge the gap. We need a new synthesis. It is not the survival of the fittest that matters. It is the survival of us all.

There has been an underlying dilemma in the unfolding of the plot. In the biospheric enterprise of man, technology corresponds to product processing in the structured context of our cultures. Spiritual insight, funded by a treasury of wonder, corresponds to product development. At the functional and supervisory levels of delegation, these two concerns—technology and spiritual insight—must be independent, just as in the example of the construction company. But now all countries and cultures have become exposed to the relentless march of technology. The movement westward has gone full circle, while the movement eastward has reached the West to kindle a spark of interest in the Eastern philosophies. The human enterprise has expanded to the limits of control that can be exercised in a three-level organization, linguistic forms and concepts being confined to the functional and supervisory levels of delegation. A global enterprise requires a four-level organization, indicating a third level of delegation. The new synthesis must therefore facilitate the refinement of energies at the administrative level, the three polarities becoming integrated into a common framework of understanding. This requires that the language of science work in concert with spiritual insight to bring cerebral function to effect a balance with our heritage.

The sun is taking a last private peek through the treetops before slipping from the stage to let the vampire night drain the colors slowly from a chameleon sky. The shoreline has taken a turn around a gradual point, where outflows of spring water cut across the sandy beach. After an ice-cold drink, the sloping bank is climbed back into the cedar grove.

There is a place to squeeze through the rails of the cemetery fence, thence through some long grass to the top of the hill, where the cemetery is maintained in fairly good condition. The plots are arranged around a very large spruce tree with branches hanging nearly to the ground. Most of the tombstones are modest, some of them are homemade, and three or four are leaning badly to one side. Some graves are indicated only by a depression in the ground.

A lot can be told about a village from its cemetery. Many people in this village are interrelated, the tombstones keeping a solemn record of the family trees. There are an unusual number of children's graves, but most of the adults have lived to very respectable ages.

There is a story associated with each grave, a story lived out but largely left untold. Each story appears to terminate here in the ground to be commemorated by terse engravings on a stone. Is this all that remains of the years of strife and struggle, searching for fulfillment with it always just one step away? Pleasures come, but so does pain, and for every joy in life, it seems an agony must be endured. Is everything just canceled out then? Do we come to this world crying, helpless, and afraid, only to leave it in the same way with no hope of answers to our questions in between?

The cyclic nature of the system indicates that death is the antithesis not of life, but of birth. If life transcends the brief episodes on earth, then there is a meaningful progression through it all. But to judge the price of progress in terms of human suffering through the ages brings wonder at the monumental value invested in the enterprise. We cannot have yet begun to glimpse the cosmic proportions of our destiny.

An ethereal thief has robbed the riches from the sky. Darkness won't be long in following in pursuit. The long hard trip ahead tomorrow will need an early start. It will take a full day to reach the intended campsite and erect the tents before nightfall. It's time to get some sleep.

Part 2
The System

9 Voices in the Wilderness

The western shoreline fades from point to point toward the north, disguised in metered increments of haze until it blends with the distant dark blanket of cloud that hangs heavy all across the northern sky. The sun is winding up another circuit; soon it will hide beyond the massive cloud bank that arches into the western horizon. The wind, unsure of its direction, favors the quadrant from the northwest, and although not strong, it has a steady perseverance. The weather has cooperated for the trip, but now uncertain threats are brewing in the north.

The lake is about a mile across at this point. From here on the northernmost tip of the island, it is visible for several miles toward the north. It lies stretched out straight and narrow from north to south with both shorelines serrated in an irregular pattern of bays and inlets, especially along the eastern side. The lake presents a very private world, with a character of its own, enclosed unto itself within the rim of the confining shoreline. The molded fluid bulk of its body searches for escape with contorted fingers reaching through haphazard gaps in the tightly laced girdle of constraining hills. The wooded hills crowd in adjacent to the shore to incarcerate the lake with a bristling picket fence. The attention is imprisoned with the lake, confined to a tiny cell of the wilderness that sprawls for hundreds of miles in all directions. Yet there is a liberation that comes with the completeness of the confinement. It has to do with sky, for each individuated world shares a common sky in a way that shows it to be representative of the whole. The common underlying pattern is whispered to the sky. The wilderness has a liberating voice.

Far to the north the distant call of a loon projects for miles across the water, echoing through the hills. It begins with a single note, clear and prolonged, that breaks and rises to a climax, then trails off softly into echoes. Another loon answers in a frenzied vibrato, then another, with calls rising in a succession of crescendos, then another. Then all wait and listen while the echoes spend their energies rebounding through the hills for miles. Not all the voices of the wilderness are whispered—none is more expressive of the resplendence of its spirit than the majestic call of the loon. There is no music more beautiful on earth than that intoned by this most talented of all the birds.

A small pail is dipped partly full of water and taken back around the rocky point to where camp has been established on the northeast side of the island. A fire has already been started. The small pail is placed across the narrow gap between two piles of flat stones that form the fireplace. The fire is adjusted a bit, and some smaller sticks are placed underneath and around the pail. A pine log, a few feet away, provides a place to sit and tend the fire, as well as a view across the channel to the eastern shore. The island is about halfway down the lake, only a hundred yards or so from the eastern shore.

A granite shelf about eight feet above the water affords an almost level campsite with just the right amount of slope for natural drainage. It comes furnished with a few pine trees and a sparse parging of earth overlaid with a carpet of moss and needles, backing on the thick forest of coniferous growth that covers the rest of the island. The main tent has been erected so that the window on one side looks out over the edge of the shelf and across the channel. The entrance opens to the north, from which the site gradually tapers into a granite ramp that renders a natural access to the lake. There is a tall, graceful white pine miraculously growing near the edge of the solid rock shelf, just a few feet from the front corner of the tent, and there are a couple of red pines to the rear. The campfire is ten or fifteen feet from the other front corner of the tent, a few feet away from the overhanging branches of the pine tree. It is an ideal setting, with a small cove, adjacent to the shelf and a little to the rear of the tent, that is a good spot for the boat.

The water is starting to boil. A stick is poked under the wire handle to lift the small pail from the fire. It is placed to one side, on the flat rock beside the fire where it will stay warm, and a couple of tea bags are dropped in. A lunch was packed for the trip—there are still some sandwiches left. Everything has been unloaded from the boat into the tent, but since nothing is unpacked yet, it isn't convenient to cook.

The last refreshment was a cup of coffee about four hours ago with Adam and Agnes. There was time for only a brief visit at their camp on the way down the lake, but it was good to see them both healthy and well. Agnes will soon be seventy—thirteen years older than Adam—yet she still keeps up with him. Until recently she used to help him run the trap line in midwinter; however, the last couple of years they have been spending the severe winter months on the reservation. A few small huts with canvas roof are hardly adequate for temperatures that sometimes get down to minus fifty degrees. They have lived in the same place for nearly twenty years, on a sandy peninsula about five miles up the lake. They will stop in for a visit whenever they get down this way.

It has been a warm sultry day, the kind that invites storm activity. A couple of green sticks are placed on the small fire to smoulder away, while the weather is checked again in the northern sky. The northwest tip of the island is stepped in a couple of weathered ledges that provide a benchlike place to sit and scan the lake. The cloud bank has advanced some. The sun has ducked its head behind it in a threatening masquerade. Filtered sunbeams are playing on the silhouettes of thunderheads that bulge above the massive hulk of cloud like gun turrets on an unknown, alien vessel. The storm is also moving to the east, still showing signs of passing like a silent ship through the coming night. The billowing turrets belch sporadic flashes with remote reports of thunder, as muffled guns wage a mysterious distant war. The breeze has mellowed slightly, breathing quietly in awe of the invasion in the north, hoping to avoid attention in the unprovoked attack.

The sky gives expression to the unity of the biosphere. Everything living on the planet shares a common sky. Even the life in lakes receives a continually renewed supply of life-giving water through the weather cycles in the sky. The biosphere is a closed, unbounded interface, a whole unto itself, but its wholeness is given in its relationship to sky. Clouds, horses, birds, flowers, crickets, trees, frogs, foxes, crocodiles, butterflies, and men, all contribute to the biosphere by sharing a common sky.

The sky itself is not something that can be known in a specific way. We see colors in it, clouds in it, the sun in it, the moon and stars in it, but we don't see the sky itself as something that can be quantified and measured. Despite this, the sky is not just empty space. The concept of space has been invented for the purpose of measurement. The space between heavenly bodies can be measured, but attempts to measure the sky can measure only the measuring device. Sky is unbounded and indeterminate—neither open nor closed. It has no specific properties. It is the passive, nonspecific aspect of being, the "yin" in yang and yin.

For a number of years prior to relativity theory, science wrestled with the question of how light can travel through vast reaches of interstellar space if it is totally empty, a vacuum in every respect. The apparent fact that light waves seem to travel through it indicates that there must be something there. Just as ocean waves are propagated through water, and sound waves through air, it seems logical that light waves must be propagated through *something*. For this reason, scientists postulated the existence of a luminiferous ether, conceived to be all-pervading, a sort of medium in which all phenomena occur. After extensive searches and subtle measurements of many kinds, they found no evidence whatsoever that such a thing exists. The search was finally abandoned, and Einstein, in postulating the basis for his theory of relativity, set the question aside, the view of a "stationary space" being superfluous. The receptive aspect to phenomena is implicitly nonspecific; yet it is *something*.

It has already been pointed out that the system unfolds in phases associated with the progression of number, that each phase is complete unto itself, and that each is subsumed by all of the phases that precede it. The first phase is manifest as the relationship of all things to indeterminate sky. In the system it is represented by the number one. It will be called System 1, just as the succeeding phases will be called System 2, System 3, System 4, and so on.

System 1 subsumes all the higher systems. All evidences of energy and substance find unity in a common relationship to unbounded sky. Everything from light to atomic particles, to molecules, to suns, planets, and galaxies, and to all forms of energy and life in all the galaxies in all the universe, is unified in sky. System 1 thus represents universal wholeness, a unity that is achieved through a common, receptive, nonspecific aspect to all being.

It should be emphasized again that the nonspecific aspect of being is not nothing. Even mathematics has been required to acknowledge that the number zero is not nothing, that it retains an indeterminate residual value. It is not possible to divide by the number zero because it can be represented by an infinitely small fraction that inverts to an infinitely large number. The inverse of zero is infinity.

Since everything must have its being within a context of universal wholeness, and since all being relates to a nonspecific aspect, being has an ambiguous quality. Being is the relationship of a specific aspect to a nonspecific aspect. The specific aspect is evidenced as an active center to experience; the nonspecific aspect, as a passive periphery. This is just a restatement of the complementary principles of yang and yin.

Being knows of the relationship between its center and its periphery in terms of the active process occurring across the structural interface between them. This amounts to a technical way of saying that everything communicates with sky. Everything finds a common unity in the sky. Everything seeks to know of this unity through the process occurring at its interface with sky.

In the system, an active interface will be referred to as a whole, but since wholes are perceived to manifest centers, it will be convenient to also call them centers. Anything that can be recognized to have an independent identity within any creative context is perceived in the system to be a whole, including galaxies, suns, planets, moons, people, plants, animals, wave fronts, objects, and manifestations of energy of all kinds.

Because being has an ambiguous quality, there is no possibility of designating a whole in any completely specific manner. Instead, the system designates it from two perspectives, one active and one passive. As with yang and yin, light will be taken to represent the active perspective, and darkness will be taken to represent the passive perspective. It is convenient to use light for the purposes of discussion, but the active aspect is intended to include all energy. The system indicates that everything is an elaboration of electromagnetic energy. A center or whole can then be represented from these two perspectives, as shown in Figure 17.

The designation from darkness is looking into the center toward light and is a passive abstracton of the system. It has no relevance to the system's operation. The designation from light is an active,

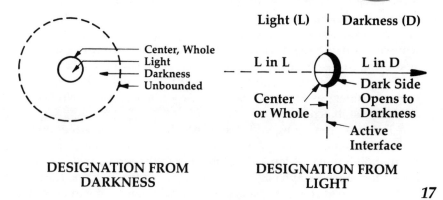

DESIGNATION FROM
DARKNESS

DESIGNATION FROM
LIGHT

17

though incomplete, illustration of the system at work. The two designations are mutually relevant; between them one may come to grasp the essence of the system. This method of designation will be used to delineate the higher systems, a single whole representing System 1. It indicates that everything manifests as a whole within universal wholeness through an unbounded active interface between an absolute center and an absolute periphery. Everything communicates with sky.

The storm is edging a little closer, but is still angling to the east. Darkness is beginning to creep cautiously out of hiding in the shadows, dissolving contrasts and obscuring fine detail along the shoreline. The haze overhead has taken on a soft, rose-colored hue, tinting everything with an artificial cosmetic to compensate for the angry furrows muttering profanities in the north. The enfeebled wind continues halfhearted efforts to decide on a direction, pushing midget ripplets gurgling into crevices along the rocky point.

A loon begins to sing a solo from the end of a long finger that pokes two or three miles into the hills to the northeast. It begins with a smooth and mellow number, the long clear note that breaks and rises to a climax, then trails off into silence, to listen as the sound comes rebounding out between the hills that confine the slender inlet. The mood-setting introduction entices a partner to lend its own interpretation to the simple tune, the two notes drifting out to blend into an aria of echoes. It is done with taste and timing, as they explore the resonant effects of the contours of the bay. Another pair of loons answers in an anxious vibrato from the broad bay across the lake, the arching shoreline acting like a band shell to project the melody out across the water. These are joined by others from down the lake, then from up the lake, by twos and fours from point to point and from bay to bay, for miles in both directions. They begin to answer back and forth in groups that join together with voices rising to crescendos, then these fall away with others answering from afar, then back again, up and down the lake in a fluid rhapsody of stereophonic movement. The impeccable orchestration proliferates across the water, cascading back and forth till calls are lost in echoes.

The hills are ringing with the wandering melodies—trees and rocks reverberating with proxy voices borrowed from the choir. The fluctuating intensities lend a composition to the whole that is punctuated for special emphasis by intermittent drumrolls in the northern sky, while gurgling ripplets play along, keeping time in crevices.

The musicians continue the performance, pausing here and there to listen for response, then join again as if on cue, so appropriate is their timing. They use the lake and hills as a uniquely constructed resonating instrument, and by their various select locations, they play it to perfection. The spontaneous concerto proceeds unbroken for fifteen or twenty minutes before the participants feel it time to let the echoes die away.

Loons have an intuitive sense of propriety, a gift for reading the many moods of their environment and giving them expression. They assimilate the whispers of the wilderness and transform them into music. They absorb the subtle energies from the sky around them, then project them once again, enhanced, into the sky. They have a spontaneous appreciation for what they do, a direct awareness of the communicative balance they effect. Each is an active interface with sky.

An active interface does not isolate a center from a periphery. Rather it relates them. All the same, a center or a whole has partitioning characteristics that define a subjective level of active intensity that is distinct from, although related to, an objective aspect. System 1 identifies the subjective active intensity as energy represented by light. Processes of all kinds are thus seen to involve energy transformations across an interface. All the evidence of our experience confirms that this is so. There is nothing that can be known with our senses, with our scientific instruments, or through the neuronal processes of our nervous system that doesn't depend on energy transformations at interfaces.

For instance, the nerve cells, or neurons, within the body of a loon maintain an electrical potential across the skin or membrane that encloses each cell. This is done through electrochemical processes that maintain the outside of the cell membrane at a positive potential with respect to the inside of the membrane. When a nerve cell is activated, this electrical potential discharges along the length of the cell to transmit an electrical impulse from one end of the cell to the other. The cell rapidly recharges itself to maintain its energy interface in a state of ready awareness.

Muscle cells exhibit action potentials in a similar way, so that the body of a loon is a highly structured pattern of energy interfaces. These mutually interact across synapses, or contact points, between individual neurons and also at terminations in muscles, all according to the manner in which the nervous system is structured. When a loon sings, there is an ongoing pattern of active intensity within its body that projects patterned energy as sound. Each nerve and muscle cell is an active interface within the body of the loon, which in turn responds as a whole, as an active interface with its environment. There are, however, two perspectives to the process.

From one perspective, nerve and muscle cells relate directly not to sky, but to an immediate environment in the body of the loon that contains and nourishes the cells themselves. The loon in turn sustains its identity within the biosphere. The biosphere is part of a solar system that is part of a galaxy that is part of a system of galaxies. In this sense the entire universe is a highly structured whole, refluxing energies on many levels that collectively communicate with sky. From this perspective, a loon is part of a succession of greater wholes.

From another perspective, the nerve cells of a loon do relate directly to sky. The electrochemical processes that occur across the cell membranes involve electronic interactions between atoms which are not just solid lumps packed tightly together. Atoms are in some respects similar to solar systems, with electrons in a series of concentric orbital shells around a nucleus. The spaces between the shells are very large compared with the size of an electron or with the size of the nucleus, just as the spaces between the planets are very large. The spaces between molecules are even larger. Solid matter, in fact, consists mostly of sky. There is a sense, therefore, in which the electronic energies that are sustained across the membranes of the nerve cells in the body of a loon *do* communicate directly with sky. There is a structured pattern of awareness, associated with a direct perception of sky, that is independent from, and yet related to, the pattern of activity in the biosphere. From this perspective the loon is a whole, complete unto itself, in a direct relationship with sky.*

These two perspectives are no different for men than they are for loons. Every living thing is a whole unto itself and also a part of something greater.** The system indicates that this common characteristic to experience is related in a fundamental way to electromagnetic energy.

These two primary perspectives to experience are delineated by

---

*The energy interface associated with the identity of the whole loon is more than the collection of its cells and molecules, yet in this context it is focused through them.

**Arthur Koestler has recognized this idea of a part-whole as a basic unit of organization. He calls it a holon and describes it as Janus-faced or looking in two directions. Arthur Koestler, *The Ghost in the Machine* (London: Pan Books, 1970).

System 2. The two wholes or centers to System 2 define two modes to a *term*, an association of two or more centers related together as one. The term in this case will be called perceptive wholeness. It has a subjective mode and an objective mode, depending on the orientation of the two centers in relation to one another. The objective mode, illustrated in Figure 18, is the perspective in which the loon relates directly out to sky. With one center inside another, their partitioning characteristics provide for two gradations of light, as shown. The second interface thus portrays a lower level of active intensity than the first, but the range of intensity from an absolute center to an absolute periphery still exists for both centers taken together. In this mode to the term, the two centers are distinct from one another, although one is inside the other, and there is a sequence or succession to the interface processes occurring at each center. The interface process at Center 2 follows that at Center 1 in a timelike succession. The interface processes at Center 1 sustain those at Center 2, which in turn relates directly to sky. Here we can think of the identity of the loon as being represented together with its cells and molecules in Center 2. Center 1 in this case represents more fundamental energy processes that are shared with the biosphere.

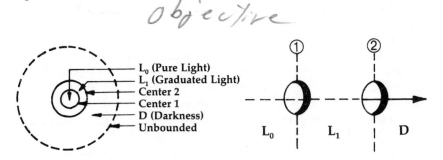

FROM DARKNESS   FROM LIGHT

18

The subjective mode to the term is illustrated in Figure 19. When two centers exist independently of one another, they mutually achieve identity through mutual perception. They are mutually perceived as one, but are two. It will be said that the two are coalesced as one, and the coalescence is designated as shown.

Each center, through its perception of identity, forms what will

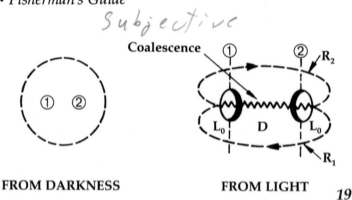

Subjective

Coalescence

R_2

L_0 D L_0

R_1

FROM DARKNESS   **FROM LIGHT**   *19*

be called a relational whole. The relational whole formed by Center 1 is designated as R_1; that formed by Center 2 as R_2. In this case the two relational wholes are simultaneous and countercurrent. Just as centers have a common periphery in darkness, this term indicates that they also find a mutual identity in light.

In contrast to the objective mode, the two processes of this subjective mode may be described as simultaneous as opposed to sequential—together they portray no subjective-to-objective distinction. There is a contraction involved between the two centers that tends to exclude a relationship to their mutual periphery in sky. The processes are indistinct. They occur together, just as a loon sustains its identity as an integral part of the biosphere.

The two modes to the perceptive-wholeness term are maintained in a state of dynamic balance through what will be called the *perceptual transposition* of Center 2. Center 2 alternately contains Center 1 to look out directly to sky, then turns around and faces Center 1 to achieve an identity with it in light. In other words, Center 2 alternately looks objectively outward, then subjectively inward. Perceptual transpositions can occur in many ways at many levels. All of the higher systems are subsumed within System 2, each exhibiting alternating objective-to-subjective perceptual modes. With this in mind let's take another look at the nervous system of a loon.

An individual nerve cell in a loon maintains a direct objective awareness of sky through the electronic interface across its membrane. When the nerve cell discharges, this electronic interface becomes perceptually transposed, turning to relate subjectively to the internal processes that are subsumed within the cell and its membrane skin. These electrochemical processes work to reflux energies, rapidly reestablishing the electronic charge behind the discharging interface, as it moves along the length of the cell. The active interface of the nerve cell thus relates alternately to objective darkness in sky and to subjective light in its own internal processes.

Within the nervous system as a whole, each perceptual transposition is effected across the synapse between one nerve cell and the next. The manner in which nerves are linked to relate to one another is thus of critical importance. Some nerve cells are very long, in a loon up to a foot or more in length, while others are microscopic in size. The job of a long nerve cell could not be properly done by several short nerve cells simply relaying an electrical impulse, because there are perceptual transpositions involved that enable nerve cells to work together in precise accord with the system. The nervous system as a whole is therefore very much more than a stimulus-response mechanism, conditioned in a series of causal sequences. A loon is an active, intelligent participant in the biosphere, independently aware of unbounded sky.

The biosphere as a whole is an integrated, intelligent system that also exhibits an alternating objective and subjective orientation with respect to light and darkness, effected through the rotation of the planet in relation to the sun. In the subjective mode of daytime, darkness is contracted through a coalescence with light at many levels, from electron orbits in the molecules of the atmosphere that make the sky blue, to various organic processes in plants and animals. In the objective mode of night, everything in the biosphere can look out to unbounded sky.

It can be seen then that perceptual transpositions occur in a wide variety of ways at various levels of organization. All occur to maintain a balance between perceptual modes oriented toward the center and toward the periphery of experience. The subjective mode represents a degree of closure in identity; the objective mode is open to unbounded sky.

The loons are silent now. The storm is rapidly approaching. A black arch has formed from horizon to horizon all across the leading edge of the cloud bank. The thunderheads, that rose like gun turrets, are now concealed by the angry rush of rolling black cloud that marks the front line of a direct attack. The billowing black arch forms a curling upper lip to a great yawning mouth, devouring the landscape whole in a single gulp. Inside the mouth is the solid dark gray of the storm itself, licking delectably with jagged tongues of lightning at choice morsels of the meal. The fire-spewing monster is belching with delight, regurgitating energies with vociferous roars, paying no heed to gluttony in an insatiable lust for more. The primal appetite is unquenchable. The storm is coming with a vicious charge. The wind, having turned decisively to the north, has gained a fierce momentum.

It is only a few hundred feet around the point back to camp, but there is hardly time enough to light the lantern and get inside the tent before the first large drops begin to fall. The campsite is well protected by a windbreak of trees, but the enraged north wind still buffets the tent severely. Fortunately it is staked down securely. A small hill on the west side of the island also gives some protection from a strike by lightning. The storm has hastened darkness. The temperature has dropped dramatically. The rain is pelting down with a vengeance now, the chill air sending shivers to the bone.

There is such a contrast to the repertoire of moods and voices of the wilderness, such a wide range to its assortment of experience. It has such varied dialogue that to understand it all is difficult. Yet all these languages share a common basis in the system.

For instance, all the terms in all the higher systems are constituted of interacting centers or wholes. All the terms within each higher system transform into one another through perceptual transpositions. Each higher system as a whole also exhibits a master interface or axis, about which there is an alternating objective-to-subjective perspective. Each higher system thus incorporates all the properties of both universal wholeness (System 1), and perceptive wholeness (System 2). The system continues to proliferate in this way, with each higher system incorporating the properties of all the systems that preceed it. This quality makes it possible to discuss the overall properties of any of the higher systems in the language of any of the lower systems.

It is somewhat like looking at a mountain from the distance. The mountain can be seen as a whole: one can talk about its overall shape and size. As one moves closer more detail is clear: one can talk about the overall patterns of forest and rock formation that constitute the mountain. The system proceeds like this, elaborating the details, but in discrete jumps associated with the progression of whole numbers. All the higher systems are there from the beginning, implicitly subsumed within the early systems, just as all the detail of the mountain is there, but cannot be seen from a distance.

The system has a related property that is like moving up to inspect an individual tree growing on the mountain: the lower systems can be used to elaborate on the detail of certain wholes within the higher systems. For instance it is possible to focus on the nervous system of a loon in the language of System 3, System 4, or

System 5 without detailed reference to the whole organism of the loon, which would require a system of a higher order. One can also focus on the digestive system, the respiratory system, or the endocrine system in a similar way. Each focus will still relate to the whole organism of the loon, but the sharpness of detail will be confined within the focus.

The first two systems transcend what we normally perceive as space and time. They subsume space and time, the origins of which will be delineated later by System 3. For now there are some further interesting points to explore regarding Systems 1 and 2.

The two modes of System 2 exhibit an alternating polarity associated with electromagnetic energy. Taken together they subsume the whole of experience, having both an explicit and an implicit component. The explicit component is commonly known as the electromagnetic spectrum. It is energy that is in a state of reflux through the creative process, as elaborated by the higher systems, being both emitted and utilized within that context. The implicit component is given by the alternating modes of the higher systems of the creative process itself.

Let's look at the explicit side first. The velocity of light, 186,000 miles per second, is a property not of light itself, but of the interaction between light and the higher systems, as these determine events with characteristics of space and time. Light waves are analogous to the waves on the surface of a lake, wave motion being an inherent property neither of wind nor water, but of their mutual interaction. Where there is no water, or no wind, there are no waves. Light cannot be seen traveling between the stars, just as one cannot see the wind alone.

The wide variance of the electromagnetic spectrum, from low frequencies with long wavelengths to high frequencies with short wavelengths, is determined by the relative partitioning characteristics of the two centers of System 2. At the low-frequency end of the spectrum, nearly all of the energy is partitioned across Center 1. Center 2 then portrays a low level of active intensity with comparatively slow cycles of perceptual transpositions, corresponding to low frequency and long wavelength. At the high-frequency end of the spectrum the reverse is true.

There is an important significance to the alternating modes in both the explicit and implicit components of electromagnetic energy. The objective mode can be described as expressive: it projects in a timelike succession to unbounded sky, with an expenditure of energy. The subjective mode can be described as regenerative, since each of the two centers receives energy from the other through their mutual coalescence in identity. The equilibrium established between these alternating modes thus effects a balance between the expenditure and regeneration of energy.

Let's now turn to the implicit side of electromagnetic energy. Imagine yourself to be hovering in a flying saucer at nighttime a few miles above the earth, which is covered with people standing shoulder to shoulder, each flicking a large flashlight on and off up into the sky. Each time they flick their lights on, energy is projected out to sky, as in the expressive mode of System 2. Each time they flick their lights off, their batteries are recharging, as in the regenerative mode of System 2. Some of the flashlights, however, are very bright, while some are very dim, with a whole spectrum in between—a thoroughly random mix. The bright lights must recharge their batteries more often than the dim ones; consequently they are switched on and off more quickly. From several miles up, individual lights will not stand out; the whole earth will appear as a universal active interface of light. Although there may be resonant patterns to the light, it will present a constant unbroken glow that fades out indeterminately in all directions. The alternating modes of System 2 across the spectrum are in this way subsumed within System 1.

The analogy, of course, is only a fabrication, for we cannot observe the whole process from the periphery. Each of us is a flashlight, flicking on and off. So are loons and fish, atoms, suns, and galaxies. On the one hand, everything projects to a common sky. On the other hand, all the recharge mechanisms are interrelated. There is only electromagnetic energy interacting with itself. There is nothing else. What's more, the whole process is intelligent. Electromagnetic energy is supreme intelligence—it subsumes all the higher systems.

The storm will be a long, protracted siege. The tent is shuddering uncontrollably, trembling in terror at the infuriated wind. Outside, the trees are straining to subdue their shrieks and sighs but can't help groaning out of grief at the misfortune of the night. Waves are smashing themselves relentlessly against an unsympathetic shore, pleading for release in suicidal plunges rebuked by cold, unmoving stone. Rain is thrashing down in sheets hurled in blind contempt, lashing out a punishment for transgressions now forgotten, but transmitted into sky. Cracking whips of lightning come searing through the air with resounding proclamations, as the raging monster that has arisen for the task of retribution takes hasty, frightful looks at the penance of its prisoner.

The lantern hisses out its light in mechanical disdain for the proceedings. It sheds a meager, moderating warmth, which rapidly disperses in the chill, damp air. The best thing to do is go to bed, with hope that the weather's mood will improve some through the night. A few things are rearranged inside the tent. The sleeping bag is unrolled on the floor along one side of the tent under the window next to the lake. The gas valve of the lantern is closed. The light gradually fades, blinking into darkness.

The darkness is total, like being stranded in a mine. The only companion is the cacophony of noise generated by the storm. Sounds have become untethered from the vision, to jostle about in independent patterns through the deep black murk. The mind tends to wander with the patterns, associating sounds, quick to focus on any strange irregularity. The night penetrates the skin and flesh to bring an aloneness that is not at all like solitude or loneliness. Everything is suspended in an indeterminate field of darkness. The whole body seems to look out independently through its cells to darkness. There is only suspension in aloneness, with wonder at a penetrating sky.

The night is harsh and cold, but the sleeping bag is warm, and tomorrow is another day.

10

Smudgy

A number of days have passed. Much of the time has been spent getting set up to stay awhile. A couple of small tents have been erected along the west edge of the site, where most of the long-term provisions will be kept. Although not strictly necessary, the small tents signify numbers and are good strategy for the many black bears in the area. They can destroy a camp in short order if they think no one is around. An island affords some protection, but once a bear swims out to it you have to share it with him until he decides to leave. The main thing is to avoid attracting bears by keeping the campsite clear of food odors and garbage.

Two or three days have been spent making a couple of small tables and a weatherproof cupboard to store cooking supplies in. The cupboard is lined with plastic sheeting, has split cedar slabs on the outside, slab shelves on the inside, and a flap in front. It stands adjacent to the pine tree. A few stumps cut from a log and set on end about chair height make ideal stools for sitting on. It's a very open floor plan, but home is beginning to look almost civilized. The toilet has been rigged back in the brush with a smooth birch pole nailed across a couple of trees. Although the mosquitoes are a little fierce at times, it serves the purpose.

Breakfast has just been finished, and the few dishes are being washed up. Here comes the hummingbird again, about the same time as yesterday. This makes four or five days in a row that it has flown in from the northeast, hovered around the camp for a couple of minutes, then darted off across the island. Its course hasn't varied by more than a few feet from one day to the next.

The camp stove and dishes are stacked inside the cupboard, and the wash water is dumped out behind one of the tents. There is still some hot tea in the pail—enough for another cup, which is carried to a stump in the shade of the white pine.

The branches overhead are animated by a gentle breeze, their tufted twigs waving sociably on limber branches, bowing slightly in a cordial display. White pines are refined and gracious trees. Their vital energies are ordered into complex branches that grow with sweeping gestures, pointing the direction of the prevailing wind. Though their trunks are tall and straight, their limbs curl in flowing clusters, like exotic arms waving in a dance toward the northeastern sky, even when the wind is still. Of all the trees in the northern forest, only these have been selected as nature's compass, in a pantomime of motion.

Red pines stretch up behind the tent with foliage evenly dispersed in bundles that are unresponsive in their pattern to the wind. Their needles are longer, coarser, and tufted into pairs collected on the ends of tougher twigs. Their arms are indistinct. They wave a multitude of hands in a fluent panoply, hinting mute messages to the breeze. Beyond, some black spruce stand like starving war-torn soldiers at attention. They have no hands, just many skinny arms with many fingers. Short needles crowd their surfaces like thick hair growing almost to the trunk. The lower branches have been sacrificed in the quest for light, to hang in ragged disarray, yet these trees are masters at survival through the frigid winters of the north.

Each species projects the distinctive pattern of its presence through its vital energies. Each has a character and personality of its own. But how is each tree linked with all trees of its species? How is each animal and bird linked with all members of its species? How is each of anything linked with all of its kind? This is the social mystery of each and all, all and each.

Within the nucleus of each living cell there is a genetic language locked up in the chemical bonds of the DNA molecule, but how does the language communicate? How does each cell communicate with all cells within each organic whole? How does the cell of a pine needle know where or when to grow, or a cell of bark, or of root? How does each relate to all? How does each electron or proton relate to all electrons or protons? How are they all the same? How is each molecule of oxygen or water the same as all the others? There is an implicit relationship between each and all, or between the particular and the universal, a social mystery. This the objective language of science is powerless to understand.

The primary activity is System 3. It portrays the general scheme by which each and all are integrated within events with space and time. All the higher systems elaborate on the scheme, and all are subsumed within this general pattern. The pattern is given in Figure

20. Two sets of alternating terms are generated. The two terms on each side of the vertical axis occur together; the two sides alternate back and forth. The two terms at the top are universal, while the two at the bottom are particular. On one side, a universal successiveness to time coincides with quantized energies balanced in eternal emptiness. On the other side, a universal identity coincides with spacelike entities with form. The alternations back and forth are synchronized through perceptual transpositions in two sets of interacting centers, each set possessing three centers. Spend a moment or two just to become familiar with the overall pattern. Then we will probe a little deeper into the makeup of each term.

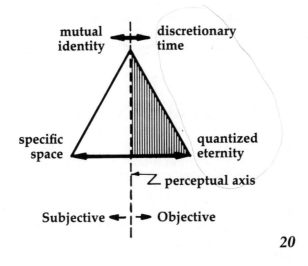

20

It's about time for the whiskey jacks to come. They are a clever bird, also called a meat bird, or Canada jay. About the same size as a blue jay, they have a grayish-blue back and wings, with a light gray breast. They are notorious camp visitors, discovering this one on the second day, and returning two or three times a day ever since. Three long notes are whistled in an attempt to call them—after a few tries, here they come. The three of them are always together. Now they swoop across the channel, one after another in long sweeping scallops, as if they were swinging along on a circus trapeze.

They all land in a dead tree behind one of the small tents, but they aren't happy with their order. They begin to jockey for position, chasing one another from branch to branch, up and down the tree.

Finally they come to rest, tentatively agreed on a pecking order, but probably out of weariness. Each of the birds has a distinct personality—after getting to know them a bit, they can be easily recognized. Number-one bird at the top of the pecking order is brash and pushy. Number-two bird doesn't like being pushed around, but displays some moderation. Number-three bird at the bottom is placid and reserved. It is just as active as the others, but less interested in a hassle.

A small pancake, saved from breakfast, is crumbled and tossed on the ground three or four feet away. Number-three bird reaches it first, but Number One barges in, then Number Two, while placid Number Three just stands and watches. Another piece is held in the hand close to the ground. Number Three hesitates at first, then hops over and takes it. Number-two bird is finally coaxed into taking a piece from the hand, but pushy Number One is too timid to risk it. All three of them eat some, then fly off to hide the rest in the branches of trees. They keep coming back for more.

A small, thin, brown bird flies in all alone, landing about ten feet away. It is a drab, impoverished-looking creature, with a couple of sooty black smudges on each wing. It looks like an orphan that's been making it on its own. Tiny wheels can be seen turning inside its little head as it takes just a moment to size up the situation. When it sees the jays eating from the hand, it runs right over and joins in, amazed at the prospect of having a human friend.

Species much lower in the pecking order often exhibit direct intuitive perceptions that are hidden from man beyond a screen of language. The creative gift of language, a mixed blessing, confines man's horizons to the bastions of his learning.

The system is a guide toward expanding horizons beyond the verbal emplacements of culture. An ambiguous wholistic approach gives the specific aspect of being polar relevance to the nonspecific aspect, in such a way that the relevance is always specific. Each higher system thus elaborates on the specific nature of being. The system is therefore both open and closed, its ambiguity requiring that insight be the fruition of personal experience.

System 3 concerns the relationship of two sets of three centers to a common periphery. There are only four possible ways that three centers can relate to one another within a term, and each will be called a relation term, so that we can speak of Relations 1, 2, 3, and 4. The four terms will be introduced briefly at first, in order to see generally how they interact in the primary activity. The discussion that follows will then be easier to understand. The terms are not complex, but their simplicity is deceiving. A comprehensive understanding of them will take some time. The following steps will be followed in explaining them:

1 Each of the relation terms will first be described in a general way. Keep in mind the diagram in Figure 20.
2 A description of nature's space-time movie of creation will follow. The primary activity can be compared to the technique of movie projection.
3 Next, organic processes and human activity will be discussed as two examples.
4 The technique of movie projection is elaborated on further, since it threads through the remainder of the book.

Relation 1

Relation 1 characterizes a timelike succession through three consecutive processes from center to periphery. It is similar in this respect to the expressive mode of System 2. As is illustrated in Figure 21, each center acts like a dam or a sieve that partitions energies that conform to a certain quality of active intensity, expending toward the periphery energies that do not conform. There is the whole range of the spectrum of experience from which to select, yet only specific qualities of active intensity are of interest to each interface. Each interface is open and unbounded. The term is universal, being unconfined by the limitations of space or spatial orientation. Since the selection of certain energies from all energies is fundamental to discretion, the term will be called the discretion term. It is also the expressive mode of the Relation 2 term.

To exemplify the term, one can think of each of the three centers as representing an interface connected with the activity of making a

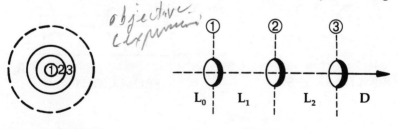

FROM DARKNESS   **FROM LIGHT**

21

table. Center 1 represents a pattern of mentation associated with the creative *idea* of the table—its design and so forth. Center 2 represents the *routine* of activity, how tools and equipment are employed in making the table. Center 3 represents the *formation* of material into table shape. From the successiveness of the three centers, it can be seen that idea gives direction to routine which in turn gives direction to formation. There is a discretionary wonder that seeks out specific table ideas, specific routines to suit equipment, and the specific formation of material. For the sake of simplicity, the three successive interfaces of the discretion term can be summarized as idea,* routine, and formation.

Relation 2

Relation 2 will be called the means term, the subjective or regenerative mode of the discretion term. The two terms alternate from one to the other through the perceptual transposition of Center 3, in a manner similar to that of the alternating modes of System 2. The term is illustrated in Figure 22. The two relational wholes R_1 and R_2 portray two identities that eclipse Center 2 between them. Center 1 perceives an identity through Center 2, but subjective to it. Center 3 perceives an identity through Center 2, but objective to it. Center 2 thus acts like a perceptual axis to a double identity, one subjective and one objective. The two identities are simultaneous through Center 2, but they cannot coalesce, because they are perceived in contrasting fields, from opposite sides of Center 2. There is a two-stage timelike succession to the subjective identity. Open and unbounded, the three centers relate in a universal manner, similar to

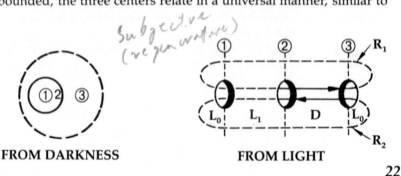

FROM DARKNESS   FROM LIGHT

22

---

*Idea is taken to include knowledge. When we get to System 4, the presumption of knowledge is not made—knowledge and idea are treated as separate centers.

the discretion term. Expended energies are regenerated through the countercurrent identities to sustain the means of activity.

To return to the example of making a table, Centers 1, 2, and 3 still represent idea, routine, and formation, respectively. It can be seen that the table idea seeks an identity with material formation through a routine of human activity that employs tools. The table idea is subjective to the routine, and the material form is objective to it, yet there is no inherent isolation of mind from matter. Both the *idea* of a table and the *form* of a table are regenerated through the *routine* of making a table. The open, universal interfaces of this term work through closed, particular interfaces of the Relation 4 term.

Relation 3

Relation 3 will be called the goal term, for it portrays the complete reconciliation of center and periphery. Two centers are coalesced as one within the remaining center. Each of the coalesced centers sees inside the other only to see outside through their common periphery. The term is illustrated in Figure 23. There is the simultaneous perception of center and periphery within the term. This perception is neither internal nor external, but both at once. It is eternal. Energies are balanced within the term such that it regenerates itself timelessly. The coalescence is a quantization or packaging of energy into discrete parcels that portray an identity in emptiness; in the primary activity it always involves the application of technique. Each coalescence is a unit of memory, worked out through experience and quantized in the void.

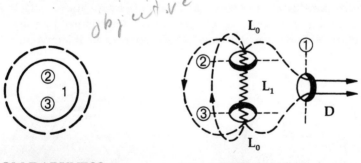

FROM DARKNESS   **FROM LIGHT**   23

The two poles of the creative dilemma find mutual balance through their mutual communion in the term. The goal to activity is thus communicative in a most fundamental sense.

When it comes to making tables, the three centers still represent idea, routine, and formation, respectively, except that in this term they represent particular fragments of each. The centers are no longer universal. Specific elements of routine become coalesced with the specific formation of material within the context of a table idea. Specific applications of technique become quantized as identities in emptiness through experience. These quantizations are fragments of the table idea, elements of memory, that include the technique for its making. They are selected and assimilated from the void by the universal discretion term.

Relation 4

Relation 4 is the consequence term, for it follows in recurrent succession from the goal term through the perceptual transposition of Center 1. It is the subjective mode of the goal term. The two terms alternate back and forth, changing into one another. The term is illustrated in Figure 24. The three centers are mutually independent, yet related. However, three centers cannot exist independently in a common sky unless each is spatially closed. Three open, unbounded interfaces must mutually interfere, so that closure is essential to their independence. Centers thus become enclosed with surfaces, which distinguish them as specific independent wholes with a spacelike quality. Each of these particular wholes is intimately re- lated to two partners through the objective perception of double identity which unites them into a single composite whole.

Each spacelike composite whole has a direct equivalence to an eternal quantization of energy as described by Relation 3. Each such quantization of memory is selected for recall into form by the uni- versal discretion term. The mutual objective and subjective identities

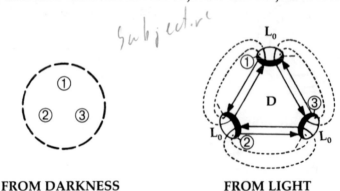

FROM DARKNESS   **FROM LIGHT**

24

of the universal means term then work through each of the particular centers of the composite whole to effect an action sequence through the double identity between them. In this way, elements of technique are compiled as a series of spatial action sequences that are synchronized with the vast multiplicity of action sequences in the projection of the cosmic movie.

Ideas become explicit in the mind and plans of the table maker; routines become explicit in his skills with equipment; the form of the table emerges from shapeless wood. Little by little, the table is compiled from the void of experience, as each quantized element is given relevance to all. The social mystery is thus implicit in the relationship between the universal set of centers, and all of the particular sets involved.

In the example of making a table, the three centers have been identified with idea, routine, and formation, respectively. It should be clear that the same three centers apply equally well to making anything. Furthermore, they are not confined to strictly human activity. The same three centers universally apply, from atomic structure, to the biosphere, to the galaxy. We will return to have an overall look at how the four terms work together to project the space-time movie of creation.

The whiskey jacks have disappeared after the last of the pancake has been stashed in the crotches of trees around a fifty-yard radius. Smudgy has stayed in camp, delighted with his new-found human friend. He runs all over camp, hopping now in figure eights around the feet.

The sun is well up in the eastern sky, projecting shadows from the pine tree against the orange-colored canvas of the tent. The branches of the pine are waving gently in a variety of rhythms, synchronized in stages with the whole structure of the tree. The slender needles are packaged together in tufts of five on flexible little twigs that join with larger twigs, which join with branchlets that are collected into branches, which reach out from the main trunk of the tree. Each stage of the elaboration of the limbs portrays a character of motion of its own, yet the rhythms of each are integrated with the rhythms of the whole. The flowing movements are not just mechanical vibrations such as a dead weed might display in passive reaction to the breeze. Each needle, each tuft, each twig and branch plays with the breeze in a living response, with vital energies yielding and resisting in an animated dance. Each has its own unique sense of timing as it refluxes energies through the patterns of its

movements within the structured hierarchy of the whole. The fluctuating energies of the breeze are brought to a dynamic balance
through the dance.

The discretion and means terms of the primary activity are like a
fluctuating universal wind that moves unseen to regulate the pattern
of a dance between form and emptiness. The stage is unbounded
sky, the stage lights are the entire spectrum of experience, yet all the
lights are also dancers in the drama of creation. Three lights are
primary for a dancing set, but the set is multifaceted, displaying
itself as two, in order to provide a dancing partner. One set dances
like a universal wind. The other set is dispersed into a myriad of
dancers that swing together with one member from each center of
the set, in groups of three. Each group of three plays ring-around-
the-rosy on its own, but interrupts the game to dance in and out of
eternity in tempo to the universal wind. This general pattern to
the primary activity is illustrated in Figure 25.

We are now in a little better position to take a closer look at
nature's movie projector. The universal driving mechanism is given
by the discretion and means terms. The expressive discretion term
is timelike and selective. Through the successive expenditure of
energy, the wheels of the projector turn, advancing the film from
one frame to the next. All the energies of the universe are sifted
through at once from inside out, and the quantized elements for the
next picture sequence are selected. At this point, regeneration of
the energies is in order, and Center 3 becomes perceptually transposed.

With the recurrence of the regenerative means term, the wheels
of the projector stall. It is still running but spinning its wheels. The
subjective identity to Center 2 is portrayed by the relational whole
R_1, still involving a timelike succession between Centers 1 and 2.
However, this timelike action sequence relates subjectively to the
content of the film, not to the advancement of the film to another
frame. The film itself stops until the energies are regenerated.

At this point, Center 3 becomes perceptually transposed back
into the expressive mode: the film begins to advance again. The
driving mechanism continues like this, advancing the film one frame
at a time, but stalling for a while at each frame.

The projection of the movie itself concerns the goal and consequence terms. As the film is being advanced past the projection
lens, it is synchronized with a blank spot on the film. In nature's
special three-dimensional projector, the discretion term advances

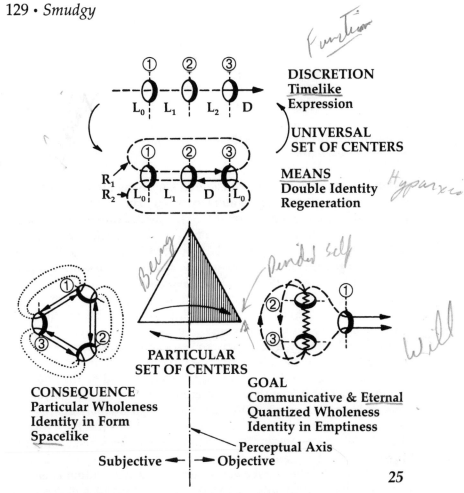

Function

DISCRETION
Timelike
Expression

UNIVERSAL
SET OF CENTERS

MEANS
Double Identity   *Hyparxis*
Regeneration

Being   *Divided Self*   *Will*

PARTICULAR
SET OF CENTERS

CONSEQUENCE
Particular Wholeness
Identity in Form
Spacelike

GOAL
Communicative & Eternal
Quantized Wholeness
Identity in Emptiness

Perceptual Axis

Subjective ←|→ Objective

25

the film while it is synchronized with the goal term, and the screen is blank. Although the film is moving, the content of the film is suspended timelessly in quantized identities in emptiness. All the content is there, quantized into little eternal energy packages, but they are balanced and void of form. Each quantized memory is like a window to a huge invisible theater that is made from sky, and each shares a common interior. The discretion term is a universal wind that sifts unseen through all the windows at once, to select those that indicate by their partitioning characteristics that they have something appropriate to offer to the content of the film.

As the film stalls with the recurrence of the means term, it is synchronized with the appearance of the consequence term. The three-dimensional form of a space frame comes into view. Particular wholes enact a memorized sequence in groups of three, each locked into the mutual perception of a double identity. The mutual identities of the universal wind now work through the particular sets of dancers to assess the linking up of each dance routine into a complete performance involving all routines. The projection of the cosmic movie thus concerns the ever-changing aspects of the social mystery of each and all.

Additional examples can be considered simply by identifying the specific nature of the three centers involved. They will of course involve idea, routine, and formation; they will form terms and interact in the primary activity in the same way. The specific nature of the centers in each example can best be identified through the relationship of the universal means term to the particular consequence term, that is, through Relation 2 and Relation 4.

Thus, for example, when we examine an organic growth process, like that of a tree, or a human being, we can expect to find specific patterns of electromagnetic energy associated with idea, routine, and formation. The pattern associated with formation is familiar to all: it is the work, entrusted to cells, of giving molecular form to a physical body. Cells in turn are supervised by the body's organs, which are more than a collection of their cells. Organs must have an electromagnetic spatial identity of their own, an energy phantom, so to speak. Some direct evidence of this has been provided by Kirlian photography, which in certain cases, using special apparatus, has been able to photograph the ghost image of a leaf after part of it has been cut away. Organs in turn are administered by a patterned energy interface associated with the idea of the whole body. This is directly evidenced by phantom-limb pain, experienced by amputee victims. Also relevant are the fleeting encounters that many people have had with ghosts. So too are "out of the body" experiences. On one occasion, humanlike faces have even been photographed in space by astronauts. Many of these phenomena deserve serious research, directed not toward their sensational value, but toward better understanding their place in the normal process of growth.

Human activity is unique; it is not confined to the organic processes of the body. It works through three major divisions of the nervous system that are committed to creative ideation, to emotional routine, and to behavioral formation. These respectively correspond to the central nervous system in the head, to the autonomic nervous

system, and to the somatic motor/sensory nervous system. Ide
links us to creative energies of cosmic origin; emotional routine
link us to our spiritual and environmental heritage; and the fori
tion of behavior links us to our social environment. Mind is all three.

From the nature of the primary activity, it can be seen that human memories involve an emotional commitment to behavior, illustrated as a coalescence within the idea interface in the Relation 3
term. In other words, memories are quantizations of experience that
have a spiritual content. Although they are keyed to the body, there
is no memory bank in the body. The memory bank is the communicative void that has been structured through commitment to activity.
Recall is effected through the universal discretion term that has
access to the history of all personal experience for each of us. Moreover, through the universal set of centers associated with the human
species, we potentially have access to all experience to the extent
we are concerned.*

All experience recalled is modified, restructured through renewed commitment made manifest in behavior, so that the communicative void, though eternal, is continually being refluxed to
reassimilate its energies. There is a continuing universal concern
with the social mystery of each and all.

Smudgy has explored the whole campsite. He comes back for attention, hopping up first on one foot, then on the other. It is time to
leave him for a while for a walk around the island, a half-hour daily
exercise that is rough going in places. The beginning of the path is
paved around the rocky point to the north, but the pavement soon
becomes sculptured into a variety of awkward ledges. In the deep
water alongside there is a large school of pickerel minnows, each a
little more than an inch long. They are all swimming in the same
direction, as if guided by a mastermind. The school extends for
several hundred feet. Masses of them coast at times, but within
large areas of the school, with very little bunching into traffic jams.
Then they move again, but all at once as if responding to a single
signal. There are hundreds of thousands of them—those that survive will provide some good fishing in a few years.

Along the west side of the island, there is a little bay with a
stony beach strewn with driftwood. The shoreline then juts out
westward into another rocky point. Around the point it angles back

---

*Note the correspondence of the three universal centers to the Hindu and Christian
Trinities.

again in solid granite that is contoured into flowing shapes, then rises into a cliff about thirty feet high. It is necessary to detour into the thick bush some distance in order to climb the small escarpment, which bulges into a ridge with tall red pines. There is very little undergrowth on top, just towering trunks reaching for the sky. The ridge then falls away gradually toward the south, sheared off into rocky ledges along the shore.

The slope toward the south is fairly open along the west side of the island—the expanse of the lake can be seen for several miles, tapering toward a narrows, then opening up beyond. The sun is ricocheting off the ruffled surface of the water in glancing bullets of energy that rebound in all directions. Each bullet is repulsed by a bullet-proof vest of electronic particles that enclose each molecule of water. Electrons are reluctant to interrupt their game of ring-around-the-rosy even though they bear a close relationship to light.

The electron is the most basic particle to behave, at least part of the time, as a hard little lump of something that can be measured.* The other part of the time, nobody knows where it is—it seems to be somewhere in the vicinity, acting like a wave motion. The primary activity indicates that the wave motion is a result of the extremely rapid little dance between form and emptiness that electrons everywhere are doing. One instant they are entrapped as packages of quantized energy that are balanced in a communicative void; the next instant, they are tiny little lumps contributing to the world of physical form and space.

The electron, however, is only one partner in the triad of ring-around-the-rosy—the one that undertakes routines in building atoms. The mentation partner is energy of a more subtle kind, encapsulated into discreet amounts, called photons, that direct the electrons into various orbital routines. The center of attention in the activity is focused on much grosser concentrations. The bulk of the material is formed into the protons and neutrons of the nucleus. The balance of double identity between the swinging triplets is monitored by the universal centers working through them to ensure that all sets are alike. The objective component of the balance is evidenced in the complementary charge between the electron and the proton.**

---

*Recent evidence indicates that a neutrino has a very small mass, about 1/10,000 that of an electron.

**The electron has a negative charge and the proton an equal and opposite positive charge, whereas the neutron is neutral. The neutron, it seems, represents a closed

The eternal dance between form and emptiness introduces harmonics into orbital routines; atoms become invested with selective discretionary powers. The primary orbit is a two-step reserved for hydrogen and helium. Higher orbits seek to complete harmonic complements of eight electron routines. Eight dance steps fit nicely with a universal beat, although the magic number is usually no more than four. By sharing up to four electrons in their outer orbits, atoms learn that they can complete a stable set of eight. Some, like husbands, give away; some, like wives, accept. Through various kinds of marriages into molecules, atoms find a more stable state in which to coexist. They conserve their mental faculties, and in the process produce an infinite range of chemical offspring from a cast of only ninety-two elementary dancers.

The system thus indicates, in a manner consistent with the scientific evidence, that the whole physical universe is a synchronous projection of sequential space frames that are vanishing and recurring millions of times a second, with and before our eyes. The timing is regulated by the alternating modes of expression and regeneration. The flow of time, as we define and measure it, comes both from the recurrence of space frames and from electromagnetic action sequences within space frames.

The ledges along the south shore of the island are only inches wide in places, yet it is easier to climb along them than to crawl through the dense growth on top. Most of the island is thickly forested, with undergrowth wherever there is light and a tangle of dead branches that make walking difficult. As the shoreline rounds into the channel on the east it becomes easier going, with more contoured granite, broken up in places into large boulders. These give way into another small point that lies out flat, slicing obliquely into the water. It is grown up with a cluster of straggly jack pines, struggling for survival on top of solid rock. The point curls back into a marshy area that is teeming with small green frogs. Then a broad ledge, smothered in moss and blueberry bushes, leads into the little cove behind the tent.

The sun is still busy projecting a pine-tree shadow dance against the canvas tent. It is something like the means term of the primary

---

relationship between proton and electron, involving also the neutrino, whereas the buildup of the orbital shells of the atom depends on an open relationship between them. These complementary modes to activity come into play in higher systems beginning with System 5. Systems 4 and 5 can provide more elaborate models of these basics of atomic structure.

activity that projects a double identity—one objective, one subjective. The same shadow dance can be seen from both inside and outside the tent.

Smudgy is still in camp and runs over to prance a little greeting. A piece of cookie is taken from the cedar cupboard; some is handed to him, the rest is crumbled up on a stone for him. It's a good time now to wash some dirty clothes and have a swim. More out of habit than necessity, the swim trunks are put on. The clothes are collected and taken down the ramp to the lake. They are soused in the water, then soaped up well and rolled up on the rock to soak for a while.

The rock is slippery as it tapers into the lake, but once the water is knee high it is possible to dive in. It feels cold at first, then moderate and pleasant. There is a vertical vein of white quartz about three feet wide in the rock ledge across the channel. Since it's only a short swim away, some prospecting suggests itself. The channel is about fifteen feet deep; on a sunny day like today, the amber-tinted water is just clear enough to see the silt bottom, punctuated with a few clams.

The channel is protected from the southwest breeze, and the waves are gliding in quietly from the main body of the lake. The surface of the water is undulating smoothly in a series of small, slick crests moving up the channel in rows. One side of each crest reflects the shoreline and the sky in distortions according to its contours; the other reveals the sunlight penetrating down into the water. It looks like a moving picture—successive frames of a continuous strip of film.

The picture side of each crest reflects a double identity that is seen in two directions. The sky and shoreline above the water are also seen reflected in the surface, as if they are beneath it. In a remotely similar way the double identity of the means term reflects a double identity through the surfaces of particular centers that dance in sets of three. One universal set reflects through all particular sets at once, lending them an integrated identity.

On the other side of each crest, the light penetrates the surface of the water as if a perceptual transposition has occurred. The particles of water no longer reflect a double identity—visually specific form is lost in balanced ambiguity. The void has a structured, quantized texture, but its energies are balanced in eternal emptiness. The timelike successiveness of the discretion term filters through it everywhere at once. Time searches through eternity unseen, integrating energies for the next picture sequence in the movie. The quantized energies required to sustain the projection of the movie are recalled back into form in the next space frame. The picture side of the next wave crest comes into view reflecting a double identity through its surface. On and on the movie goes, stepping timelike through eternity.

There is a place where it is easy to climb out of the water beside the vein of quartz. The shoreline is a ledge about ten feet high that is broken into steep steps, chunks of the vein having fractured off into boulders that have tumbled down next to the water. The quartz is fairly good quality, but unfortunately it is not laced with gold. The top of the ledge rounds up into a ridge about thirty feet high with red pines of various sizes. The ground is fairly clear, with scattered patches of blueberry bushes. There are a few green berries coming, but the soil is too acid for a good crop. They thrive best after a fire. The ground is too hard on the bare feet to walk very far. After enjoying the sun for a while, it becomes quite warm. The swim back to camp is refreshing.

The clothes are rinsed out and hung up on a line between the two red pines behind the tent. Smudgy, who has been ignored, hops up on the table to attract some notice. He isn't pretty, he doesn't sing, he doesn't even chirp, but he sure is friendly. After a short visit, it's time to catch a fish for supper.

There is a good fishing spot in front of the bay on the west side of the island. The canoe is slipped into the water and paddled out around the point to the north. The breeze is not strong—about right to drift back across the bay. The canoe is paddled down to the rocky point beyond. Pickerel feed near the bottom, preferring a clean bottom, so a jig is generally the best pickerel lure for casting. This jig has been made by an old friend and fishing partner from Pennsylvania. It is slightly heavier than commercial models of the same size and a little better for casting. The head of the jig is a lead casting that weighs about a quarter of an ounce, with a single hook that protrudes to the rear, surrounded by a nylon skirt. The jig is fastened to the line on its underside so that the hook rides facing up.

A cast is taken toward the rocky point, and the jig is allowed to sink to the bottom. The slack line is then taken up, and the tip of the pole is jigged up sharply. The tip is lowered again as the line is reeled in a turn, then another jig up, and so on, with an even tempo. The speed of retrieval is adjusted according to the depth of the water and the movement of the canoe, so that the jig goes through a series of rhythmic jumps along the bottom.

The third cast brings a heavy strike—the fish is taking line. It soon stops but continues the fight with heavy tugs, taking line again in the usual pattern of a pickerel. Gradually it tires—in about five minutes, it is close enough to net. It is a nice pickerel of about five pounds, much too large for supper. The hook is removed from its upper lip, and the fish is placed back over the side. Uninjured it swims away immediately.

Another few casts bring supper, a pickerel about eighteen inches long. Its neck quickly broken, it quivers as it dies. Its patterned energies are doing a final transposition into the void, to wait there until recalled in another spawning season. The void is a repository of experience that is structured, refluxed, and restructured through experience. It embraces energies on every level of organization, from atomic and molecular processes, through celestial and organic evolution, to complex patterns of human mentation, and to levels of experience with which we are not familiar. The void is a timeless master sensorium of patterned energies, a master eternal memory bank that is available for recall at will.

Will is exercised on every level of organization. Discretion fishes through the void discriminating appropriate energies, that they may be recalled and identified in form. Each of us is implicitly aware of the process in the intuitive aspects of our own mentation, as we search to give form to idea and thought. It works in a similar way on every scale and level of organization.

The paddle is placed across the canoe in order to clean the fish on the broad part of the blade before returning back to camp. Pickerel come in to feed regularly in the late afternoon in front of this little bay. It is very convenient. This school comes in a variety of sizes up to six or seven pounds, but most run about two pounds. In an unspoiled lake like this one, different schools tend to develop different patterns within certain broad limits. Some schools of the same spawning season stick together year after year for a few years, all members of the school running about the same size.

On rare occasions a school will be encountered where every pickerel caught will weigh five to seven pounds. Schools of large pickerel like this are more diverse in their feeding patterns. They range more. They don't usually come back consistently to the same place, and they also tend to get broken up, with members dispersing into other schools, or ranging in smaller groups. Sometimes schools will have a variety of larger members, from three or four pounds upward, with a few as large as ten or twelve pounds. Pickerel larger than this are very rare, even in this lake. It is a special event to catch one of fifteen or sixteen pounds.

Each school tends to exhibit a collective will, tempered by the experience of its membership. This interplay between each and all provides for a wide spectrum of social variations in different schools.

Apart from the two fillets and one small fin, the fish still remains intact. The float hasn't been broken, and a couple of seagulls nearby already have their eye on it, so it is tossed over the side. It will drift slowly toward the long bay to the northeast—the seagulls will get most of it long before it reaches shore.

The canoe is paddled back around the northern point of the island. Three long clear whistles come from the campsite. After a pause they come again. Whiskey jacks are gifted mimics, and now it is their turn to do the calling. The three whistles come again.

The canoe is pulled up and tied. The fillets are rinsed a final time, then taken up to camp. There are some fresh vegetables stored in a couple of coolers buried in the shade—a few are collected and prepared. They are put on to boil on the camp stove while a fire is started for tea. The fillets are then put on to fry while Smudgy hops around observing everything.

The jays are less interested in what is going on. One of them flies into an overhanging branch in the pine tree, anxious for attention, chirping softly. A woodpecker flies into the dead tree and shrieks out a loud, shrill call. Pushy Number One immediately accepts it as a challenge and flies to a branch about two feet away, then screeches out an identical note just as loud. The woodpecker looks at him dumbfounded for a few seconds. Then, not knowing what else to do, it flies away.

Supper is placed on the table and a stump pulled up looking out toward the channel. A few small pieces of fish are tossed out for the jays; they come and peck at it, but they like pancake better. They accept a biscuit, though, and seem satisfied. Meanwhile, Smudgy has occupied one corner of the table to eat a few crumbs of crust from the fish.

The jays leave shortly. Smudgy goes back to exploring on the ground and hopping around the feet. The dishes are cleaned up, and the garbage is burned. The leftover fish is wrapped up for a snack later on. Some birch poles were cut the other day for firewood. After a while a few of these are sawn up into lengths and split.

Smudgy stays around until later in the evening. He leaves unnoticed. There is the feeling that he is never to return. Perhaps he has a rendezvous to keep. Perhaps the obligations of his species require him to journey. Whatever the nature of the energies that motivated his departure, we have had a friendship for a day, perceived through the relationship of each to all.

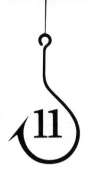

11 Dance Halls and Spaceships

White pines sometimes favor growing on rocky points where there is very little soil. Their root structure, like their limb structure, seems more highly developed than that of most trees—they can find sustenance and cling to rock where other species fail. They grow other places as well, of course, but a rocky shoreline gives them a freedom of expression they do not enjoy when crowded in by neighbors.

To the northeast of the camp the shoreline juts out into a couple of points as it turns northward on its contorted journey up the east side of the lake. Each point is graced with genuflecting pines. The boat is drifting slowly near one point, a good spot for jigging, although pickerel usually feed here later in the day. A lone white pine is standing some distance apart from a couple of others, its branches licking at the sky, like frozen green flames. A slight breeze betrays the pantomime with gentle movements, just as slightly moving lips sometimes betray the voice behind the ventriloquist's dummy. On windy days the mimicry of motion is all but forgotten in order to accentuate the wind, with dancing limbs tugging at their trunks to join the rhythm.

There is another unseen dance going on within the tree, though it is all part of a master choreography. Like a brilliant Sherlock Holmes, science has done a great deal of diligent detective work, identifying many of the characters in the cast, but still has not glimpsed the surreptitious plot. The motive and the modus operandi remain a lurking mystery, concealed by the collusion of the dancers. The detective work proceeds in the belief that the universe is nothing more than a gigantic thermodynamic bakeshop.

The Sherlock Holmes of science sees a pine tree as a recipe for a cake. The masterful detective is very earnest in this belief, going to great lengths to convey the opinion to a trusting public. In this ongoing dialogue, the public is Watson, the long-standing assistant and faithful companion to detective Holmes.

"You see, it is all very elementary, my dear Watson. Certain chemicals are being drawn up with moisture from the soil and circulated through the vascular system of the tree, which runs in a complex maze—like tiny arteries and veins—to carry the lifeblood of sap to every portion of the tree. The foliage of the tree contains special cells with green structures within them called chloroplasts. These give the foliage its green appearance, but they are also the main kitchen for the tree, where the primary ingredients for a carbohydrate cake are baked. As the sap is circulated through these special cells in pine needles, water from the soil is combined with carbon dioxide absorbed from the air to produce the carbohydrate sugar. This cooking process requires energy, just as any kitchen stove requires energy. In the kitchen of a tree, the energy comes from sunlight. Because the process of cooking or synthesizing sugar from water and carbon dioxide requires sunlight, we will call it photosynthesis," proclaims the brilliant Sherlock, confident that the central culprit in the recipe has been apprehended.

"You see, it is all quite elementary, my dear Watson. Light energy from the sun is essential for the chemical bonding of water with carbon dioxide, to produce sugar. In this way, light energy becomes stored in the chemical bonds of sugar, and it is carried in the sap to various parts of the tree. Some of this energy is then released and used by the tree to build the more complex substances needed for its trunk, roots, limbs, needles, cones, and seeds."

"But how do various cells know how to do this?" pries the inquiring Watson.

"This was rather puzzling for quite some time," replies the brilliant sleuth, "but now you may rest assured that it all has to do with a secret code."

"It sounds frightfully diabolical," says Watson.

"Not at all, my dear fellow," reassures the famous detective, with his usual air of confidence. "It sounds a little complicated, but really it is just a simple matter of elementary chemistry. You see, the code is locked up in a safety deposit vault, the nucleus of every cell, and it is really nothing more than chemical bonds between four rather simple chemicals. These four chemicals join hands in pairs to form the rungs of a very long ladder-shaped molecule, called DNA, that gets twisted into a helical shape revolving every nine or ten rungs, like a winding staircase. The genetic code is transferred through the rungs. The sides of the ladder sometimes come apart like a zipper, each side of the zipper retaining half of each rung. Each side of the zipper then acts like a template to build a new, identical zipper. In this way the secret code can be transferred into a new cell when the cell divides."

"Amazing!" says Watson. "The energy for cooking the recipe is collected from the sun and stored in chemical bonds, while the recipe for mixing the ingredients of the cake in a proper sequence and in proper proportions is stored in chemical bonds as well. That *is* amazing! If the rungs of the ladder contain the secret genetic code, then the language of the code must be written in the sequence in which the different kinds of rungs occur. The DNA molecules are sort of like the chief cook, then."

"Very observant, my dear Watson," says the sleuth masterfully. "That is basically it. The code is written in three-letter words, or groups of three rungs in the ladder. Although there are more than sixty words possible, only a third of them are necessary to designate the amino acids in the proper order for assembling protein molecules. The code has already been cracked in this regard, although related questions remain."

"How about all the other complicated processes going on in the cell, outside the nucleus, in the cytoplasm that surrounds it?" asks the curious Watson. "If the chief cook is in the nucleus, how do his instructions get passed along?"

"I thought you would ask that, Watson. The chief cook has helpers or messengers, called RNA, that are copied from the pattern of DNA. They are like sections from one side of a zipper. These shorter templates go out into the surrounding cytoplasm with piecemeal instructions on how to mix various constituents in the cake. The whole thing is run like a bakery. There are other workers as well, enzymes and so forth, but the secret is in the code."

"Fascinating," replies Watson, "but how do all these messengers know where or when to go with their instructions, or whom to give them to? How is it that they can move through the batter of the cake to the right place, at the right time? How about cell division? How about the code itself? Where did it come from?"

"One question at a time, my dear Watson. It is all very elementary. There are electromagnetic energies at work in many ways that are associated with the molecules within a cell, and no doubt work in some way to explain their migrations through the batter. We don't have all the evidence as yet, but no doubt some satisfactory explanation can be worked out, given a little more time. As for the code itself, it is just a fortuitous accident."

"An accident!" exclaims Watson, showing some surprise. "You mean a pine tree is an accident? That is remarkable!"

"Precisely, my dear Watson, although it is really a series of accidents, occurring over hundreds of millions of years, that have produced pine trees, and you and I as well, for that matter."

"You mean I'm an accident too!" blurts out Watson, a little horrified.

"No need to get upset, Watson, it is all very elementary. You see, the secret code got started a very long time ago through fortuitous circumstances and a happy coincidence of certain molecules in just the right configuration. It was more like a soup than a cake in those days—with all the molecular collisions going on, and with a little help from radiation and lightning, it had to happen. The chances were reasonably good that it would happen somewhere in the world, and once the secret code got started, there was simply no stopping it. The code got revised and changed through more accidents—caused by cosmic radiation and so forth—and through these mutations different recipes got started for different cakes. Some cakes had a more successful code than others and could survive better, so natural processes selected in their favor, while other cakes died off. In this way, the secret code gradually built up into more and more sophisticated versions. Everything happened in a very natural way. You see, it is all really just a big bakeshop. Pine trees and people are just successful cakes."

"I don't mean to impugn your brilliant detective work, Holmes, but my confidence is frankly shaken. Is it not possible that some evidence has been overlooked or misinterpreted?"

"Nonsense, Watson! All the evidence is coming together beautifully! The case will be wrapped up as soon as we tie up the loose ends."

"But maybe there is something we don't understand about energy. It seems very important to the case. After all, isn't it the sun's energy that is stored in chemical bonds, and don't chemical bonds have to do with electrons, and aren't electrons and molecules just special forms of energy, much the same as the energy from the sun? Maybe the secret isn't in the code, but in the organization of the energies involved?"

"Of course energy is involved, but how does that affect anything? We already know all the major events in the case, and the evidence is clear!" retorts the masterful Sherlock, a little perturbed.

"But maybe energy works in an organized way that we don't suspect," persists Watson.

"What are you suggesting? That energy knows what it is doing? That it's intelligent?" shouts Sherlock, getting more upset.

"That might explain why we bother working on the case," replies Watson, with a little sarcasm showing through a grin.

"Preposterous," roars the sleuth angrily, "and most unscientific!"

"Perhaps not if we could learn to understand how it works," comes a timid reply.

"Quit interrupting while I'm thinking about the case," snaps Sherlock.

"But maybe we are looking in the wrong direction and will never . . ."

"Be quiet!" interrupts Holmes sternly.

"But . . ."

"I *said* be quiet, Watson!"

Are we to believe, with the brilliant Sherlock, that we are just accidental happenings, mere users of energy to manipulate dead matter to prove our mastery? Or are we intelligent participants in an intelligent universe, seeking a responsive understanding as a living realization of our being? Must the deficiencies of language forever divorce us from a spiritual identity with our own understanding? Why must it be so?

The boat has drifted down the shoreline, without a strike. It is a good day to try a couple of fishing spots toward the north, then drop in for a visit with Adam and Agnes. There is a long bay about a mile to the north that is sometimes good for big northerns.

The boat is steered out around a peninsula, followed by sheer cliffs forty or fifty feet high. These curve into the bay that is about three hundred yards wide at its mouth. The bay tapers down to a narrows at an island, opening up again beyond, into a long finger that curls about three miles into the shoreline to the east. It is the mouth of the bay that is of interest today, however. The motor is stopped well out, as soon as some scattered weeds become visible ahead. The boat will drift slowly toward the island in the narrows. It is an ideal spot for pike. Sometimes they come up to thirty pounds in size. The lure is changed, and casting begins.

There is a large white pine standing on the island like a traffic policeman giving direction to the breeze. An accidental pine-tree cake indeed! Soil, sun, wind, and rain are fashioned into a living dance of energy through the agency of a single seed. What kind of magic is at work?

Since the conjuring of a pine tree is linked to its cells, let's look into the activity hierarchy of a cell. *Idea* is translated genetically, through the agency of the nucleic acids—DNA and RNA; *routines* are enacted through the agency of organelles in the cytoplasm—mitochondria, endoplasmic reticulum, ribosomes, golgi complex, etc.; *formation* of metabolic end products—molecular synthesis—is regulated through the agency of enzymes. Although each agency has a molecular form, the interface processes that work through them are concerned with electromagnetic organization.

The action sequence in each space frame is confined to electromagnetic activity, recalled as elements of learned technique from quantizations of experience in the void. Each quantization is a timeless coalescence of routine with formation, as an idea. The idea of a cell thus exists as a composite pattern of electromagnetic organization—a timeless collection of quantized elements in the void. These gathered elements are mutually committed to the being of a cell: they span the complete growth sequence of its molecular history, from birth to death. Furthermore, their mutual commitment itself has a pattern of electromagnetic organization provided by the universal centers. A cell is more than a random collection of particularized elements of technique; the elements must come together in a certain way.

To get back to the pine tree, cells are its chemical factories, producing the molecular *form* of its physical bulk as it matures. The *routines* of the tree are enacted through the agency of its organs—its vascular system, foliage, reproductive system, etc. Just as with cells, trees have evolved through the mutual commitment of diverse quantizations of technique, organized together into the integrated *idea* of a whole tree, complete in all of its interdependent aspects. The universal centers of a tree span the growth sequence of its molecular history, as it dances to elemental tunes perfected through its ancestry, and eternally preserved as memories in the void.

Thus, although the musical score may be written in genetic code, the code is neither the music nor the musicians. It is a referent to the music—like notes written on a printed page—a discretionary guide for the universal centers to select the appropriate patterned energies from experience. Each sprouting seedling interprets the musical score according to its own environment.

Cells read the code through their own hierarchy of activity, but each cell relates to all through the hierarchy for the tree. Each cell thus interprets the code in the context of the tree, while the tree has no access to the code except through cells. The lineage must be transmitted through a seed. Nevertheless, the structured energies of each new tree emerge under the tutelage of its parentage, spanning generations of space and time through the dance.

Don't be misled by the apparent simplicity of the action. Visualize the complexity if you can. Atomic dancers jostle in a molecular Mardi Gras through the maze of avenues circulating within the tree. The streets and alleyways are lined with myriads of cells, like dance halls of various designs, complete with ionized facades. Certain performers are enticed to enter certain halls, while others are ejected by bouncers at the doors. Inside, what a show! Dancers far more populous than people are induced by enzymes to join hands in complicated patterns, while others are broken up, to form again renewed. Exotic energies are wafting everywhere, sifting through the dancers as they two-step to and fro into eternity, waving as they come and go. The hall is rocking with the beat, the organelles sustaining the rhythms of routines. Observe especially the mighty mitochondria. These energy sustainers for the show are separately delegated their own DNA, at the supervisory level of the eukaryotic cell.

The maze of streets and alleyways lead on to limbs and twigs, reaching out to halls in needles with special energy-fixing organelles—the chloroplasts, too, have DNA. It is here the favored triplets enact their star performance to a caroling chorus of chlorophyll. Triplets beckoned from the moisture of the soil are joined in wedlock with triplets coaxed in from the breeze. The parson comes from ninety million miles away. The nuptial festivities are sanctified with sunlight. The six-member ring of glucose resonates the wedding march. Sweetness and light prevail. Space and time are bridged through light. The energies of lifetimes are bestowed. The whole tree strains for this event. The bride of light, its life is light.

The boat has drifted into thicker weeds close to the island. The pike aren't feeding either. From close up, the pine tree has a matronly appearance, stout trunk, broad bushy boughs, but not so tall as many. The soil is better here. The pine hasn't had to rise as much to gather light.

The main festive period for pine trees is earlier in the season, after winter slumber. The air is alive with vital energies then, the celebrations being at their peak. Long tentacles clutching into the breast of mother earth sustain new growth struggling out for light. From roots, to trunk, to limbs, and twigs, space and time are bridged through countless marriages with light in needles. The tree is given spatial continuity as a living form through light. The tree is not caused by events in space and time. The tree itself is space and time. Space and time are life.

The hosting hierarchies of the creative process are a dance of light that spans the broad range of the electromagnetic spectrum through nanoseconds, minutes, months, and years. Each life incorporates its music from across the keyboard, selecting notes for their harmonic interplay. Life, refluxing energies through the void, evolves eternal species that reach across the epochs to span the whole of history. The world of form reshapes itself through life, to perfect the cosmic orchestration.

Elementary? Preposterous! It's not a big bakeshop at all. It's an incredible country-dance to celestial music wafting through the heavens. It's intelligent and alive. It's all a mind. Our mind. Yours and mine.

The boat is pushed out of the thick weeds into deeper water. The motor is started and the boat maneuvered slowly through the shallow water back out into the main body of the lake, then north again along more rugged cliffs, crowned with a thickly wooded hill that rises steeply for a couple of hundred feet. It is about a mile and a half to another long narrow island close to the eastern shoreline—sometimes a good spot for pickerel. The pike lure is exchanged for a jig along the way.

The boat is stopped off the south corner of the island. After a few casts, a nice pickerel is caught and put on a stringer for supper. The island is relatively flat, very rocky, and quite open, falling away into boulders, bathing in the shallow water at the shoreline. There may be some blueberries on the bushes that blanket the rocks, so an open spot is selected between the boulders and the boat pulled up on shore. A handful is collected, then a smooth boulder is chosen for a stool beside the water. It's like a fast-food place with seats outside for customers.

In the shallow water the slight ripple is warping sunlight into refracted patterns that move in bands across the bottom, rebounding off other boulders in complicated designs. The sandy amber bottom is only a few inches deep with tiny crystal surfaces glistening in the sunlight. There is mossy brown algae growing on the rock surfaces, covering them with a dense fine hair a few millimeters thick.

At first glance the shallow water looks lifeless, apart from the few small weeds. On closer inspection it becomes apparent that it is a teeming invertebrate jungle. Hundreds of water beetles are flitting endlessly over the bottom, scouring it for food, only occasionally coming up for a hurried gulp of air. They are burrowing at the bottom and through the mossy algae, in a tireless energetic plight for food.

Out a little further, in six or eight inches of water, is a school of small minnows, almost transparent in color. About two hundred of them are just basking in the sun in an irregular pattern, as if each had deliberately selected a random orientation to the others. Occasionally a notion overtakes the school to move a foot or so, as if to cool off a bit. It is as if an invisible magnet polarizes them all in one direction, all at once. They are riveted in one direction, move about a foot, then all at once they again resume a random orientation. There is a collective will at work through which the whole school moves and stays together, yet within this constraint, individual behavior is just as mandatory.

Activity in the invertebrate jungle is not so highly organized. Countless thousands of tiny gnats, hardly visible, are swarming through the algae, and straying out from it freely through the water. Although so small it is a marvel they can incorporate all the functions required for such an active life, incessant motion seems to be their main defense.

On a sandy patch of the bottom, a small bundle of tiny water-sodden twigs, about half an inch long, intermittently moves. The wormlike larvae stage of the cadis fly has built itself a shelter to carry on its back. Nearby a small patch of sand on the bottom makes a little jump. Another cadis larva has built a shelter from grains of sand. Many of them are scattered over the bottom, while water beetles sometimes try to burrow underneath to get the worm.

Near a small stone, a large leech is sucking on the empty shell of a crawfish. Many leeches are skulking about, searching under one stone, then the next, using a methodical process of reaching out in front, then bunching themselves forward, retrieving the tail end for another push.

A crawfish emerges from under a stone with pincers out in front, ready for the kill. It can move quite quickly, trying constantly to use the element of surprise to trap a victim. Sneaking up to the edge of a rock, it rushes around the corner with its pincers spread out ready, but it isn't having any luck.

Nearby a strange-looking creature, an inch long, moves out very slowly from under a stone. The naiad stage of a dragonfly must survive in this jungle for about three years before crawling out of the water to attach itself to a plant or log. In the spring and early

summer, it is common to see them clutching corpselike to twigs or
driftwood along the shore, while the dragonfly within matures.
Unfortunately this naiad will never know its final metamorphosis. A
crab comes on it quickly from behind, making no mistake about the
catch. Pincers excitedly crush it again and again, especially near
the head end. The crawfish wastes no time in tearing into the meal.

A few feet away a small snail floats up to the surface, turning
upside down. Its vulnerable side rests against the surface, with the
shell giving protection from predators beneath. Skating around on
top are long-legged water bugs, interspersing figures with jumps,
while others churn around like an act of clowns. It's a regular insect
ice capades with a bird's-eye view of the jungle underneath. There
is more drama here in half an hour than in going to the movies.

Like pine trees, each of these little creatures has a maze of
streets and alleyways, but from there the divergence widens: roots
and limbs have been exchanged for legs and feelers; the trunk has
been restructured to house digestive organs; the crown of needles
has been exchanged for a motor/sensory apparatus. Nonetheless,
the new devices remain dependent on the dance with light in
plants—the source of all food transmitted through the food chain.

The great mobility the invertebrates display has not been easily
won. Cells have had to learn to cooperate in large numbers to perform complex activities—a feat extending far beyond the evolution
of new capabilities for single cells. The difficulty of the chore is
evidenced by the many primitive invertebrate colonies that collectively exhibit plantlike traits. At first they could do little more than
copy. Collective animation only gradually gained momentum as
these creatures plodded plantlike through their lifetimes. Each major
tier of delegation requires a great gathering of experience in the
void.

In the higher invertebrates, dance halls themselves collude as
dancers, nerve and muscle cells animating the linkages of limbs.
The slow-motion movie of the plants is speeded up a billionfold.
Space and time are bridged anew, as each new tier of invertebrate
technique in the refinery matures.

The delegation of the discretionary tiers is not a happenstance
affair. It is effected by a discretionary gathering through the timeless
energies of the void. Experience is assimilated from across the ages,
then recommitted to expression in the world of form. The musical
score of certain select cells is intelligently and intentionally rewritten. Major changes in the code come through mindful intervention,

with a concomitant universal set of centers. The branches of the evolutionary tree return as roots into the common trunk.

The invertebrate jungle of activity explores the limits to sensitive experience through a dance of intermingling elemental minds, working out the details of ever more complex routines. Every water bug, leech, and crab is on a treadmill of activity prescribed by the species, with little room for individual interpretation. Individuals are sacrificed for survival of the species. In contrast, the school of minnows is calmly basking in the sun, quietly reflecting on their mutual association. An autonomic nervous system invests these simple vertebrates with a limited capacity to individually reflux their sensitive experience into conscious reflection. This reflective interplay, while indebted to invertebrate exploration of sensitive response, spans these patterns of space and time anew.

Adam and Agnes live a little more than two miles to the north, on the west side of the lake. The stringer is pulled in and the boat steered out around the island. The eastern shoreline falls away in the distance as the lake widens a couple of miles in that direction, providing an enhanced view to the north as well. The small peninsula where they camp juts straight out into the lake a couple of hundred yards, like a rocky fist, joined to the mainland by a wrist of sand. It is on the north side of this neck of sand that Adam and Agnes have their camp, nestled in a grove of tall poplars and white birch with a wide beach extending down to the water's edge.

The boat is kept well out from the shallow water at the end of the peninsula, then circled in a wide arc into the sandy cove on the north side. Their boat is at the dock so they must be home. There's Adam working on his canoe, in a shady spot on the beach. He waves, then walks over toward the small dock. The motor is slowed to a troll, then shut off as the boat coasts past some weeds in toward Adam on the dock.

"Hello, Bob, glad you came." He catches the front end of the boat and secures it, then we exchange greetings again.

"Come on over while I finish with the canoe," says Adam. "It'll only take a few minutes.

"What are you doing to it?" I ask.

"Just a coat of paint. It needs some new ribs, and a new canvas, but this will last the season out."

The canoe is upside down on two sawhorses, most of it shining with a fresh coat of green paint. Adam picks up the brush to finish the small area left. An old canoe, it has been kept in good repair. "These old canoes are good, but they take a lot of maintenance." I stoop down to look up underneath.

"Plenty heavy on a portage too, especially when it soaks up some water. Too much for Agnes anymore," he adds with a grin.

Just as I am about to ask where Agnes is, she steps out from the kitchen up in the woods, shouts a greeting, and waves. Then she speaks a few words of Indian to Adam and goes back inside.

Adam finishes the canoe, puts the lid on the paint can, and cleans the brush. "Come on up and sit down, Agnes is making coffee."

The sandy beach slopes up gradually to a level area, where a few armchairs face out toward the lake to the north. Behind them, in the poplar grove, are three small huts, and a larger one that serves as the kitchen. Two of the small huts are used for sleeping, the third for storage. There is an unfinished fourth hut some distance beyond the kitchen. Log walls have been completed four or five feet high, with a pole framework above that has not yet been enclosed. All the huts have a pole framework with fabric roof. Everything is very neat and tidy. It's like a large house with kitchen, bedrooms, and storage, there being no need to enclose the family room.

"Let's sit outside," says Adam, pointing to the chairs. "Agnes will be out in a minute."

On the beach, to one side in front of the chairs, a low fireplace has been constructed, using the top of an old stove. Cooking is usually done on the large wood stove in the kitchen, while this one is used for keeping a continual supply of warm water. There is a very large cast-iron pot sitting on it, simmering away nearly full of water.

Agnes comes out carrying a small tray with three mugs of coffee, some canned milk, and a few homemade biscuits. She is a heavy woman, with straight gray hair, cropped in page-boy style, framing her distinctive Indian features. It is easy to tell that she has been an attractive woman in her youth. She has raised eight children by a previous marriage and has many grandchildren. Adam is taller, but thin, straight, and wiry. He has never been a candidate for a beauty contest. In fact there is nothing noticeably outstanding about him. He just gradually grows on you, until you start to find yourself a little surprised at the quality of his wisdom. Adam speaks English better than Agnes, who often mixes in some Indian, sometimes throwing in a few French words for good measure. Her first husband spoke French well.

Both Adam and Agnes grew up in the wilderness, close to the old traditions. Agnes is from a lake about sixty miles by water to the east, while Adam is from another lake, a similar distance to the north. In the old days Indians lived in small groups and bands dispersed all through the shield. Where conditions were especially good, there were villages of a few hundred, or even a few thousand. Lake Nipissing, for instance, supported a few thousand Indians in several large villages around its shores.

Agnes likes to talk about her family. She tells about her daughter from the city, who came to visit for a few days with her husband and children.

"Not enough room to sleep," says Adam. Then, nodding toward the partly finished cabin, he adds, "Need to fix up another sleeping camp."

"Too many grandchildren," chuckles Agnes.

"Did you know she had such a big family when you married her?" I ask Adam with a smile.

"Yes, I knew them all a long time," comes the reply.

"After first husband died and family gone, we know each other good, so I marry him," explains Agnes.

"She wanted me because I was so young and handsome," laughs Adam.

"We got married in town," says Agnes.

"Where did you go on your honeymoon?" I ask.

"Came here," says Agnes.

"We've been here ever since," adds Adam.

"Still on honeymoon," giggles Agnes—then we all laugh.

We sit for a while, talking about this and that, enjoying the view to the north. There are several loons on the lake doing takeoffs and landings, getting in their daily flying practice.

Agnes begins to say something in English, but it trails off into Indian.

"Speak English," interrupts Adam.

"What language is it?" I ask.

"Algonkin, different nowadays from most Indians on Nipissing."

"I thought Algonkin Indians lived in the area from Lake Nipissing to the south." I am a little surprised.

"Long ago," says Agnes. "Then Iroquois came. Much fighting."

"You mean the Indian wars? But that was over three hundred years ago!" I am fascinated that she should know anything about the event. Neither of them has ever read a history book. Even if they had, this is a story that has never been properly told.

"Yes, long time ago," Agnes confirms. "Many people come here then to escape Iroquois. Some stay here ever since."

"How do you know about this, Agnes?"

"From old stories when I was young."

Long before the white man came, the Indian nations had a broad perspective of the continent, with limited trading contacts extending from James Bay in the north, all the way to Florida. This was one of the first things to be disrupted by the appearance of the white man on the continent. In those early days, the white man's most extensive trade route was established up the St. Lawrence and Ottawa rivers, then across via Lake Nipissing to Lake Superior and beyond. This trade route was direct and skirted most Iroquois land. The Algonkin, Cree, and Ojibway peoples wanted the benefit of trade with the white man, while the much-feared Iroquois felt threatened by it.

Ironically, it was the Indian, not the white man, that subdued the Iroquois, clearing the way for the settlement of their territory. The continued massacres of trading parties by the Iroquois finally brought retaliation from the great Ojibway nation. They came by the thousands from north and west of Lake Superior, from Wisconsin, and Minnesota. For hundreds of miles they paddled their war canoes, their numbers gathering with the tributaries of the river systems, gaining in momentum like a storm. Like a cleansing scourge, they fanned out through the water systems to the south and east to totally destroy the Iroquois peoples as an organized nation. This all took place about 1650, when the white man's numbers were still quite small. Had the Ojibway shared the feelings of the Iroquois, the course of history might have been very different.*

Adam and Agnes know something of these events through remnants of their folklore—legends transmitted from generation to generation. Fragments of their culture still persist with those that sense its living spirit.

"Do young people on the reservation still learn the language?" I inquire after a while.

"When the family speaks it," Adam explains, "but many not interested. They must learn English and French in school also. Young people forget about the old ways."

---

* A brief account of these events, taken from early missionary correspondence, is given by Murray Leatherdale, *Nipissing from Brule to Booth* (North Bay, Ont.: North Bay Chamber of Commerce, 1971).

"Will you stay for supper?" asks Agnes.

"By the looks of that dark cloud, I should soon head for camp."
I indicate the large thunderhead encroaching from the north.

"A storm's coming, all right," Adam agrees. "Many storms come
from the north this year."

"Time enough for another coffee before you go." Agnes collects
the cups and scurries off to the kitchen. She returns in a few minutes
as Adam and I exchange estimates on when the storm will arrive.

"When are you coming down to see me?" I ask.

"Gasoline a big problem," Adam explains, "but we have to go
down the lake in about a week or ten days. We'll stop in on the way
back."

The coffee is gulped down quickly, with apologies for the hasty
departure. With some luck, there should be time enough to make
it back to camp before the storm.

As the boat is turned out around the point toward camp, the
sky exchanges its somber shroud for a translucent veil of light across
the south. The lake is serene—a pool of molten silver, alive with
scintillating shimmers. Light is playing through air and water, rocks
and trees, in the endless game of spanning space and time. Sunlight
is only a messenger in a living solar cell that is itself a massive dance
of energy. Eight minutes from the sun, it comes to show the way, to
lend space and time to pines and poplars, spruce and birch, reaching
out of rocks in ancestral celebrations. The hills are rejoicing in a
boisterous silence, as the boat skims like a spaceship through a
timeless fantasy of form. Everything seems suddenly like a splendid
dream.

Nightmarish undercurrents are working through the dream,
recalling spaceship protégés of light to action, from energies gathered through the eras. The woods and water are full of tiny cannibals, exploring techniques of bridging time and space. Fish are
cannibals as well, but the vertebrates bring a refinement of reflection
to behavior, from minnows to loons and men. Sensitive activity is
given perspective through spiritual reflux into consciousness. Behavior becomes manifest as conscious action. The suitability of technique can be perceived, assessed, and modified.

Man has been equipped with a special apparatus for spanning
space and time. Folklore and legends are woven on a loom of language. The threads are spun from words, but words are not the
experience transmitted through the tapestry. Words, like secret
codes, are neither music nor musicians. They are a discretionary
guide, to summon the spirit of the tapestry to a rebirth in the minds

of men. Cultures are given continuity. The benefits of hard-won insights through experience are preserved for generations, yet more nightmares come to haunt the splendor of the dream. Words tend to become the message, not the messenger. Insights are exchanged for vested interests untailored to the circumstance. Conflicting spirits in the tapestry clash for total dominance. Mind is lost in massacres and wars.

The spirit is neither the object nor the subject of the mind. It is the axis of experience, through which mentation and behavior are mutually reflected. Through discretion, spirits are entertained in spirit on a hierarchy of levels. The spirit hosts a dance of many spirits that come through invitation, then seek a way to participate and stay. Each must submit to tailoring, to find relevance to the tapestry of experience through the void. Space and time through all eternity are ours, according to how we weave the fabric of our mind.

The spaceship fleets over the slick silver surface, through the light-drenched splendor of the dream. Memories of a lifetime pale to insignificance before those of eons, dancing from suspension in an ageless sea of emptiness, to enact the imagery of nature's drama. As the boat moves through the scene, it seems the scene is moving through the being. Space has lost objective relevance to time in the reflection of identity through a universal spirit.

Behind the boat, the dark cloud is gaining quickly in the chase, but the race will easily be won. The island is already visible against the shoreline, discarding camouflage as the distance shortens. The fish will get to live another day. Tonight there will be time only for a hasty can of stew prepared inside the tent.

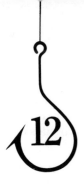

An Onion Dance

There is a disturbance in a patch of grass near the pine-log bench. A garter snake about eighteen inches long has captured a frog by one hind leg. Its jaws disengage so that it can swallow the frog which is considerably larger in diameter than its body. The frog, however, has no sympathy for the snake's appetite. It is struggling as best it can to escape, uttering squawks and little cries with a curious, human, pleading quality.

A few small sticks are tossed in the direction of the snake. When one of them hits, the snake releases the frog who immediately recognizes its benefactor and the direction of safety. It takes several rapid hops, jumping up on the log about eighteen inches away. The snake, obviously angry, has no sympathy for the frog's freedom. It too recognizes who has robbed it of its meal: after a frantic search through the patch of grass, it crawls right over in a plain display of agitated defiance. It seems to sense that the frog is in hiding near the intruder who has so unjustly interfered. It crawls around quite close, with angry rapid movements that show its avowed intention to recover its meal. A motion with the foot to chase it away doesn't frighten it in the least—it returns with increased determination. Meanwhile, the frog sits quietly by, safely perched out of sight on the top of the log, not anxious to go anywhere.

More sticks are tossed and poked at the snake, which persists even after it is hit a number of times. For a while, it becomes even more agitated and determined, but gradually it moves away a little. It is only after more sticks strike it that it finally gives up and crawls away. The frog, who doesn't move for quite a few minutes, finally senses that all is clear, hopping off in the opposite direction.

Even the reptiles and amphibians have a capacity to rapidly assess their situations and respond according to their needs, despite the fact that a creature so strange to them as a human being is involved. There is a common basis to perception, assessment, and response that spans the entire vertebrate series. Anchored in a common pattern of reflux through the autonomic system, it provides a certain limited basis for intuitive communication.

The invertebrates are more remote from us. We share the sensitive energies with them, which doesn't extend to a common organization of perception, assessment, and response. Many variations of organization are explored by the invertebrates, each projecting a different pattern of sensitivity that we can intuitively perceive. We have little appreciation for creatures with compound eyes, a multitude of legs, and mandibles, yet we pick up their projected energies of patterned sensitivity. Just to see a millipede is enough to make the skin of many people crawl.

We have an affinity for plants that we don't experience with the invertebrates. The vitality we derive from the air we breathe and the food we eat we owe to plants, but we also share their vital character in the energies they project. Who that is human and has wandered deep into an orchard dripping with cherry blossoms has not sensed more in the spring air than fragrance? The air is alive with a vitality that invigorates the human spirit.

Plants have transformed the biosphere, the air, the soil and sea. In the course of their own evolution they have had a major influence on the evolution of the planet. They have drastically altered the chemistry of the atmosphere, with a regulatory effect on such things as cloud cover, precipitation, solar radiation, mean temperature, polar ice caps, ocean levels, and the plate tectonics of continental formation. Whatever the complexities of planetary evolution, plants have exerted a major influence for over three billion years.

What is the planet then? Is it another living tier in nature's energy refinery? Is it a structured hierarchy of interrelated energies engaged in a self-regulating activity? Is it an intelligent being functioning on a scale with which we are unfamiliar? Or is it just a big, round mud cake that somehow happened to collect itself together near a kitchen stove? Sherlock has something to say on the matter, you may be sure.

For the last few days the kitchen stove has been warming things up beautifully following another cold, wet spell. Today is a lazy, sultry day caressed by a soft, intermittent breeze, like a lover's warm, sweet breath casually stirring a quiet excitement deep within. The whiskey jacks have come and gone, the hummingbird has made its hasty inspection, and there has been a visit from a spruce partridge. This morning six loons came through the channel, stopping to give a brief serenade. A red squirrel is rummaging through the cupboard now, looking for something to eat. The cupboard may be waterproof, but it is not squirrelproof—the pancake flour and oatmeal must be kept inside the tent. Living alone in the wilderness involves quite an active social life once the neighborhood accepts you.

Across the channel, tree trunks are reflecting in the surface like long snakes trying lazily to slowly work their way to shore, never quite succeeding. The dimpled surface is slicing off the images of treetops, as if preparing vegetables for an imaginary stew. The kitchen stove, soaring overhead, is warming up the water—a swim just finished felt more like a dip in a simmering pot than a plunge in the waters of a northern lake.

It is the kind of day that stirs a desire to fish, whether the fish are biting or not. The gasoline budget can afford some trolling. This is an excellent way to learn a lake, to find the weed beds, and to explore the patterns of shallows and depths to get a feel for the contours and quality of the bottom. The nature of the shoreline and shape of the lake provide many clues as to the quality of the bottom as well. Knowing the general habits of a species, one can then begin to appreciate the feeding patterns in a lake. The experience gained by trolling is therefore never wasted, whether fish are caught or not. It all adds to a master sensorium of lake experience, a spontaneous feel for the many subtleties of its character.

In general this formless field of awareness evolves according to the way in which experience is assimilated. As the current stream of circumstance unfolds, discretion sifts through this fund of history, spanning space and time, to select elements of current relevance. The elements of relevance that are recalled and tailored to the current stream of needs contribute to the specifics of ongoing behavior. Through the relationship of each and all, the specifics of a particular course of behavior are then perceived against a background awareness of all experience. This background awareness is, however, qualified by overriding frameworks of understanding involved in the process of assimilating experience. We tend to develop favorite fishing spots that are selected through biases rather than through a clear perception of experience.

Trolling helps to inject new experience into the awareness to keep it up-to-date with the changing patterns in the lake. A new feeding ground may be discovered, or a ranging school of larger pickerel may be encountered.

Today trolling is begun right from camp, through the channel toward the south. The spare fishing pole is better for trolling, as it is a little shorter with slightly stiffer action. A regular trolling rod is not necessary for this kind of trolling which is very slow, and close to shore. A popular minnow-shaped lure is being used. It has a quivering sort of action that is very effective for pickerel. A wire leader is used in case of a big northern, and a good-sized rubber-core sinker is placed four or five feet up the line from the lure. To find the pickerel, it is necessary to stay close to the bottom. The lure is a floater and will tend to ride up slightly from the sinker, which helps avoid snags along the bottom. Toward the south, the water gets a little deeper, and more line is fed out. The boat is turned east a bit, past the first point. There are some rocks in the water beyond, with half a dozen seagulls standing in a row, as if they were waiting for a bus. Past another small point, the boat is turned south again, heading across the mouth of quite a large bay that extends about a mile to the east. The boat is kept just off the edge of a rocky shoal that extends across the mouth. Then it is turned out around a large point.

Around the point, the granite slides into the water in a solid sheet, with hardly a crack in its weathered facade. With clean-flowing lines, it slips gracefully beneath the surface to seek shelter for its naked form within the depths below. Above the waterline, the lichen clings for life as it has done for centuries, while further up the slope more developed, mosslike forms of lichen grow. These give way to moss, then to low bushes that provide scant covering for the otherwise naked skull of rock. At the fringe of the bush, there are some small pines with a thick stand of moderately sized red and white pines beyond.

A broad outline of the evolution of plants is written on the rock near the waterline, from the algae growing below the surface, through the lichens and mosses, to the higher plants. But what about the rock itself? What about the evolution of the planet?

The eminent Mr. Holmes has been busy on this case as well, certain of a link to the mystery of the organic cell. For one thing, he is convinced that there isn't any motive in either case, that everything has just happened according to fortuitous accident. Second, he is convinced that the modus operandi is the same. Everything is essentially just a big thermodynamic bakeshop that most probably began with an unthinkable explosion over ten billion years ago. As the universe expanded and cooled, it condensed into clusters of matter that eventually formed the galaxies, stars, and planets. There are several variations as to how this could have happened, and there are even some alternate ideas, but essential to them all is the notion of the bakeshop. Third, he is convinced that there is a common corpus delicti. He believes that there is only a mindless body, a corpse of molecules, particles, and radiation that is shared alike by cells, people, planets, suns, and galaxies.

The ingenious Mr. Holmes has done some admirable detective work in exposing many pieces of the puzzle; still, he is firmly entrenched in his methods of interpretation. He has regained his composure from his earlier disenchantment with his good friend Watson, and they are on speaking terms again.

"You see, my dear Watson, the evidence from dating the most ancient rocks in the Precambrian shields in different parts of the world, and also from dating moon rocks and so forth, indicates that the planet probably had a birth going back over four billion years ago. Now all of the major planets revolve around the sun in very nearly the same plane, and in nearly circular orbits, in the same counterclockwise direction. With the exception of Venus and Uranus, all of the planets and most of the moons also rotate on their own axes in the same direction. This suggests that the solar system evolved from a swirling disc of gas and dust that came to surround a central concentration of gas and dust in a large protosun. At this point, however, the sun was not luminous. The cookstove hadn't been ignited yet."

"Interesting," replies Watson, "but I have become more skeptical of your ideas. You mean that the solar system evolved from a big cloud of gas and dust, shaped something like a huge, spinning flying saucer? This turbulent cloud then condensed into a central sun and the nine major planets with their moons. I suppose gravity, turbulence, and electromagnetic forces can account for all of this, can they?"

"Despite your unruly imagination, you really are quite a clever chap, Watson. Yes, that is essentially how it happened. It is all quite elementary. The sun became compressed into a nuclear cookstove, and the planets condensed into big buns whirling around on a rotisserie in a solar oven. There are some problems yet to be worked out, but, given more time and more evidence from space probes and so on, all these things will fall into place. You see, the five outer planets are separated by an asteroid belt from the four inner planets, and except for Pluto they are much larger and less dense. It is like two very different kinds of planetary worlds, but this can be explained by the factors involved as the planets condensed. The four inner planets are very close to the sun compared with the outer planets. For instance, earth is the third planet from the sun, and it is thirty times closer than the eighth planet, Neptune."

"It all sounds plausible enough on the surface," comments Watson. "I suppose that ever since the planets were formed, they have been held in orbit by a balance of centrifugal and gravitational force, whatever these are, but how about all the other problematic evidence you have collected? If more than ninety-nine percent of the mass of the solar system is concentrated in the sun, then why is more than ninety-eight percent of angular momentum in the planets and satellites? How about the clockwise rotation of Venus on its axis? Why is the spin axis of Uranus nearly in the solar plane instead of approximately perpendicular as in the other planets? Why is Pluto so small compared with the other outer planets, and why is its orbital plane inclined? Why do a few of the outer moons of Jupiter and Saturn orbit in a clockwise direction? Why is there an asteroid belt containing material of all sizes up to minor planets instead of a regular planet? Is it just an accident that a planet didn't condense in an orbit where one might have been expected? How about some of the minor planets, Hidalgo for instance, with an elongated orbit astride that of Jupiter, but inclined forty degrees? Also, the space probes seem to be turning up more new questions than answers to old ones."

"Of course there are some disturbing questions yet to be re-solved," replies Holmes between puffs, while lighting his pipe. "Nevertheless great progress is being made, and there is no reason to suspect a different modus operandi. Furthermore, there are many contingency factors that could explain some of these anomalies—collisions and near collisions, comets, and so forth. Also, since we are just beginning to gather evidence from space probes, many of these questions must be deferred."

"Can you explain more about the planet Earth, then, Holmes? Space probes aren't as essential here. I really do have a great respect for all the work that you have done on the case."

"Be glad to, my dear fellow. As you know, gravity was a primary factor in the physical consolidation of the planet, although turbu-lence and electromagnetic factors came into play. In this way, the initial orbit of the planet and its angular momentum became estab-lished. A geothermal consolidation followed, in which the main cookstove was the heat produced through radioactive decay pro-cesses going on within the earth. Earth became organized with a molten metallic core with solid center, surrounded by an essentially solid, but somewhat pliable, mantle, and overlaid with a primary crust. Electromagnetic consolidation then occurred, probably related to internal convection currents in the predominantly iron fluid core, and magnetic poles formed in an approximate alignment with the axis of the earth's rotation. The earth's magnetic field in turn no doubt exerts something of a regulatory effect on internal convection and also on rotation of the planet, crust formation, and atmosphere. A magnetosphere came to surround the planet in a vast envelope that interacts with a solar wind of charged particles* ejected from the sun. This magnetosphere was important to an atmospheric consolidation that followed."

"It all sounds so organized," remarks Watson. "From what you say, there have been four successive stages to the development of the planet: a gravitational consolidation, a geothermal consolidation, an electromagnetic consolidation, and an atmospheric consolidation. Why, it is as if each of these has been worked out in successive stages of delegation, almost like a manager delegates work in a hierarchy of levels as a business enterprise grows."

Holmes pauses for a moment, making an effort to control himself, then he takes a puff on his pipe and says sternly, "It is all perfectly straightforward, I tell you. There is no need for these inane ideas you keep coming out with."

"I'm sorry, Holmes." Watson is genuinely apologetic. "The thought just happened to come to me. Can you tell me more about the magnetosphere, the atmosphere, and solar wind? This sounds quite mysterious."

"It's very elementary, Watson. The solar wind is related to sunspot and solar-flare activity that propels high-energy radiation, electrons and protons, toward earth. This has a major effect on the magnetosphere. For instance, electrons and protons become trapped in what are called Van Allen belts within the magnetosphere. Two belts, one with electrons and one with protons, surround the girth of the planet like the shells of two doughnuts, one inside the other. The proton belt is closer to earth—less intense than the electron belt—but both are far above the atmosphere at the equator. Within each belt the electrons and protons spiral around the magnetic lines of force very rapidly, traveling back and forth from one polar region to the other. The two belts also drift in opposite directions around the girth of the planet. Their intensity varies greatly, depending on solar activity. In addition, the shape of the whole magnetosphere

---

*Electrons and protons. The solar wind is a very rarefied ionized gas or plasma.

is distorted by the solar wind. Some of earth's magnetic lines of force are unable to close in the direction away from the sun. They are swept into a long tail that trails out indefinitely into the planetary disc for at least several million miles. A simple diagram will help to clarify all this." (See Figure 26.)

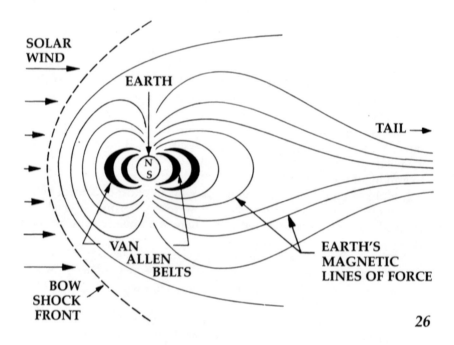

26

"Fascinating!" exclaims Watson. "Why, the tail is like an electromagnetic hand on a solar clock that sweeps around the planetary disc as the earth revolves around the sun. Do other planets have tails as well?"

"Don't get carried away again, Watson," snaps Holmes curtly. "This is only of incidental interest to the case. The important thing is that once a magnetic field had become well established, organic life could begin to evolve on the planet. The magnetosphere and atmosphere filter, sieve, and select specific radiation from the sun—this is essential to the development of life in the biosphere, since much radiation is very harmful. Portions of the upper atmosphere are particularly structured in this regard, since radiation levels are higher at more elevated altitudes. As you know, at the low altitudes we are normally exposed to, the atmosphere is mostly a mixture of the two gases nitrogen and oxygen, with only small concentrations of carbon dioxide and other gases, together with various amounts of water vapor, depending on the weather.

"For about the first fifty kilometers above earth, the gases in the atmosphere are all mixed up because of the turmoil of weather and whatnot, and for this reason it can be called the homosphere. Above fifty kilometers, the atmosphere becomes sufficiently thin for the various gases to tend to separate into layers, one above the other, according to their density, though they are still somewhat mixed up. This heterosphere extends up for another several hundred kilometers. Nitrogen predominates near the bottom, in the layer on top of the homosphere, then oxygen, then helium, and lastly hydrogen dwindles out on top.

"Now, when high-energy radiation comes soaring into the atmosphere, it encounters these layers, especially the more dense oxygen and nitrogen layers. This high-energy radiation bombards the molecules, ionizing them by knocking electrons free from their outer orbits. Positively charged ions become separated from some of their negatively charged electron partners—these charged particles interact with the magnetosphere. This forms what is called the ionosphere. It too is organized in four layers, each characterized by its ability to reflect different frequencies of electromagnetic-wave propagation. This is very important for long-distance radio transmission."

"Very interesting," interrupts Watson. "The way you describe it, earth is like two different kinds of concentric onions, both inside a doughnut. There is the material onion of earth, with layers of core, mantle, crust, and then atmosphere, which in turn has layers of homosphere and heterosphere. The onion of the ionosphere is constituted of electronic layers within the heterosphere. This is all enclosed by the doughnut-shaped magnetosphere with its long tail reaching out toward Mars."

"Hmmm, an onion doughnut. I'd wager that would taste quite good," muses Holmes thoughtfully to himself.

"Please tell me more about the ionosphere, Holmes. If it is caused by radiation, does it change from night to day, or from season to season? Do the tidal influences of the sun and the moon on the atmosphere affect it? Do fluctuations in the ionosphere cause changes in the strength of the magnetosphere? Does this in turn affect electrical currents and convection currents in the center of the earth? Is the ionosphere related to the weather? There are so many questions that come to mind when one starts thinking about electric currents wandering about in the upper atmosphere."

"It is rather complicated," agrees Holmes. "Yes, there are air movements in the ionosphere that generate electrical currents through the interaction of the electrically charged particles with the magnetosphere. At low levels in the ionosphere, there is even turbulence. In general, however, air movements in the ionosphere tend to conform to patterns of gravity waves and tidal influences. Temperatures over polar regions are similar to those over equatorial regions, which also indicates a polar movement of air. Possible relationships between the ionosphere and weather systems at lower levels in the atmosphere are tenuous and difficult to assess, but the strength of the ionosphere has a certain influence on the magnetosphere. This undoubtedly has an effect on internal events in the core and mantle of earth. Changes in the strength of the ionosphere are dominated by the sun—both by solar activity and by the daily rotation of earth in relation to the sun. In the daytime, there is an equatorial bulge in the ionosphere toward the sun, while at night the layers fade. Some tend to disappear altogether."

"It sounds as if most of the layers wake up and go to sleep with the rest of us through the daily cycle," remarks Watson jokingly. "Is it not correct that the ionosphere has evolved with changes in the chemistry of the atmosphere, brought about by the evolution of life in the biosphere?"

"An astute observation, Watson," compliments the sleuth, thinking that he has regained the confidence of his long-standing companion. "Yes, the oxygen in the atmosphere is primarily the product of photosynthesis in plants, although it is possible that the disintegration of water vapor into hydrogen and oxygen by cosmic radiation may have contributed. The presence of oxygen is definitely a key factor in making the ionosphere what it is."

"That is remarkable!" exclaims Watson enthusiastically. "The character of the ionosphere is indebted to plants. The ionosphere in turn selects radiation, which enhances organic life while preventing harmful levels of radiation from penetrating the biosphere. If I understand you correctly, the ionosphere also regulates the strength of the magnetosphere to a significant extent, therefore also influencing electrical and convection currents in the mantle and fluid core. It seems that this could even have an effect on events in the crust of the earth. Who would have thought that microscopic algae and their gentle descendants could wield such immense power on such a massive scale? Why, it is as if the ionosphere and its relative, Van

Allen belts, sustain mentation processes that reflect the needs of the biosphere and have a complementary effect on the behavior of earth as well. Could the planet be a living being?"

Holmes begins to puff furiously on his pipe, then blurts out angrily, "There goes your unruly imagination again! It's all a big bakeshop, I tell you, and the planet is just a big bun going round on a rotisserie!"

"I'm terribly sorry, Holmes," pleads Watson, "I just can't help it! These seditious thoughts keep coming, and before I know it I've spoken them. It's as if I'm possessed by the devil himself."

Holmes glares at him for a moment or two, puffing compulsively on his pipe. Then he turns abruptly and walks away.

Science is extremely reluctant to entertain thoughts of an intelligent motive or modus operandi. It regards that perspective as filled with superstitions, yet its own view has itself become a superstition, with an unreasonable belief in an accidental corpse as the only reality. There seems to be a feeling that to admit that intelligence is at work in the universe is to abandon the possibility of understanding the natural order, as if order and intelligence were mutually opposed. There is no doubt that the fishing hole of science has produced a few nice catches, but there is a whole lake left unexplored.

The outboard motor sounds out its incessant muffled chugs with monotonous regularity. The turns of the propeller are synchronized with nature's movie to smoothly slide the scenery along in a script that has been unfolding through eternity. Even the early chapters of the story, long since told, linger to maintain a dialogue in mute words of sculptured granite along the naked shore. The gallery of hills rises in irregular variations, forested with throngs of spectators that keep returning to the show.

A broad flat point has been shattered into large pieces that rest intact, a little weatherworn, yet still assembled like a jigsaw puzzle. Around the point, the granite has been scraped into grooves by a great claw of glacial ice. Approaching up ahead is a small marshy bay rimmed with yellow water lilies. The bay harbors a grove of poplars, tall and lean, wiggling a smattering of leaves as a standard salutation to every passerby.

Beyond the bay the granite becomes marbled with skinny veins of white and orange running through it in complicated road-map designs. The nude stone shoreline keeps modulating the tone and texture of its complexion. In places there are outcrops of feldspar

z, or regions of metamorphic rock, full of seams, twisting
ng in various directions as a reminder of pained contor-
...e awkward plastic stages of its youth. The acid water has
patiently eaten out some of the softer veins into ragged ruts that
meander with the convolutions of the grain.

Beyond another marshy spot, the rock resumes a regularity of
appearance. It has cracked in parallel divisions that angle upward to
the left, assuming an even, reddish hue. The rock has sheared away
between some of these divisions to expose vertical faces up to twenty
feet in height, rising cleanly from narrow, angling ledges. The slope
of the land begins to rise sharply from the waterline into a very large
hill, with faces growing to greater heights on angles up the incline.

The narrow ledges between the faces descend steeply in a sloping shelf and steplike pattern. Pine trees are growing on them out of
solid rock. One tree has lost its hold and fallen outward, but then
taken root again. Other pines have adapted to their meager sustenance with a stunted, dwarfed appearance. A few have outgrown
their food supply and died. Still others are quite large, thriving from
a few small cracks in solid granite.

The hill has now become a series of cliffs in tiers, with ledges
running up on inclines. It rises nearly vertically from the water the
first couple of hundred feet, then continues to rise steeply another
couple of hundred feet before it rounds off into a large knob, elongated parallel with the shore. The hill plunges into three hundred
feet of water.

Momentous happenings on a grand scale must have resulted in
this rugged terrain that has survived for hundreds of millions of
years. The trials these tortured hills have endured are unrecount-
able. Erosion, quakes, and crumbling through the ages have tumbled lofty peaks, mutilating stately forms. Then great walls of ice
came crunching through, pulverizing pieces, scouring away debris,
and spreading it in granulated layers hundreds of miles to the south.
Again and again the ice receded, only to come crushing down once
more, a mile deep, with great teeth munching off the tattered tops
and raking out the valleys. Robbed of noble stature and regal bearing, these tormented hills huddle in the memory of the grandeur of
their youth.

The ice has all receded now. In repentance it has melted into
valleys, like a myriad of teardrops that trickle in never-ending mur-
murs to the sea. Oppressive giant walls of ice have capitulated in
remorse, to wash and sooth inflicted wounds and mend pained

memories. This water wonderland is born from the sorrow of what these martyred hills have suffered long ago.

In compassion, great forests have sprouted forth from barren cracks and meager beds of bankrupt soil. They offer consolation to these hunched monuments to the past, clothing their disfigured forms beneath a cloak of cover, that they might rest in slumber. What a tale these hills could tell! Only fragments of the story can be pieced together from anguished words written in scattered glimpses of their faces. Stuttered sentences of broken language cry out at the heinous improprieties of their misfortune. But even here, colonies of lichen grow in soft, gray-muted tones of pale greens and blues to veil the starkness of distress from exposure to the world. Only at the surface of the water do windswept tears continue to erode at wretched memories of the past. Here the words are read the clearest, yet sometimes still, these hills can rouse to utter audibly a word or two. They have not spoken harshly now for many years, but when they do, all creatures shudder as they listen, such is the awesome tremor in their voice.

These persecuted craggy knobs and ridges are elder members of an honored family of pioneers. Their origins reach back to the early days of continents, when the planet's primal crust was busy making stages in order to enact an animated drama. Precambrian shields are from a family of protocontinents, with members scattered with their offspring now, in continents throughout the world. But what about the building of the modern continents? Has there been a method and an order to it, or have they just happened along, in a random chain of events?

Watson's curiosity has been piqued as well; he has chased after his good friend Holmes with profuse apologies.

"Please forgive my irritating remarks, Holmes. You simply must believe that I have a profound interest in the case and the highest admiration for the fine detective work that you have done. What you have to say is of great relevance to the case. There are many questions that I wish you would clarify for me."

Holmes continues walking for a few moments, reflecting on their long association—on the support and assistance that Watson has given on so many cases over the years. Then he stops. Turning to look directly at Watson, he says politely, "Very well, my good fellow, what is it that's on your mind?"

"It's all this business about the continents. I've heard rumors about strange tectonic movements—continents floating about like rubber rafts—but it hardly sounds credible to me."

"I found it rather difficult to get accustomed to the ideas also, Watson, but the evidence is very convincing. From the earliest geological record—the Precambrian shields in various parts of the world—the most ancient rocks have been dated at more than three and a half billion years old. In contrast, the oldest rocks in the ocean floor are only about two hundred million years old. This strongly suggests that the earth's crust under the oceans is continually being consumed and renewed from the mantle beneath."

"You mean that the solid crust that supports the oceans is constantly being spewed up and formed from the mantle in certain places, and devoured back into the mantle in other places? How can such a thing occur?"

"Be patient, Watson, I'm coming to that. These activities occur at junctions known as tectonic boundaries, that often coincide with major earthquake and volcanic activity. They divide the earth's crust into a number of major areas known as plates. Since the continental plates are less dense and much thicker than the crust under the oceans, they tend to ride above an ocean plate when the two are thrust together. The ocean plate is turned back into the mantle of the earth, where it tends to melt, producing volcanic activity. New ocean crust is formed at ridges that run through the oceans of the world, like spines of parallel mountain ranges with a trough between them. For instance, there is a spine ridge that runs through the center of the Atlantic Ocean, from the Arctic to the Antarctic, where it shifts around the southern end of Africa. At these ridges, magma is forced up from the mantle of the earth beneath and drawn out into new crust as the ocean floor spreads. Although these movements are very slow, at most only a few inches a year, they have been sufficient to replace the entire oceanic crust in about two hundred million years. In contrast, the continents have drifted and changed through a variety of processes."

"But if the mantle is solid, how are such movements possible?" puzzles Watson.

"Well, it seems that the top layer of the mantle, known as the lithosphere, is quite solid. It supports the crust and, in fact, moves with it. Beneath the lithosphere, however, the mantle can assume a plastic consistency owing to high temperature and pressure. It can permit these very slow, massive types of movement. There are probably even patterns of thermal convection through it, accounting for the forces that move the plates in relation to one another. Where the ocean crust is forced under a continental plate, generally there is a trench, such as the one that extends in an arch from the Aleutian Islands in Alaska down the west side of the Pacific Ocean to Indonesia. More complex processes at tectonic boundaries, such as mobile belts, have resulted in the mountain building along the west side of the Americas. The Himalaya Mountains seem to be the result of collisions between the continental plates of India and Asia."

"But how do the movements of the ocean crust adjust to the complex shape and movements of the continents?" interrupts Watson. "Surely the ocean floor is not made of rubber."

Holmes is not amused by Watson's comment, but he continues. "Indeed not, my dear fellow. Movements of the continents are accommodated through what are called transform faults. The crust of the ocean floor shears past itself in lines that radiate laterally out from the spine ridges. A simplified diagram will help clarify the general pattern." (See Figure 27.)

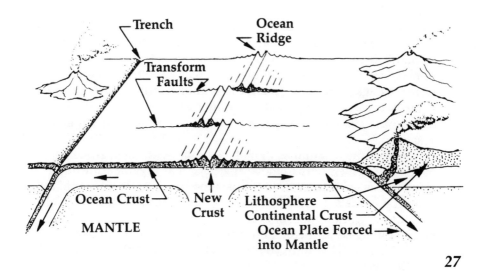

27

"Very fascinating, Holmes. Your analysis is beginning to sound quite plausible," commends Watson. "The ocean crust is like a system of conveyor belts that shift the continents around from place to place over very long periods of time. Explain more about the movements of the continents."

Holmes pauses for a couple of minutes to refill his pipe. Then

he continues. "The geological record indicates that the early protocontinents got started about three and a half to four billion years
ago, the first crude beginnings of organic life probably coming along
shortly thereafter. Conditions were very different then; volcanic
activity expelled huge amounts of carbon dioxide and water vapor
into the atmosphere. In fact much of the volume of water in the
oceans could be of volcanic origin. Things must have been in quite
a dreadful state, but as organic life got a foothold, a more orderly
pattern began to consolidate. Tectonic activity became established—
associated with the protocontinents—but a very different configuration of activity existed than the one we find today. Unfortunately,
the primary crust of the ocean floor has long since been gobbled up
and replaced, so that we are left with only meager evidence of early
events in the Precambrian shields of the world."

"That is unfortunate," agrees Watson. "I guess it means that
you aren't able to tell much about the movement of the continents."

"Not at all, Watson. There is strong evidence that as the protocontinents evolved and grew, they moved into a confluence with
one another. They all came together into one massive supercontinent
called Pangea, a little over two hundred million years ago. By this
time organic life had also matured enormously. The bony fishes and
amphibians had been around for quite some time. Reptiles were
coming into their heyday, but the mammals hadn't yet entered the
scene. At this point, new tectonic boundaries formed; Pangea began
to break up, dispersing into the continental pattern that we find
today. Australia broke away from Antarctica only sixty-five million
years ago."

"You make it sound as though the continents have grown and
bounced together, only to move apart again as organic life trotted
along into ever more evolved forms. One supercontinent would also
tend to provide a distribution of the various reptile species over all
parts of the world, a sort of even mix, from which evolution could
branch out again as the modern continents separated. In heaven's
name, Holmes, how have you been able to deduce all of these earthshaking events?"

"It is all quite elementary, my dear Watson. You see, it is possible to date the formation of the earth's crust through trace radioactive elements. It is also possible to determine the initial orientation
of the crust at a given location, in relation to the earth's magnetic
field, because trace magnetic minerals become permanently magne-
tized in a north-south direction at the time the crust solidifies. With

this knowledge of age and orientation gathered from points all over the world, together with other evidence, it is possible to gradually piece the story together. For instance, portions of the continental crust from Africa and America can be accurately matched, indicating they were once together in the supercontinent Pangea. Transform faults also give many direct clues about movements since Pangea. Furthermore, the earth has reversed its magnetic polarity from time to time. This has helped a great deal to assimilate the evidence."

"I'm flabbergasted," gasps Watson. "You mean the earth can just reverse its magnetic polarity? Change the North Pole to the South Pole, and vice versa? Why, that must be a cataclysmic event!"

"No need to get excited, Watson. It's no big deal. It has happened hundreds of times throughout geological history, although I admit that it is difficult to understand *why* it happens. As a matter of fact the sun reverses magnetic polarity about every eleven years."

"You mean that massive giant, the sun, does it too? And so quickly? That must have some profound significance!"

"You really are a very excitable chap, Watson, and you keep getting carried away. You must learn to get hold of yourself," says Holmes, puffing a little more rapidly than usual on his pipe.

"I suppose you are right. I'll try to be a little more objective. Perhaps you could expound some on the development of the continents prior to their confluence into a supercontinent. Continental growth seems to have had a relationship to the evolution of organic life. Is that so, Holmes?"

"In a manner of speaking, I guess you could say that. You see, the huge amount of carbon dioxide in the early atmosphere has been disposed of by two main processes. About three-quarters of it has been dissolved in sea water and deposited as calcium carbonate in the extensive limestone and dolomite formations of the earth—a process assisted by life in the sea. Today nearly all calcium carbonate is precipitated in the tiny invertebrate skeletons of ocean plankton. The remaining quarter of the atmospheric carbon dioxide has been transformed by plants and animals into sedimentary deposits in the coal beds, oil-bearing structures, shale formations, and soil. Nowadays, concentrations of carbon dioxide are very small. Plants and invertebrate animals have played a major role in effecting this transformation."

"Then plants and the invertebrates have participated directly in the building of continents. Is that correct, Holmes?"

"In a manner of speaking, I suppose so, Watson, but other

factors—crustal movements, erosion, ocean levels, and so on, come into play. For instance, carbon dioxide levels can affect the average temperature of the earth—a change of only a few degrees can alter the size of polar caps substantially, which can change ocean levels dramatically, thus altering the pressure distribution on the earth's crust, which affects plate movements."

"But aren't carbon dioxide levels regulated by organic life?" inquires Watson.

"Yes, but also by volcanic activity, although organic life has gained the upper hand. For example, man's enormous use of fossil fuels can increase carbon dioxide levels."

"Then are you answering my question in the affirmative?" persists Watson.

"Well, I suppose so, in a manner of speaking, but there are other things—for instance patterns of thermal convection in the mantle influence crustal movements."

"But aren't these in turn influenced by the magnetosphere, which is influenced by the ionosphere, which is the result of changes in the chemistry of the atmosphere brought about mainly by plants?"

"In a manner of speaking, I suppose so, but solar radiation is involved as well," replies Holmes with a forced air of confidence, while puffing much more quickly on his pipe.

"But hasn't organic life been an essential instrument behind the regulation of solar radiation as well?" insists Watson, excitement mounting in his voice.

"In a manner of speaking, yes. But so what? You are going in circles and beginning to make me feel like a prime suspect in the case," retorts Holmes, with his annoyance beginning to show again.

"Perhaps we are all prime suspects in the case," replies Watson, with a wild and fiendish glint in his eyes as the words begin to spill out rapidly. "At every turn since its first appearance on the planet, organic life has been busy working out a balance between cosmic energies and the behavior of the planet. There are not just two onions to the planet, but three. The third onion is a biospheric onion with layers of organic life, from plants and invertebrates to vertebrates and man. The biospheric onion works out a balance with the material and electromagnetic onions, and it . . ."

Watson is fired up and about to continue, but Holmes cuts him off.

"I know what you're thinking, Watson, but don't say it!" he bellows.

The two men stand looking at each other sullenly for what seems an eternity. A new perspective to the case has gripped Watson's mind. He wants desperately to explore it. At the same time, he has a great respect for his longtime companion and is repulsed by the thought of jeopardizing their friendship. Finally, discretion prevails; he perks up with a cheerful suggestion.

"Would you fancy a pint of bitters at the local pub, Holmes?"

Holmes is a bit startled by the sudden change of mood, but after a moment's reflection, he is taken by the idea. "Yes, I believe I would, Watson. That sounds like a brilliant proposal."

The two men agree on a familiar haunt. As they walk down the street, the conversation changes to the dismal weather.

Science after all has been zealously pursuing its mode of inquiry for more than three centuries. It isn't likely to drastically alter its attitudes on the spur of the moment. We have all acquired a tremendous vested interest in science and its technological implications. We depend on science every time we brush our teeth or read a newspaper, yet we cannot escape the need for a more meaningful interpretation of the evidence. We are more than an accidental corpse of molecules in a cosmic bakeshop. Like the earth, we are onion beings with three different kinds of layers that seek a mutual balance. Moreover, we have begun to manage the animated spirit of our planet—this dear earth is as much our home as our individual bodies are; we can't forever treat it as a mindless accident of good fortune and expect impunity.

When fishing for a new perspective, thoughts often come in schools, some with little ones, some with large. They are seldom found in old familiar fishing holes—we must change our tactics to do some trolling. The waters of our understanding must be explored with different tackle and new techniques.

The boat is turned out around a jagged point as the shoreline strays outward from the steep rise of the hill. Another series of low cliffs follows, cracked and eroded deeply, some cantilevered over the surface of the water, with big chunks missing from their faces. These also begin to rise into another hill, but the contour of the land takes them inland from the shore. Next, an avalanche of gravel and large boulders gives way to a sandy beach, where the shoreline curves out to a point at the big narrows.

If you have a good arm you can throw a stone across the big narrows. There is usually very good fishing here—always a current from the flow of water southward, which keeps the channel clear. The water is about forty feet deep in the center. Schools of fish moving up or down the lake must pass through the narrows; it is worth some special attention. The motor is shut off, the trolling line reeled in. There is already a jig on the other pole. Casting is begun as the boat is carried along by the current toward the channel. There is time for ten or fifteen casts as the boat drifts slowly through the narrows, but there isn't any action. Even the best of fishing holes is disappointing at times.

A couple of miles to the south, the lake widens into a maze of islands, with arms at the south end reaching out east and west for two or three miles in each direction. The prospects for pickerel are better there. The boat is headed down toward a narrow channel on the east side of the lake.

The sky is almost cloudless. The spendthrift sun is squandering its energy, with indifference for its reserves. Light leaps in all directions into boundless sky, toying here and there with distant relatives of form, spanning space and time. Our lumbering planet scavenges through the radiating wealth discarded like small change by an eccentric billionaire. It circles and filters through the emanating streams, transforming some, selecting some, rejecting some, according to its needs. An electromagnetic apparatus has been fashioned to exercise discretion. Huge haloed layers of energy enshroud the earth in a meditating womb, reflecting a maternal vigilance for a biospheric fetus. Deep within her bowels, our Mother Earth is churning with concern. Turbulent fluid spirits are disciplined by a brain of interacting ions gyrating through the sky. Seething, restless currents are shaping her behavior to ensure a place and opportunity for her child.

Shifting breasts have heaved and spread to nurture a suckling infant that has been weaned in stages toward maturity. Vital, sensitive, conscious, and creative spirits are entertained in a resonating biospheric song. Each intermingling elemental mind refluxes energies, dancing through the void to seek harmonic balance with the whole. Discordances are introduced as the drama of exploring experience in tiers unfolds, but gradually they are singled out and tailored to the master orchestration. Gradually, the maturing adolescent learns its part and place. The lessons are imposed through resonating limitations ringing through a planetary bosom.

Our whirling lady is a living being dancing round a living solar cell. She has a brain, a body, and a spirit that have mutually evolved, yet she had a primal spirit before the biosphere was born. In her youth, she was a wild unruly wench, lost in constant stormy moods. Lacking a refinement of discretion, she was given to volcanic eruptions of behavior and flashing lightning thoughts, as if she knew it all. Impetuous and impressionable, she was easily influenced by the tide, reveling with her dancing partners, a satellite and sun. Rhythm was her regularity. Maternal instincts came with pregnant seas, then life took root on land while her atmosphere and moods were tamed, steadily transforming into a womanly concern. Our gracious lady has blossomed into beauty. She still dances to a tidal rhythm, but she has learned to sing a melody of life.

She dances through a solar wind, part of her magnetic mental apparatus blowing out like skirts into the breeze. The outer layers of petticoats perceptually transpose on every revolution, opening to trail off into the wonders of the planetary disc. She relates to her environment to keep from getting dizzy. Her twirling tilted head and her magnetic personality maintain an equilibrium. Her axis wobbles slowly through the epochs to modulate her moods and the currents in her core, while magnetic polar transpositions occasionally record the ages of developments. Her whole molecular bulk is itself a syncopated clock pulsating with the galaxy as it tiptoes to and fro into eternal emptiness.

The timing of the complex melding of music into mind spans vast extremes. Our seasoned spaceship earth has memories with referents recorded in her continental crust, reaching back four billion years. Within the grasp of recall she has wandered with her beaming escort around the galaxy twenty times or so, yet spanning space and time on such a scale is not the greatest of her achievements. Along the way, she has reared an offspring that has been fathered at intervals by a Universal Being.

Recall from the void is effected through discretion delegated in many tiers—from planets and plants, to bugs and men. Each has a capacity for recall according to concerns of circumstance, but each major stage of delegation requires a gathering from throughout the void by a being that transcends all limitations of space and time. Our cosmic father is such a being. The roots of his mentation remain unborn in a steadfast center that spans the vast extremities of his electromagnetic rainbow.* We share the roots of his mentation with the most distant suns and galaxies—the span of all lifetimes is determined by the complements of his extremes. He gathers his spirit from the void of all experience as he wishes, for his discretionary access knows no limitations. Then he recommits his spirit as he

*Center 1 in System 2 does not perceptually transpose.

deems appropriate. He is endlessly regenerated through a living
spiritual commitment enacted through behavior in the world of
form, spanning all space and time through tiers of delegation.

In the evolution of the biosphere, each major stage of delegation
has been entrusted like a newborn child to the care of Mother Earth.
She has nurtured it, modifying its nature through her biospheric
song, teaching it to sing in harmony. Again and again the energies
of the void have been gathered and recommitted to her care. She
has suffered, as every parent suffers, learning through experience to
adjust to her family's needs.

Most recently, however, she has reared a problem child with a
strange perceptual handicap: the ability to speak. His name is man.
Two halves of man's brain have been delegated special functions.
The half that organizes speech is naturally concerned with social
endeavors; through cultural developments, man has learned to
provide quite well for his material needs. The other half, which
concerns esthetic appreciations and structural relationships, sometimes catches intuitive glimpses of his spiritual nature and his vagrant cosmic father. As if two sides to his brain were not enough,
man's autonomic system, which refluxes emotive energies into his
mentation, is anchored to his evolutionary origins in the biosphere.
Mother Earth had great hopes that man would one day help her
manage her affairs, but through the use of words, man has learned
to reflect on experience in abstraction. He sees in his death the
transience of life; at the same time he is taunted by a timeless cosmic
intuition. The creative gift of language has thus presented man
with a spiritual dilemma, bringing much consternation and disruption to the drama.

Man's cosmic father is something of a philanderer, but though
he entertains many wives in his massive harem he is responsible
and faithful to them all. He keeps a watchful eye; when help is
needed, he intervenes to assist in family matters. Man's education
has been of prime concern—long ago both parents agreed upon
a curriculum. The two aspects to man's mentation have received
independent attention through the divergent streams of East and
West, as man has explored the extremities of the world and learned
his limitations. All the while, our Mother Earth has tried to complement the divergence of attention through biospheric resonance,
while our cosmic father interjected considerable direction.

The lessons have frequently been misconstrued and very painful, being compounded by a twist to the dilemma that has ripened
with the play. The language of technology is flatly inconsistent with

the dialects of spiritual concerns. The divergent lessons appear to be in conflict, yet man cannot ignore them, and cannot shake loose his ancestral biospheric roots. Resonance requires a reconciliation as the divergent streams of education move full circle to converge on one another.

Learning is not confined to individual concerns. It embraces the evolutionary destiny of the human species—our "wholey" spirit. We don't create the master plot or write the master script in such a drama, but we are obliged to be performers in the play. Obliged to interpret and contribute, we find a part and place according to how we fish for understanding. Expansive pressures, confined by limitations, move us inexorably toward a climax, yet, despite the most profound predictions, we cannot appreciate the details of the drama until they are enacted. Likewise the Christian message of the Western stream has not been without its share of deficient contributions, gathered along the way on the shirttails of an essential core of truth.

The channel on the east side of the lake is only a few yards wide. The motor is slowed down to navigate carefully through the shallow water that continues on the other side for some distance. Once out beyond a couple of small islands the water deepens again toward a long jagged point at the entrance to the arm of the lake that reaches eastward.

The north shoreline of the arm looks best for trolling. As the boat slows down, the lure is fed out about seventy or eighty feet. Taking into account the speed of the boat, the weight of the sinker, and the drag of the line through the water, this gets the lure down about twenty feet deep. The depth of the water is then judged by the slope of the land as it enters the water. The distance from shore is adjusted accordingly.

There is a smooth rock ledge a few feet high at the water's edge. It supports a thick grove of cedars with boughs reaching out over the ledge, in an effort to conceal it. This is a character trait of cedars—both sociable and secretive. They often cluster into groups, their foliage growing together into a solid mat that conceals their trunks and limbs from view. Their tops stick up like pointed heads protruding from a common body. It is an attractive style they have, both shy and friendly.

Approaching ahead is a skinny island, about a hundred yards from shore. The boat is angled out to make a pass along its northern side. The water is not quite as deep between the island and shore—

fifteen or twenty feet of line is reeled in. The island is an extension of a low ridge from a point a couple of hundred yards beyond. Off the far end of the island the bottom is visible; there is only ten or twelve feet of water. As the submerged portion of the ridge is crossed, the motor is speeded up a notch to avoid getting snagged. As the lure follows across the ledge there is a heavy strike. The motor is shifted into neutral—the fish is taking line. It is fighting like a pickerel, a nice one. After a few minutes it is close enough to net. Several other nice ones can be seen following behind. A school is feeding along the underwater ridge.

The pickerel, a couple of feet long, about five pounds, is unhooked and released. The boat is positioned on the outside edge of the ridge, a little over a hundred feet from the end of the island. The anchor is lowered and snubbed in place near the front of the boat, with only a few feet of slack rope. There is not enough breeze to drag it, and the position of the boat will not be inclined to turn or shift. Poles are changed, and the jig is cast over the ridge toward the point beyond the island. The water is even shallower in that direction, but there is another nice strike. It's another pickerel, about as large. The next cast brings another and the next another.

There is a pickerel for almost every cast for a while, then a very heavy strike. This one takes a long run before it stops, fighting hard. It runs again, heading for the deeper water off the ridge, then swings from one direction to the other. It is too soon to work one this size in close to the boat, but it is coming in anyway, conserving energy. It is dragging in slowly like a northern, but hugging the bottom. It's a big pickerel. When it sees the boat, it dives under it like a torpedo. The tip of the pole is quickly plunged into the water—about three feet—in order to swing the line under the motor at the rear end of the boat, playing the fish on the other side. Almost lost it on that maneuver! It swims forty or fifty feet away again, circling around the point of the boat. A few steps are taken down to the front of the boat as the big pickerel moves back into deeper water, fighting hard. It keeps slanting back and forth, trying desperately to tear loose. As it begins to tire, the tension adjustment is eased up a bit to keep it away from the boat. It continues to make sporadic runs, staying deep. Gradually, its strength is waning. On the way back to the rear of the boat the net is placed nearby to have it ready. Now it is coming up, very weak. It is approaching the boat from the rear. The tension is tightened up again—the direction is ideal for a net attempt. It's in the net on the first try—a big one, measuring a little over thirty-one inches, about ten pounds. It is well hooked, but not injured; soon it is back in the water and on its way again.

Casting is continued. The fish are still hitting hard and fast. In a couple of hours, fifteen to twenty pickerel are caught, most of them five or six pounds. Fortunately, a couple are smaller—one about eighteen inches long is kept for supper.

Trolling paid off well today, although only a small one is needed for a meal. The rest are like ideas clearly grasped then released again to range unseen through the waters of our understanding. We can never catch or keep them all, yet our discretionary access matures with each experience.

Although the fish are still biting, it is ten miles back to camp. Time to get started. It has been a rare delight to find a school of large ones feeding in shallow water on a sunny summer afternoon. One may try this spot again a hundred times and have very little luck.

An Indian Dance

The morning is quiet, not serene, just an earthy sort of quiet. The wind will get up after a while—often the breeze doesn't feel like doing much until the afternoon. Across the channel, the vein of white quartz is reflecting in the water, as if an unsteady hand is trying to duplicate its image in the surface, patiently erasing unsuccessful tries.

Six loons glide silently into view around the point from the north, moving with an easiness that's magic. There is no working movement to their bodies to reveal the paddling of their feet. The power of their unaided will appears sufficient to propel them through the water. There is an aura about them, as if they were space visitors from another planet.

Loons choose one mate for life, never congregating into flocks, although they sometimes get together with their neighbors. They like to go for occasional strolls together; a cruise through the channel is often on their route. They know that a human being is living here, and entertain a passing curiosity. They are very discreet about their observations, as they are an exceptionally refined and independent bird. They don't like intruders and wouldn't think of intruding themselves. You won't find these birds crowding into parks in cities as ducks and geese so often do. They won't accept a human diet and would never abandon their migratory habits. They migrate to the oceans, but their love is the lakes throughout the wilderness of the shield. They never overcrowd them—small lakes may have only a lonely pair. They stay until freeze-up in the fall, returning again as soon as spring break-up lets them land. Each year they raise a brood of only one or two.

Through time, these birds have learned to accept and trust the stranger living on the island. They swim by only fifty feet away, volunteering a couple of quiet hoots of acknowledgment as they pass. Now six more loons come cruising around the point from the south. More soft hoots are exchanged as the two groups slowly coast together. As they are about to merge, a wild vibrato call is uttered, shattering the silence in a shock that spreads for miles. Another loon joins in, then another and another, until all revel in a chorus of fervid celebration, rejoicing in reunion through their ritual of song. Once in the mood, they can't seem to stop the music. It gushes unrestrained in waves of runs and trills that keep climbing to climax after climax. As they mingle into a single group their vocal volleys are paced and timed to proliferate a modulated medley. They pause in turn for breath to join again in chorus, while as a group they slowly turn gliding back toward the campsite. There is no leader, no loon that strives to distinguish itself apart. Responding in spontaneity as they sing, they seem to sense together the awe-inspired admirer sitting on the island. What better thing to do than perform a special show that I might better know the music of their spirit?

They approach like a group of carolers dressed up in Sunday best with freshly laundered shirts and collars and ornamented coats. About fifty feet in front, they stop. All turn to face their honored audience of one. Beaks are quivering with the vibrato of their voices immersed in ecstasy of song that hastens on and on in a command performance, as for a privileged king. Verse after verse ensues, with every loon attentive and enthused in the opera, rejoicing at the marvels of rejoicing. The infatuation of the theme is transfiguring the scene into a mystic medium of enraptured sound. Calls chasing after calls careen up through the chorus into crescendos that follow with crescendos. Enchantment swells into exhilaration to saturate the senses with enthralling wonder at the virtuoso spirit flooding through a mind transformed to music. Ancestral echoes are answering these birds from deep within this human being's breast.

These charismatic creatures have an uncanny sense of showmanship: very casually they turn together to add some magic movements to the music. They circle slowly out toward the center of the channel, moving as a single bird but with a dozen voices. Very graciously they execute some turns and loops, in a flawless flow, as if they had rehearsed it all a thousand times before. Their fluid movements sweep round in a circle to return the lyrical melisma for a curtain call in front. More vibrant verses of the opera are offered before they turn again to once more wend their way through a glide of magic grace back to the center of the channel.

Suddenly the music stops, and so do they. As the echoes fade, a deafening quiet rebounds to fill the vacuum. The silence is suspenseful. They sense it too. Still in a close-knit group a couple yards across, they begin to mill around, as if crowded in the lobby at intermission time. Then all at once, without anything to trigger the event, they burst away from the center of the group like maniacs. The water churns to a froth as they all fan out like fragments of shrapnel from an exploding shell. They slam their wings ferociously into the water as they swim and shriek out calls, as if something terrible has gone wrong. Most of them don't go far, about twenty feet. Then they stop quickly and poke their heads under the water to look around. They all seem to have gone crazy at once. They bring their heads up at random, look around, let out a giddy laugh, then stick their heads back under to look around again.

One especially affected loon doesn't stop with the others after the initial burst, but keeps on swimming like a mad fool trying to kill the water with its wings. It swims away from the group a hundred feet or more before it stops and pokes its head under the water like the others. The next instant it turns and flails the water back through the center of the group again, then stops again to hide its head, look up, and laugh. It makes another long, feverish rush back and forth, then rejoins the group in their idiotic game of look-and-tell. They look around underwater, then look around on top, then make a mockery of the difference between the two with their giddy calls.

Gradually they close the circle once more, regrouping as they cruise toward the north. Continuing with the game, they then start to take turns diving. They just go under and pop up again at random within the group as the others play look-and-tell. The whole group goes down, then comes up again together and continues with the game. They keep up these antics like a group of clowning kids until finally they disappear from view around the point.

A group of loons has often paused before to serenade in passing, yet this has been an unusual performance, spontaneously conceived, sustained, and varied. They delight in teasing with their common spirit, each creatively exploring its relationship to all, in song and dance and play. Despite their talent for social harmony, these majestic birds are not caught up in flock behavior. They don't perpetuate their gatherings into closed and automated social patterns. They exercise discretion with an eye and feel for what is fitting to the circumstance. They each regulate their responses in perspective, translating the moods of nature into music. The majority of their time is shared quietly with their mates.

The sun is playing peek-a-boo with cotton clouds. Shadow

phantoms are creeping in scattered patches across the contours of the landscape. Denied a surface of their own, they grope and feel their way over every hill and treetop in their path, each shadow phantom exploring a lane in a procession directed by the breeze. Sometimes the lanes overlap, and if we watch the parade for long enough we may find that the surface of the landscape has been thoroughly explored.

Unlike the language of the loon, our words and signs and symbols are shadow phantoms—they must borrow surfaces from the landscape of experience. They are more than social servants; we use them to explore. But the question is: if we succeed in mapping out the whole terrain, what will we accomplish? Can we understand it from a borrowed externalized perspective? What about the idea clouds that shape the shadows? What about the discretionary breeze that aligns them with specific patches of the landscape? What about the cosmic sun that casts all the shadows? What about the complexities of the landscape itself that underlie its surface? We may be familiar with the phantom mapping of the whole terrain yet not appreciate the projection of a single shadow, or the splendor of a cloudless day.

It is time to do some fishing. The embers in the campfire are doused with a pail of water, the tent is closed up, and the gear is taken down to the canoe. A trolling lure is dragged along behind, as the canoe is paddled slowly north across the bay, then northeast along the granite shore. The rock slopes steeply into the gaping mouth of water in timeworn weathered veins, parched withered lips quenched and soothed by lapping wavelets. The canoe slides silently along toward the narrow inlet at the end of the bay.

The trolling line is reeled in as shallow water approaches. A pike lure is selected for the casting rod. The inlet is about fifty feet wide with a slight current. The character of the bays beyond is quite different. They are ringed with dense beds of lily pads that extend out fifteen or twenty feet from shore, teeming with minnows and small fish. Northern pike often scout around the edges of bays like these. The canoe is kept out a moderate casting distance from the edge of the weeds, and paddled along at intervals. A stretch of weed bed is cast thoroughly from one position, then the canoe is moved along to the next stretch, and so on along the shore.

A shadow phantom passes as the sun peeks out from behind a fluffly cloud. The trailing edge of shadow fingers through the trees, counting off their numbers as it manipulates its way along the shoreline. The added warmth is welcome, since the shade is cool today.

The sun and planets have still not been thoroughly investigated by science, much less understood. This of course doesn't dismay the undaunted Sherlock Holmes. He has supreme confidence in his methodology and theories about how all the evidence fits together. Watson remains quite inquisitive, especially since the evidence also pertains to the intermittent insights that he gets into a new perspective. The other evening at the pub, the two men solidly reconfirmed their friendship. Watson got a little tipsy, and Holmes trounced him consistently at darts. Bolstered by his fine performance, Holmes is once again responding to Watson's queries, expounding on his findings about the mystery of the solar system.

"You see, my dear Watson, the four inner planets, Mercury, Venus, Earth, and Mars, are called terrestrial planets because they are all similar in their basic structure to earth. Not only are they similar in size and density, but they all have a distinctive rocky crust with comparatively little atmosphere. In contrast, the four outer planets—Jupiter, Saturn, Uranus, and Neptune—are very much larger but less dense, and their atmospheres are extremely thick. They are called Jovian planets because they are similar to Jupiter in their basic structure. Pluto is a maverick, since it is smaller than a terrestrial planet, yet has a density similar to the Jovian planets."

"Strange that there should be such a sharp distinction between two basic types of planets," comments Watson. "They are even separated by an asteroid belt, a continuous circle of debris like a stone fence between them."

"You can scarcely think of it as a stone fence, Watson. The asteroid belt is a broad band of widely scattered planetesimals and smaller bodies and boulders, down to the size of dust. Ceres is the largest, with a diameter of about a thousand kilometers, there being more than a thousand asteroids larger than thirty kilometers in diameter. Smaller ones are increasingly numerous, yet they have presented no serious obstacle to space probes passing through the belt. A number of factors have probably contributed to preventing the asteroids from condensing into a planet. During the accretion process, they may have been too close to the sun to retain sufficient gaseous material to become a Jovian planet, yet too far from the sun to collect into a terrestrial planet. Combined with the disturbing influence of massive Jupiter, this probably accounts for why the asteroids remained dispersed in a broad belt. The balance of factors involved as the planets condensed can also account for the sharp transition between the terrestrial and Jovian planets. After all, the innermost Jovian planet, Jupiter, is nearly three and a half times farther from the sun than the outermost terrestrial planet, Mars.

"Whatever the apparent reasons for the belt, it is still an outstanding structural feature," remarks Watson. "But, of course, the planets within each group are not identical. Can you describe some of the prominent differences between the terrestrial planets?"

Holmes pauses to reflect for a moment before continuing. "We have learned quite a lot from the space probes but, yes, the major contrasts can be summed up briefly. Mercury, as you know, is the closest planet to the sun, and it has no moon. In fact, the planet resembles our own moon in many of its surface features. The plane of its quite elliptical orbit is inclined seven degrees to the ecliptic plane, which is about the same as the inclination of the sun's equator. We used to think that tidal influences kept the same face of both Mercury and Venus toward the sun, just as our moon does toward the earth, but for some reason it doesn't work that way. Mercury rotates once on its axis in almost exactly two-thirds of a Mercury year. This means that each year the planet exposes opposite faces toward the sun. A year is precisely half a day on Mercury. Since the planet's axis of rotation is perpendicular to its orbital plane, there are also no seasonal variations apart from very hot days and very cold nights. Mercury has only a slight trace of atmosphere, with a magnetic field sufficiently strong to produce a shock front with the solar wind and a magnetosphere. The general pattern of the magnetosphere is similar to that of Earth, but it is not strong enough to produce Van Allen belts.

"It sounds as if Mercury is halfway between a sun satellite and an independent planet," interjects Watson. "Is Venus similar to the moon as well?"

"In only one respect, Watson. It has little or no general magnetic field. In the case of our moon, the particles of the solar wind impact directly with the moon's surface, and there is a long, cone-shaped plasma void on the downwind side of the moon. Venus, on the other hand, is perpetually enshrouded in dense, thick clouds of carbon dioxide to such an extent that its atmospheric pressure is about ninety times that of Earth. The solar wind is prevented from reaching the surface of the planet through interaction with an electrically conductive ionosphere four hundred kilometers above the planet's surface. This induces magnetic eddy currents, and a well-developed bow shock front is produced; thus, the electromagnetic environment of Venus is intermediate between those of the moon and Earth. There is a wind on Venus that always blows in the direction of the planet's rotation, encircling the entire globe like a dog chasing its tail. At the cloud tops it reaches velocities of more than two hundred miles per hour. The slow rotation of Venus is retrograde. The sun rises in the west and sets in the east every one hundred and seventeen earth days. An interesting feature is that Venus exposes the same face to the earth at every inferior conjunction, when it is directly between Earth and the sun. Venus is nearly as large as Earth; radar soundings indicate the surface topography to be comparable to that of Earth—the planet may still be geologically active. Only about one percent of the sun's radiation can penetrate the dense clouds, but they retain the heat. The surface of the planet is even hotter than that of Mercury in daytime. Lead would melt on the surface of Venus. There are also continual intense discharges of lightning on the planet. It is a regular planetary hell."

"I sure don't want to visit Venus," says Watson with a shudder. "Is Mars any better?"

"A little better, perhaps. However, it is very cold. As on Venus, the atmosphere is mostly carbon dioxide, but unlike Venus's atmosphere, it is very thin. Atmospheric pressure on Mars is only about $\frac{1}{150}$ of what it is on Earth, but it is sufficient to create dust storms that sometimes engulf the entire planet. Mars has some unusually prominent surface features. The densely cratered southern hemisphere stands up to three kilometers higher than the sparsely cratered northern hemisphere, with a complex boundary between them. There is a major ridge amid the lowlands that is eight thousand kilometers wide, rising ten kilometers above the surrounding terrain. Called the Tharsis region, it contains four enormous volcanoes. The largest one is twenty-five kilometers high, about twice as high as Mount Everest. A huge equatorial canyon system, extending radially away from Tharsis for four thousand kilometers, is up to four times the depth of the Grand Canyon. These features indicate an active volcanic and tectonic history, displaying a vertical character as compared with the horizontal variety on earth. There is widespread evidence of water erosion in the past, particularly in the channels that indicate flows from the southern highlands to the northern plains. There is no longer liquid water on the planet, but there is a permanent north-polar ice cap. Both poles become topped with dry-ice* caps that come and go with the seasons. Mars is larger than Mercury but much smaller than Venus. It has two very small moons, roughly twelve and twenty-two kilometers in diameter. As with Venus, the solar wind interacts directly with the ionosphere, producing a weak bow shock that trails off down wind. The length of a Martian day is similar to that of an Earth day, but the year is nearly twice as long. It is a strange land with magnetic iron soil, peach-colored skies, and purple sunsets."

"It sounds like an exotic place to visit, but I wouldn't want to live there. Our Earth is certainly the most fortunate of the lot," proclaims Watson like a typical tourist. Then he ponders, assuming a very professional tone of voice as he begins to comment on Holmes's brief account. "The terrestrial planets exhibit definite relationships that seem to be of fundamental significance to the ordered behavior of them all. Mercury, for instance, exposes opposite faces to the sun on each revolution, which provides a precise datum for the relationship of night to day. Of related significance is the retrograde rotation of Venus. Every time it is directly between Earth and the sun, it exposes the same face toward earth, even though exactly five Venus days elapse between such conjunctions. The length of a Venus solar day coincides with two axial rotations of Mercury. A Mercury day, however, is two complete orbital revolutions of the sun, which is three axial rotations of Mercury. On the other hand, the axial rotation period of Venus is two-thirds of an Earth year. The same ratio of two-thirds keeps recurring between rotation periods and revolution periods. There seems to be a triadic character to the behavior of the terrestrial planets that is reminiscent of the triadic relationships of particle physics."

"You are stretching the point more than a little, Watson. Where does Mars fit into your tidy scheme?"

"Just give me a moment to recapitulate." Watson pulls out his pocket calculator, scanning a tabulation of data on the solar system and scratching his head. "The rotation period of Mercury (58.65 days) is two-thirds (0.6667) of its revolution period (87.97 days). One Venus solar day (117 days) is two-thirds (0.665) of a Mercury day (175.94 days). The rotation period of Venus (243.17 days) is two-thirds (0.666) of an Earth year (365.25 days). Now, a Mars solar day is 24.6587 hours. That means there are 666.80 Mars days in a Mars

---

*Carbon dioxide freezes at $-123°$ C ($-190°$ F) and sublimates back to vapor at warmer temperatures without a liquid phase between.

year. The ratio of a Mars day to a Mars year is therefore also two-thirds, except that there is a factor of one thousand involved."

"Then how about the rotation period of Earth? An Earth day is about forty minutes shorter than a Mars day and doesn't exhibit any special ratio to revolution periods."

"But an Earth day is nevertheless of the same order of magnitude as a Mars day. Both the Earth and Mars have seasons distinct from days, whereas Mercury and Venus do not," retorts Watson. "Perhaps Earth is allowed some flexibility in its rotation period to compensate for the influence of organic life. Earth is also the only terrestrial planet to have a major moon—tidal influences have played an important role in the evolution of the biosphere. Is it just an accident that the rotation period of the moon coincides with the average rotation period of the sun? With the single exception of Earth's rotational period, all terrestrial rotational and orbital periods display a resonance that cannot be explained by laws of mechanics. Only Earth displays a degree of freedom in its rotational period."

Now it is Holmes's turn to scratch his head as he takes off his hat and walks slowly in a circle. Then he stops, replaces his hat, looks up at the dreary sky, and says in a condescending tone, "What are you suggesting, Watson? Are you implying that the laws of mechanics aren't valid? Are you saying that gravity and momentum don't work according to the time-tested laws of physics?"

"Not exactly, Holmes. I am merely pointing out some remarkable coincidences that indicate a more comprehensive system of order to things. Since electromagnetic energies are involved as well, perhaps our understanding of physical laws is incomplete. It could be that nature doesn't work in exactly the way we think it does. The formulation of so-called physical laws is built on empirical observations. There is no proof for them."

"Nonsense, Watson! All this talk sounds more like astrology than science. You mustn't try to make so much of a few coincidences. None of the Jovian planets shows any kind of resonance between rotation and revolution periods. They all have rotation periods of nine to eighteen hours."

Watson observes that this is very rapid and consistent, considering their enormous size, but he doesn't pursue the question. More interested in other evidence that Holmes has collected on the Jovian planets, he continues with his inquiry. "The Jovian planets display global winds, complex satellite systems, and rings. Can you tell me more about this and about their magnetic properties?" Watson is especially curious about electromagnetism.

"Very well, Watson. The space probes have told us quite a lot about Jupiter and Saturn, the two largest of the Jovian planets. Jupiter alone is about seventy percent of the total mass of the solar system—excluding the sun—while Saturn is about twenty percent. Both planets radiate roughly twice as much energy as they receive from the sun; both have numerous moons resembling miniature solar systems in themselves. Both planets have dense atmospheres and turbulent winds that encircle them like huge hula hoops in banded patterns. On Jupiter, the winds reach speeds of several hundred kilometers per hour at the cloud tops, alternating their direction from band to band relative to the planet's interior. Giant hurricanes like the red spot on Jupiter can last for hundreds of years. Saturn's upper atmosphere is dominated by a broad equatorial jet stream that covers more than forty degrees of latitude, reaching velocities of eighteen hundred kilometers per hour, four times the maximum wind velocity on Jupiter."

"I thought Venus was windy, but Jupiter and Saturn are even worse," spouts Watson. "Are the interiors of the planets so turbulent as well?"

"Unfortunately, we don't have much direct evidence about the interiors of the Jovian planets apart from speculations. Jupiter is enclosed in a vast envelope of hydrogen and helium gas about one thousand kilometers thick, gradually transforming to liquid molecular hydrogen. Internal pressures become so great that the liquid hydrogen becomes stripped of its electrons to produce a sharp interface where it transforms to liquid metallic hydrogen—an electrically conducting fluid closely associated with Jupiter's magnetic field. At the very center of the planet, there is probably a rocky core. Saturn is similar, except that internal pressures are not quite so great. The atmosphere should be thicker, with a proportionately smaller metallic hydrogen interior."

"Interesting," replies Watson pensively. "A similar pattern exists as with our Earth. There is a layered structure with a fluid metallic core associated with a magnetic field. In this case, however, there is a fluid layer of molecular hydrogen instead of a crust and mantle separating the metallic core from the atmosphere. This must lead to interesting interactions between convection patterns in different layers, with equally interesting electromagnetic effects. Do Jupiter and Saturn have strong magnetic fields?"

"Yes, indeed! Jupiter has a huge magnetosphere about 1,200 times the dimensions of earth's magnetosphere, and the magnetic moment of the field is 19,000 times stronger. The magnetosphere flares out in a distended disc shape, like a doughnut that has been flattened outward around the edges. This is due to the influence of a plasma, or ionized gas—within the magnetosphere—which co-rotates with the planet and so is thrust centrifugally outward. The tail of the magnetosphere probably extends well out beyond Saturn. The size of Saturn's magnetosphere is intermediate between those of Earth and Jupiter. While our moon passes through the tail of Earth's magnetosphere for only a couple of days every month, the major satellites of both Jupiter and Saturn revolve within their respective magnetospheres, creating some interesting effects."

"That sounds very intriguing. Moons are more completely under the umbrella of planetary influence. Please continue." Watson is anxious for more information. "How many moons does Jupiter have?"

"At last count there are sixteen, Watson. Galileo first discovered four of Jupiter's moons in the year 1610, using a primitive telescope. Called the Galilean moons, these are as large as or larger than our moon. Closer to the planet are four much smaller moons and a faint ring within the innermost moon. These eight moons closest to Jupiter are in the equatorial plane, revolving within the magnetosphere. Much farther away from the planet are eight more moons, most of which are only a few kilometers across. Four of them are about 11,000,000 kilometers from the planet, with orbits inclined about twenty-eight degrees to the equatorial plane. The remaining four are about 22,000,000 kilometers away, with orbits inclined about a hundred fifty degrees. The outer four revolve in a retrograde direction."

"That number four does keep cropping up, doesn't it, Holmes? Sixteen moons arranged in four groups of four. That is remarkable. Do they display any special resonant effects?"

"Don't get started up again, Watson. The outer moons, which are held very tenuously in their orbits, could be captured asteroids. The Galilean moons are of greatest interest because they have certain similarities to terrestrial planets. The inner two are of rocky structure, while the outer two, though larger, have an icy crust and probably water or water-ice mantles. There are some interesting geological phenomena. The innermost Galilean moon, called Io, has active volcanoes, which spew sulphurous material into Jupiter's magnetosphere, resulting in some powerful electromagnetic effects. Io seems to be the primary source of the plasma within Jupiter's magnetosphere. Interestingly enough, the inner three Galilean moons do display a simple type of orbital resonance. Their orbital periods double from moon to moon, moving outward. Of course, nearly all the moons of both planets are in synchronous rotation, just as our moon is. Tidal influences always keep the same face toward the planet."*

"The electromagnetic effects of Io sound fascinating. Are there similar effects with any of the moons of Saturn?"

"Not in the same way, Watson," says Holmes, lighting his pipe again. "Saturn has seventeen known moons, many of them of intermediate size between 300 and 1,500 kilometers in diameter, most of them having a large water-ice component. The largest moon, Titan, is the largest moon in the solar system, the only one to have a dense atmosphere. Titan is larger than Mercury, with an atmosphere over ninety percent nitrogen, the remainder being mostly methane gas. Orbiting through the outer fringe of Saturn's magnetosphere, it produces substantial plasma and magnetic effects. All but the two outermost moons, Iapetus and Phoebe, orbit in Saturn's equatorial plane, Phoebe having a retrograde orbit. The equatorial plane of the planet is also the equatorial plane of the magnetosphere. Saturn's magnetic axis very nearly coincides with its spin axis, whereas Jupiter's magnetic axis is inclined ten degrees. The magnetic poles of both planets are also reversed in relation to the earth's present magnetic polarity."

"It is unusual that the magnetic axis and the spin axis of Saturn should coincide," Watson observes, casually moving upwind from Holmes' pipe. "Does this have any relationship to the rings of Saturn?"

"It is difficult to say precisely in what way electromagnetic energies may affect ring formation, Watson. The rings of Saturn are very complex, consisting of thousands of intricate ringlets. Water ice seems to be the main constituent. Particle sizes average as much as ten meters in some rings, down to the size of dust particles in other rings. Some rings display precise proportions of different particle sizes, even though particle populations vary from place to place in the rings. One kinky ringlet consists of braided strands. The rings are also very thin, less than four hundred meters thick, with surprisingly sharp edges. There are various resonant effects between rings, as well as gaps in the rings, with different moons. Electromagnetic influences may predominate on very small ring particles,

---

*The theory is that tidal bulges become permanently fixed on opposite sides of a moon as it consolidates, so gravitational torque keeps it in co-rotation. Our moon is slightly egg-shaped.

but there are other curious electromagnetic effects with both moons and rings."

"Tell me about the resonant effects with moons first," requests Watson, showing a special interest.

"There is no great mystique about them, Watson. It is all very elementary. Gravitational resonances occur between orbits whose periods happen to exhibit ratios of simple whole numbers or simple fractions. It has to do with regularly recurring patterns of gravitational perturbation. This type of resonance is very common. Material tends either to collect in such orbits, or to be absent from them. For instance, the three inner Galilean moons of Jupiter exhibit this type of resonance, which was probably instrumental in the accretion of these moons. On the other hand, there are gaps in the asteroid belt, known as Kirkwood gaps, where asteroids are absent. These gaps occur at distances from the sun where orbital periods are simple fractions of Jupiter's orbital period. The reverse situation also exists, as in the case of the Hilda asteroids, which have orbital periods two-thirds that of Jupiter's period. To get back to Saturn's moons, Tethys has an orbital period exactly double that of Mimas. Dione's period is double that of Enceladus. A major gap in the rings known as the Cassini division has diffuse ringlets with an orbital period one-half that of the satellite Mimas. There are a variety of other resonances and near resonances between the rings and satellites."

"It all sounds like a fascinating dance of rings and satellites, performed to resonating musical rhythms—like a big phonograph record driven by a planetary turntable. The rings meter out the music in the grooves according to resonating patterns. Are there any clues as to how electromagnetic energies might participate?"

"A few, Watson. There are sporadic radio emissions associated with the rotation of the magnetosphere—perhaps also modulated by Dione—but the source of the emissions hasn't been identified. Apart from this, there is an unusual pattern to the absorption of inward-diffusing electrons and protons of the magnetosphere's plasma. At the orbit of each of the larger inner satellites, electrons moving at the same rate as each satellite diffuse freely across the orbit, whereas nonsynchronous electrons have a probability of absorption by the satellite. This alters the energy spectrum of the electrons similar to the way that light is altered passing through successive color filters. A selection takes place at each satellite, until the surviving electron population at Mimas has a nearly monoenergetic spectrum. This effect does not occur with Jupiter. In contrast, inward-diffusing protons are strongly absorbed. Electron density drops off dramatically at the outer edge of the "A" ring owing to the further absorption by ring particles, so that the region closer to the planet is nearly free of energetic particles."

"That is quite peculiar," asserts Watson. "The result is a succession of different electronic energy levels between the satellites. Each energy level bears a specific relationship to the orbital rates of the preceding outer satellites. The orbital behavior of the satellites is thus monitored by electronic energies. It is as if the planet is able to keep track of them. Are similar patterns apparent in the outer planets Uranus and Neptune?"

"We haven't gathered sufficient evidence from space probes as yet, Watson. These planets are considerably smaller than Jupiter or Saturn, though still much larger than Earth. It is likely that they are similar to one another in structure, with a central rocky core surrounded by a liquid mantle of water, methane, and ammonia. Both are enveloped in atmospheres of hydrogen and helium gas. Uranus has five known moons of intermediate size and nine slender rings. Neptune has two known moons, one of which, Triton, is very large, with a highly inclined orbit. Both Uranus and Neptune probably possess extensive magnetospheres. That of Uranus will be of special interest if its magnetic axis is closely aligned with its spin axis, because the latter lies close to its orbital plane. Twice per orbit, its axis points toward the sun, and the rush of solar wind down its magnetic poles may affect the magnetosphere in surprising ways. With luck, the *Voyager 2* space vehicle will provide more information on both planets when it reaches them in the late 1980s."

"The solar wind certainly has an extensive and varied pattern of interaction with the planets. Does it continue out indefinitely into interstellar space?"

"The *Pioneer 10* space probe has already confirmed the wind's presence beyond Uranus, and it is likely that it extends well beyond Pluto. It is remarkably constant in velocity, but it diminishes in intensity. At some point several times the distance of Pluto from the sun, the solar wind should encounter an interstellar wind and lose its identity. This limit is called the heliopause."

Watson, who finds Holmes's account intriguing, continues to question him on many details. The master sleuth patiently obliges him, responding on different aspects of the evidence in the case. He elaborates on the character of Jupiter's ring, on the shepherding moons of Saturn, as well as on the twin co-orbital satellites, which share the same orbit by less than the sum of their diameters, changing places by jostling past one another every four years. He

expounds on the high refractive index in the dense atmosphere of
Venus that bends light around the planet, such that one standing on
the planet might see the back of his own head. He fills out the picture in many other aspects, from Kepler's law of orbital mechanics to
proposed space missions. Watson absorbs it all attentively.

Through it all, Watson finds a basic intuition more and more
confirmed. He sees a pervading relationship between gravity, electromagnetism, and cyclic patterns of angular momentum, all
brought to a mutual balance through successive tiers of consolidation in the solar system. He sees in this the analogue for behavioral
form, mentation, and an animating spirit that have mutually evolved
in stages over great periods of time. He sees an intelligent relationship, a triad of mind dancing at many levels to a cosmic tune, but
out of deference to his colleague, he strives to keep his silence. Time
is on his side. However much Holmes may try to confine his attention to shadow phantoms, the evidence will require him to do some
different fishing. Holmes will have to diverge from his old familiar
fishing holes and begin to explore the lake.

The canoe has been worked in a circuit around the first bay, through
a narrows into the second. Three or four northerns have been
caught, but none of trophy class. Down the bay to one side, a
moose, feeding in a marshy area, is facing the other way and doesn't
notice the canoe. Casting is continued along the ring of weed beds.
The round green pads congregate in close formation like thin cook-
ies floating on a fluid grill to synthesize their sugars. A few white
and yellow water lilies turn pretty faces upward to flirt with passing
insects. Low bushes crouch along the shoreline, leaning against the
water's edge. Behind them, a black spruce army stands up straight,
with long, lean spines crowded in congested ranks.

The dense weeds end abruptly to demarcate the edge of deeper
water. Each cast is placed at intervals of ten or fifteen feet, as the
canoe is moved along in stages. Up ahead a patch of weeds is clustered farther out from shore. A cast is taken along one side. As
the lure approaches the canoe, a monstrous northern hits it in a vicious swirl. The line snaps on impact. The fish is gone! The line is
reeled in, tested with a couple of tugs, then another leader and lure
are attached. Sometimes a northern will stay in the vicinity and
strike a second or third time. The area is thoroughly cast again but
no luck. This northern has learned its lesson.

The moose finally looks up with a vacant stare, then ambles
slowly into the thick brush out of sight. The sun is moving west-

ward—time to think about a fish for supper. The fishing hole beside the island is still a dependable spot; the canoe is turned and headed back.

After supper the campfire is kept going. A final cup of tea is sipped while shadows lengthen out across the channel. The sun is sinking in the west. The clouds have nearly disappeared.

The sun is naturally of central concern to the mystery of the solar system. Holmes and Watson have continued their review of the evidence in the case, Watson having exhausted his questions on the planets and their satellites. He turns his attention now toward the sun.

"As I understand it, the sun, like most stars, derives its energy from the nuclear fusion of hydrogen atoms into helium, the same process that releases the terrifying energies of the hydrogen bomb. Is that correct, Holmes?"

"Yes, that's correct, Watson. The sun is a huge nuclear cookstove, a huge sphere of burning gas, nearly all hydrogen and helium, with only small amounts of heavier elements. Only in the central core of the sun are temperatures and pressures sufficient to sustain the nuclear conversion of hydrogen into helium. Surrounding this is a huge radiative zone where energy migrates slowly outward to a convective zone. Here, the outward flow of energy becomes turbulent, creating bubbling streams of rising gas, detectable as fluctuating patterns of granulation in the photosphere. The photosphere is the normally visible surface of the sun from which the great majority of its energy is released as light. The more diffuse chromosphere above it is normally invisible because of the much greater brilliance of the photosphere. Extending for about 19,000 kilometers above the photosphere, it can be photographed when the photosphere is masked, such as at times of solar eclipse, to display a pattern of supergranulation. Needlelike spicules of rising gas jet upward in complex configurations dominated by magnetic forces. Above the chromosphere is the corona, which is influenced by sunspots and related phenomena known as plages, solar prominences, solar transients, and solar flares. The corona radiates outward in the solar wind, bathing the planets in a stream of particles.

"Fascinating indeed!" exclaims Watson. "The sun is also organized in layers. There is a central core of nuclear energy generation, a radiative zone that disperses energy outward, a convective zone that takes over out to the photosphere, a chromosphere of magnetically dominated activity, then a corona that radiates particles out to the planets. Some of the solar activity associated with sunspots and so forth sounds frightfully awesome. Can you fill out the picture a little more?"

"Happy to, my dear fellow. Sunspots are often heralded by plages, which are bright spots due to magnetic concentrations in the chromosphere. Beneath the bright spot a dark sunspot may appear in the photosphere. Sunspots are areas of lower temperature that tend to appear in pairs of positive and negative magnetic polarity. Solar prominences most often form along the boundary between regions of opposite magnetic polarity associated with sunspots, some types extending more than 500,000 kilometers into the solar atmosphere. Others take on the shape of a huge arch or loop which indicates the presence of a strong magnetic field. Solar flares likewise tend to occur along the boundary between positive and negative sunspots, sometimes causing radio blackouts and intense aurora activity through their effect on earth's ionosphere."

"These truly awesome phenomena all seem to be associated with sunspots and magnetic fields. Do you as yet know how all the evidence fits together?"

"The more we learn, the more things are gradually falling into place, Watson. A remarkable feature of the sun is that it displays differential rotation. The equator rotates in twenty-five days, while the poles take thirty-three days. Since the sun is an ionized gas, the magnetic lines of force become linked to the differential rotational movements, spirally wrapping around the girth of the sun many times. The spiral pattern converges from both poles toward the equator, the lines of force popping out in loops when solar activity occcurs. X-ray photographs of the sun reveal that the lower corona is dominated by loops laced between regions of opposite magnetic polarity. High above these, the sun's outer corona radiates in long-tailed streamers shooting outward from the arched bulbous bases. The corona consists of very hot but widely separated atomic particles, mainly electrons and protons, whose high energy carries them away from the gravitational pull of the sun. As they strive to escape into the solar wind, many are bound by the magnetic arches of the lower corona. Where there are no loops, the solar wind seems to flow more freely into space along open magnetic field lines."

"I see," says Watson. "The solar wind begins as a sort of tug-of-war between high-energy particles and solar gravity. Magnetic lines of force reach up in loops to regulate a balance between the recapture and escape of particles. The solar wind streams outward from this balance of factors, taking with it a portion of the sun's magnetic field along open magnetic field lines."

"That's the general picture, Watson. At the same time, the great majority of solar radiation is in the form of a nearly constant stream of light."

"Then the fluctuations of the solar wind are related to special features of solar activity, which display recurring patterns in about an eleven-year cycle. This certainly suggests a high level of internal order to the sun. Can you tell me any more?"

The sleuth strokes his chin pensively, then takes a puff on his pipe and continues. "Surface observations of the sun tell us quite a lot, Watson. For instance sunspot activity always begins at middle latitudes, between twenty and thirty-five degrees, at the start of each eleven-year cycle; the activity migrates toward the equator as the cycle progresses. Close observations of surface velocities on the sun reveal that there are also traveling torsional waves that begin at both poles, converging toward the equator about twenty-two years later. Around both hemispheres there are two slightly faster and two slightly slower zones symetrically superimposed on rotational movements; a new set begins the twenty-two year migration toward the equator every eleven years. Sunspots appear to occur along the poleward shear lines between fast and slow zones, joining the migration at middle latitudes."

"Then there is a direct correlation between the fluctuating patterns of the solar wind and the internal organization of the sun?"

"Yes. The evidence points to this, Watson. During quiet periods, the solar wind radiates outward at about 400 kilometers per second, but the speed and intensity of the wind can vary drastically, depending on solar activity. As fast streams overtake slow streams, there are a variety of harmonics, all taking the form of an Archimedes spiral because of the rotation of the sun. This is illustrated more clearly by a diagram." (See Figure 28.)

"It is extraordinary that patterns of activity in the sun should be translated into an electromagnetic sphere of influence outward to the heliopause, where it succumbs to an interstellar wind whispering through the galactic community of stars." Watson stops for a moment and struggles to contain the words, but they come out anyway as he continues on.

"It is like an enormously complex mentation system that both influences and monitors the behavior of a planetary family and has done so from the beginning. The resonances of the solar system are

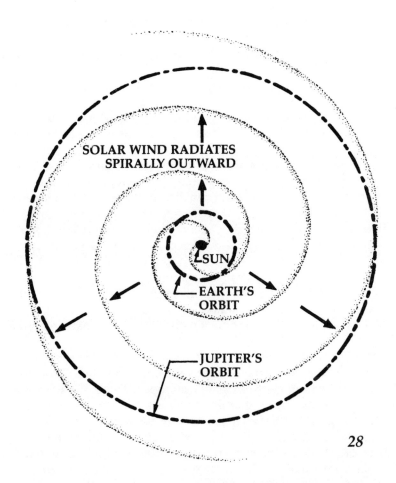

**SOLAR WIND RADIATES
SPIRALLY OUTWARD**

SUN

EARTH'S
ORBIT

JUPITER'S
ORBIT

28

but one expression of an underlying system of order that seeks harmonic balance between ideation and behavior through an animating spirit. These three factors invariably have their analogues in electromagnetic phenomena, gravitational formation, and routine dynamics of motion." The words have tumbled out almost against his will, and Watson himself is a bit shocked.

Holmes takes a couple of quick puffs on his pipe. Then in an effort to be casual, he removes his hat again to scratch his head. "Very well, Watson, then *you* tell *me!*" he says disdainfully. "What is

*Adapted from a drawing by James A. Van Allen in Beatty; O'Leary; Chaikin, eds., *The New Solar System* (London: Cambridge University Press, 1981).

this mysterious system of order that you imply masterminds the behavior of the solar system?"

It is Watson's turn to scratch his head. "Well, I don't know exactly, Holmes. It just seems to me that it is not only intelligible, but intelligent. The polar relationships exist within the solar system in order for it to know of its own behavior, and even to compensate according to its needs within discretionary limits worked out through its history. As the sun and planets consolidated, they didn't just gather into dead lumps at random. The accretion process occurred through gravitational forces that were accompanied at every step along the way by dynamic patterns, as well as by electromagnetic energies. The solar system can't be understood by considering these factors in isolation, for they have always been inseparably related. Furthermore, they don't bear a linear causal relationship to one another, but rather seek a mutual balance through cyclic patterns."

Holmes is becoming more disgruntled and assumes a stern demeanor. "You speak of the motions of the planets and their satellites as if the motions were something independent. *Of course* they exhibit dynamic patterns, but to consider this an animating spirit is quite preposterous, Watson."

"Why is it preposterous?" insists Watson. "The kinetic energies of moving bodies are something quite distinct from their gravitational bulk, or from electromagnetic energies. This is not to say that they aren't related, but rather that there is a distinctive routine of kinetic energies that has evolved through their mutual relationship. Furthermore, it is a routine replete with resonances of many kinds, as harmonic balances have been worked out on a time scale that strains the imagination. The solar system is a veritable symphony of movement playing through the unique orbital coincidences of the terrestrial planets, the many resonances of moons, the extraordinary intricacies of Saturn's rings, and who-knows-what beyond. The global winds of Venus, Jupiter, and Saturn reflect resonances of another kind, not to mention the performance going on within the sun. One can only speculate on the dynamic patterns boiling within the bowels of sun and planets, or on the related significance of magnetic fields. To think that motion can be understood in terms of causal forces through a mystical belief in time and space is what seems to be preposterous. Where do we find time and space without reference to our solar system? We determine time by regularities of solar-system movements and space by measurements of its form.

Our solar system itself offers the basis of our verbal definitions. How can we hope to understand its causal origin in terms of concepts that are dependent on its nature?"

"Then the alternative you suggest is that it is all intelligent," retorts Holmes, raising his voice and getting a little red in the face as he makes a grand sweeping motion with his arm. "You're proposing that the massive bodies of the solar system are animated by a spirit, reflecting an evolutionary balance with electromagnetic energies. Where on earth do you get the notion that electromagnetic energy is intelligent, or that it engenders mental processes?"

"In heaven's name, why not?" blurts out Watson in rebuttal. "Aren't our own mental processes engendered by electromagnetic energies? Don't we employ the electronic potentials of microscopic nerve cells in our brains to formulate our thoughts and integrate our experience? Through an evolved hierarchy of organization, don't these same insignificant energies mobilize the bulk of our bodies according to fostered patterns of performance that enable us to walk and run, drive cars, or send rockets to the moon and Mars? By comparison, the mentation possibilities in an electromagnetic body like the sun are staggering. It is highly organized in tiers of turbulent cells, with overriding cyclic patterns associated with magnetic-pole reversals. Its sphere of influence extends beyond the planets. Each of the planets in turn displays a personality of its own—a unique magnetic character—effecting a balance with the organization of its form through its dynamics. Massive though it may be, given that the solar system has had five billion years to get its house in order, why shouldn't we consider it intelligent? Don't you see, Holmes? The case takes on a whole new complexion. We are not just accidents of chance striving for blind mastery over a celestial corpse. We are intelligent participants in a living world."

Watson has glimpsed beyond the shadow phantoms confined to borrowed forms. He has glimpsed the clouds that formulate the shadows projected by a universal sun, but he is thwarted in his efforts to give it clear expression. Holmes stands firmly on his record, asserting himself with an overbearing confidence.

"Whether you like it or not, Watson, we must provide for all our needs through knowledge gained directly from the evidence. The laws of physics work to meet our material requirements."

"They may work within limits, but we try to extend them far beyond those limits. For every question answered, there is another left unanswered. We suffer from our ignorance of our ignorance."

This time Watson will not be put down. He goes on. "What is space or time? What is gravity, momentum, mass, or light? Why are orbits or spins or magnetic fields inclined to one another with inconsistent variations? Why do some resonances occur and others not? Why do magnetic poles reverse? What are they anyway? Why do we seek to understand it at all beyond our immediate needs? I don't mean that all your patient efforts have been a waste of time. I'm not suggesting that rampant superstition replace a disciplined pursuit. I'm suggesting that the language of our scientific laws is piecemeal and deficient. There is a more fundamental, all-embracing system of order to it all that we should try to understand."

"Very well, Watson, then where do we begin?" asks Holmes snidely.

"Don't you see, Holmes? The triad offers an alternative approach to that of cause and effect in a space-time continuum. I can't singlehandedly reformulate all the language of science in a few minutes, and you can hardly expect me to. You have had the resources of the whole department working on the case for over three hundred years. The point is simply that the present course is riddled with deficiencies. We will never explore the rudiments of intelligent order unless we try."

Holmes is fatigued and exasperated by Watson's persistence. He is hardly in a position to get angry, since he has invited Watson's comments. He stares blankly into space for a few moments, then, turning to his colleague, smiles and says, "I believe it is my turn to suggest a pint of bitters."

Watson smiles back and answers, "A brilliant suggestion, Holmes!"

A drizzle has started. Both men put up umbrellas.

"Next thing, you'll be trying to drag me off to church," growls the detective.

"Oh, I'd never go that far. May heaven forbid!"

"I wish the sun would shine sometimes," grumbles Holmes, changing the subject as they turn the corner and walk up the lane toward the pub.

The campfire is stoked up with two sticks of white birch. Another pail of water is put on for tea. It is almost dusk. The sun has set but there is still enough light to see clearly. The fire eats hungrily into the fresh birch wood. The bark curls and fries into tar as flames lick up around the pail. The water is already beginning to hiss. The bed of red-hot embers sporadically erupts, sending sparks skipping out of the edge of the fire. A small toad approaches in volleys of short hops. It positions itself near the stones where it can get some warmth, but not too much.

The sound of a motorboat becomes audible in the distance to the south. As the noise gets a little louder, it is easily identified. There is only one outboard motor that sounds like an automatic weapon. It must be Adam and Agnes. The exhaust housing on their motor has been broken off for years.

The water is boiling vigorously—the pail is set to one side on the stones. Another large stick is added to the fire, and a couple of tea bags are dropped in the pail. Daylight is fading quickly now.

As the outboard motor enters the channel from the south, the racket is amplified into a full-scale invasion. When they come into view past the point, Agnes throws up an arm and shouts out a whoop. I wave back and go down the ramp to meet them. Adam steers in carefully, and I catch the point of the boat, holding it while Agnes scrambles out. She is quite nimble for her size and age. The boat, a very old cedar skiff that has been nursed along for years, is loaded with camping gear, a chain saw, and heaps of birch-bark sheets about two feet square. I pull the point up on the rock as Agnes ties it. Then Adam climbs out over the load.

"I haven't seen you for a couple weeks or more. Where have you been?" I shake hands with Adam and give Agnes a hug.

"Camping trip down the lake," answers Agnes. "We camped on Sandy Island."

"Camping trip! Every day is a camping trip for you folks."

"We went to cut some wood and do some work at a cabin down the lake," explains Adam as we walk up to camp. "A man from the city owns the cabin, but he only comes for a few days in the spring and fall. He wanted me to cut wood last fall, but I told him, 'Sap not up. Wood not burn right. No good now.' This spring he asked me again but I forgot what I told him last fall and I said, 'Sap up now. Wood too wet. Not burn right. No good now.' I didn't want to cut wood in black-fly season. I should have cut it last fall when it was cool and no flies, but we wanted to go and visit family. I tried to fool him, but only fooled myself. I had to agree to cut it in summer. 'Sap just right in summer,' I told him."

"I see that you stripped and saved the birch bark. What are you going to use it for?"

"We'll use birch bark to finish new cabin," says Agnes, as we sit down beside the campfire. "We'll chink logs with moss and line cabin with birch bark. Make nice and warm for grandchildren."

"There is fresh tea. Excuse me while I get some cups."

"We'll have Irish tea," says Adam as he produces part of a bottle of whiskey. "Man from the city is not so bad. He left part of a bottle of whiskey behind for us."

"Sounds like good medicine for a cool evening." I use a stump for a coffee table to pour out the tea, while Adam adds a little whiskey to each.

"Saw a bear down at the narrows," says Adam as we settle back to sip tea and look at the fire.

"Which side was he on? Maybe he's headed this way."

"He was on the other side, but he might cross there where it's easy."

"Have you been bothered much by bears at your camp?" I ask.

"Not too much," replies Adam. "They know us pretty good and don't bother us so much. Usually, when I chase them they stay away. I have only had to shoot two or three in twenty years."

"One broke into camp two years ago," Agnes points out with a trace of annoyance at the memory.

Adam laughs. "Yes, when we were away on a trip to town. He broke into everything. It took us a week to straighten up the mess and fix things up. He even punctured and emptied every can of outboard-motor oil. He must have drank it all, because there was none spilled on the ground."

"He would have a good laxative."

"That's maybe why he never came back," says Adam.

I add some more wood to the fire as Adam pours out some more Irish tea. It is dark now; the moon should be coming up shortly. After a while Adam returns to the subject of bears.

"We came across a bear hibernating one year in March. Agnes and I were working the trap line on snowshoes near a small lake west of our camp."

"Yes, after a thaw," confirms Agnes. "Adam tried to wake him up."

"He had dug himself in under an overturned tree root, and his head was laying out on the snow. I got right up close and shouted in his ear, but couldn't wake him up."

"It's a lucky thing for you he didn't wake up. Have you ever tried to climb a tree on snowshoes?"

We laugh, then sit watching the fire, sipping tea and exchanging a few more bear stories. After a while the subject of the stories changes to moose. Then suddenly Agnes jumps up and begins to sing and dance around the fire.

Adam begins to chant along, stopping a moment to explain. "It is an old Indian song about a hunter who kills a moose."

Agnes treads lightly on her toes in time to the rhythm, gyrating around in traditional Indian fashion as she slowly circles the fire. The flames lick up in pulses to augment the rhythm with a flickering shadow-giant, mimicking the performance along the ground and through the branches of the overhanging tree. The setting is hypnotically transported to another time, to bygone days of campfire dances after a successful hunt. The atmosphere is suddenly psychic, infused with ancestral presences returning to enjoy the song. Their energies can be felt. They are almost visible sitting cross-legged in an outer circle, their interest focused intently upon the dance.

Adam interrupts his chant occasionally to describe the song: "The young hunter has killed a moose and is making many trips to carry it back to the village."

He joins again in a refrain between the verses.

"There is a big hill on the way back to the village. The refrain is about the hunter struggling up the hill with a heavy load. It's a funny song."

At every refrain Agnes adds some body movements to the dance to dramatize the struggle up the hill, while Adam tells parts of the story in between. The hunter is very proud to have killed such a big moose, and he wants everyone to see it. He is not satisfied to carry home just the meat. He comes back for the head, to show it off. Then he returns for the hide, and then the hoofs, to show them off as well. Finally he tries to carry home the guts. He ties them all up in rawhide, with a tumpline over his forehead, but as he struggles up the hill, they keep slipping out and sliding down his rear end.

Agnes finishes at last, sitting down out of breath, while Adam chants another chorus.

"Do you dance too?" I ask Adam.

"Only do sun dance," he jokes. "Like to keep the rain away, but this summer not too much power in my dance. Rain spirits sometimes very strong."

We continue telling stories and sipping tea. After we finish up some fish left over from supper, they decide it is time to leave. It's quite late—the moon is well up in the sky. I take the lantern to show the way as we head down to the boat.

"How long do you plan to stay?" inquires Adam.

"Another few weeks. Until it gets too cold."

Adam scrambles in over the load to the rear, and I lift the boat off the rock before Agnes climbs in the front.

Skillfully turning the boat around with a paddle, she giggles and turns to Adam. "Let's hurry home, Adam. Not sure, but think I feel sexy."

Adam laughs as he wraps the starting rope around the flywheel and gives it a pull. The motor coughs and spits a few times, deciding whether to explode or run. Then it catches. We wave good-bye as they head off in a cloud of blue smoke up the lake.

The lantern is taken back to camp and another stick put on the fire. It doesn't feel like bedtime yet. The night is still and clear, and the moon shows ample light to walk around the shoreline to the northern point.

The racket of the outboard motor is already fading into the distance. For some reason, the noise doesn't seem out of place. There is a quality to Adam and Agnes that compensates. They are saturated with the spirit of the land. As with their ancestors for generations before them, their spirits are attuned to the earth spirit and her moods. You sense this in their presence. You rarely sense it in a white man's presence, for in his culture, the earth has no spirit. It is something to be used. The Plains Indian summed up the problem many years ago: "The white man doesn't know where the center of the earth is." He doesn't sense it in his being.

The moon looks like an aperture seen from inside a cosmic camera. Images stand out as phantasmal forms projected on celestial film. Everything is smeared with the mystic pallor of the moon. The sky is adorned with a silken veil that mutes the messages of stars, reminding them that the moon is mistress here tonight. The influence of the moon on the earth spirit is profound, eternal—like a heartbeat and breathing both. Similar influences pervade the solar system, like a celestial Indian dance around a campfire—a tradition that recalls ancestral patterns to the resonant performance.

There is another resonance which Holmes neglected to elucidate. It was discovered by a man named Jean Foucault in 1852. Suspending a weighted pendulum on a long wire from the dome of the Pantheon in Paris, he carefully observed it swing. He found that the arc of its swings gradually rotated such that its motions back and forth were independent of the rotation of the earth. If the Pantheon were situated at the North Pole, the direction of the swings would go through a complete circle every twenty-four hours. It was reasoned that only gravity acted on the pendulum—that it was independent of the rotation of the earth. This was taken as proof that the earth rotates. The fact remains that the direction of motion of Foucault's pendulum is governed not by its proximity to the earth, but by the fixed stars in the galaxy, thousands of light-years distant.

This is obviously not the result of causal factors operative in space and time. It is direct evidence of the social mystery of each and all, implicit in a synchronous dance of energies between form and emptiness. The alternations of matter between the particulate and quantized modes are regulated by universal centers everywhere at once. Gravity is a manifestation of this implicit unity. The resonating dance of the solar system is superimposed upon an eternal atomic jig throughout a living cosmos. The dynamic patterns are independent from the gravitational mass.

It is quiet now. Even the loons are silent, listening to the moon. It whispers hush across the land. Faded stars are winking in the water. The hills have lost their features, themselves becoming like shadow phantoms. Everything is filled with a common emptiness. The great mystery is transparent.

Thoughts of the experience return. The world of form vanished in the void. There was an immediacy to it, as there is tonight. The whole of history is now. Patterns of the past work to shape the future through the void, but not in causally determined ways. The future is not a runaway expression of the past. The two must ever find a balance in a never-ending present. It is a work of mind.

Old fears come back to grip the heart, memories of the terror and all the questions in the years that followed. Nonsense! It's been worth it. There was nothing malicious in the Cosmic Being. He gave an insight that transcended his creation.

The granite point has donned a faint fluorescent glow. The pallor of the moon paints its cracks and folds as lines and wrinkles in an aging skin. Deep cracks with weathered edges are mapped in bold relief, while gnats and bugs creep unseen through the dark lanes and narrow alleys. They find it risky to be too conspicuous. Some cautious crickets are the only muted voices, their squeaking squelched by cracks.

Spruce trees are poised like rockets on a launch pad. There is a tautness to the hollow night. The trek back to camp is like a space walk across a prehistoric monster's hide. In places rocks have flaked like flecks of dandruff from the scalp. The monster's face is hard and cold, unflinching, yet tensed toward the moon to hold it captive in a tidal staring match. There is no rest for the watchman over regularities of life.

14

Black Bandits

It has been raining steadily for several days. Everything is damp and miserable. For a couple of days there were strong north winds with whitecaps rolling on the lake. Now the winds are light, but a solid mass of sullen gray cloud keeps moving in from the north. Sometimes the rain lets up for a brief respite; then it starts again. Temperatures in early morning have dropped near freezing. The only reprieve from the bitter cold is in the sleeping bag at night.

The fish have stopped biting. The little cove beside the island hasn't been providing supper. Fortunately, a few strays are still biting across at jam-bag rock and down at the big narrows, but it takes time to work for them. All the clothes are damp. They will not dry on the small clothesline strung up in the tent. This morning the drizzle is fine, yet it keeps peppering down without a sign of quitting.

Much of the time has been spent reflecting on the system. System 4 is a little more complex than System 3, but it is no more difficult to understand. Since the general pattern can be conveyed in a simplified way, it is worth some patient attention. System 4 has already been briefly introduced in the geometric form of the enneagram; we have seen how it applies to the three polarities of a business organization. The nine terms of the enneagram are generated from five sets of four energy interfaces. Before discussing the individual terms, we will explore how the active centers are divided into universal and particular sets, and how these sets transform from term to term in a specific way.

You may recall that there is a six-pointed figure and a mediating triangle to the enneagram. The six-pointed figure consists of three sets of particular centers following one another in succession through the six-pointed sequence. The mediating triangle consists of two sets of universal centers, each set with a sequence of transformations of its own. A total of five sets of centers thus participate in three sequences of transformations. This creative matrix will be called the primary creative process, to distinguish it from the primary activity of System 3.

Let's take a brief look at the sequence of transformations in the six-pointed figure first. The three sets of particular centers each transform through each of the six terms in succession. Since they follow one another at every other position in the sequence, only three terms manifest at once. The pattern can best be illustrated by a series of diagrams in which each of the three sets of centers is designated by a roman numeral. (See Figure 29.)

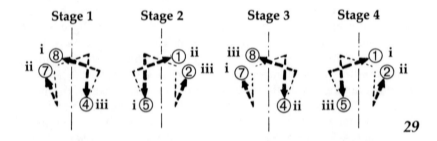

29

The sequence of transformations is shown by the arrows and by the numbers 1, 4, 2, 8, 5, 7 in the positions of the six-pointed figure. The three sets of centers (i, ii, iii), which delineate terms, are shown at successive stages of transformation, like successive frames in a movie.

Two points can be noted. First, terms alternate between positions 8, 7, 4 and positions 1, 2, 5 indefinitely. Second, at every four stages of transformation, the three sets of centers are in mirror-image positions across the vertical axis. Compare Stage 1 with Stage 4.

To turn now to the mediating triangle, two sets of universal centers are operative. They each go through a cycle of transformation that repeats with every four stages outlined above. This can be illustrated by another series of diagrams in which one set of universal centers is designated by "O" and the other set by "X." A fifth stage is shown to illustrate the beginning of the next cycle of four stages. (See Figure 30.)

The perceptual axis of the mediating activity has been shown in

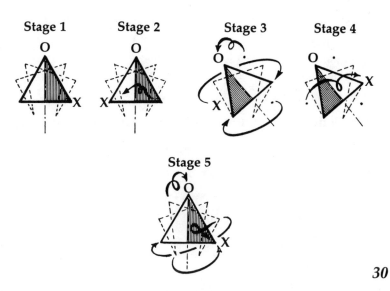

Stage 1   **Stage 2**   **Stage 3**   **Stage 4**

Stage 5

30

each stage. Like a master mirror for the matrix of activities, it is associated with the "O" term. It can be seen that the "O" term remains unchanged for two stages, while the "X" term transforms; the "X" term then remains unchanged for two stages, while the "O" term transforms. The transformation of the "O" term inverts the perceptual axis in Stage 3, as if to flip the whole triangle over into an alignment with positions 8, 2, 5. This new alignment of the perceptual axis directs the transformation of the "X" term to Position 2 in Stage 4, rather than back to Position 3. Between Stage 4 and Stage 5, the triangle flops back again as both terms simultaneously transform back to their original positions. Stage 5 is the first stage in a new cycle of four stages.

This time, three points are significant. First, within each cycle, the "O" term does not transform between Stages 1 and 2, nor between Stages 3 and 4, while the "X" term does not transform between Stages 2 and 3. Thus, there is a continuity of reference within each cycle through a mutual bridging of transformations. Second, between cycles this bridging is lost, since both terms simultaneously transform to begin the next cycle. This introduces a degree of discontinuity between cycles. This discontinuity will be called a shift transformation to indicate the shift in the perceptual axis. Third, the form of the activity inverts midway through each cycle, between Stages 2 and 3. The mediating triangle flips from an independent

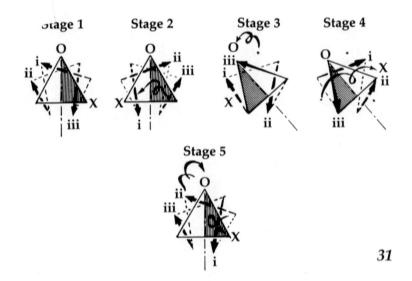

Stage 1   Stage 2   Stage 3   Stage 4

Stage 5

31

alignment to an inverted alignment with one-half of the six-pointed figure. Between cycles, it flops back again, to begin each new cycle in an independent alignment.

When the two sets of diagrams are put together, an integrated picture is provided of the pattern of transformations. (See Figure 31.) Although this may look a little complicated, it is as simple as learning a little rhyme. There is a rhythmic spirit to the pattern.

> *Particular sets take alternate steps*
> *to see themselves in the mirror,*
> *Universal sets take double steps*
> *to flip themselves round with the mirror.*

The creative activity of a business enterprise can again be used to exemplify the pattern. The particular sets of centers in the six-pointed figure are associated with specific cycles of product activity. The universal sets are associated with the overall policy of a company as it integrates specific product cycles. The three polarities of a business enterprise are mirrored across the medial axis within each cycle, since each product set is in the opposite position across the axis every four stages. Another diagram will refresh the memory. (See Figure 32.)

Sales is mirrored in the market. Product development is mirrored in the treasury. Product processing is mirrored in the organi-

32

zation structure. Each stream of product activity is assessed on its own merit, according to one of the polarities within each cycle. The universal company-sets of centers commit resources to each product stream on this basis. In practice, this may take the form of periodic reviews, but such reviews reflect changing conditions in three groups of streams.

There are two other significant factors involved. First, it is obvious that each particular set of energies associated with each product stream must take six stages to complete the sequence through the six-pointed figure. Second, energies cannot be endlessly committed to production without replenishing resources. The ability of a company to perform in the market must be sustained. Each particular set of energies must therefore also go through a regenerative sequence, in addition to the expressive sequence associated with production. An expressive mode and a regenerative mode come into play for each term, except that the sales term in the sequence acts as a pivot between expression and regeneration. It always occurs in the expressive mode.

From these two factors it is apparent that twelve stages are required to complete the creative sequence of each particular set of energies. There is an expressive sequence of six stages and a regenerative sequence of six stages. Three cycles are involved. In each cycle, each particular set of energies progresses from one polarity to the next. This pattern can be represented in tabular form, the letters "E" and "R" in the table representing the expressive and regenerative modes of specific terms in the six-pointed sequence. (See Figure 33.)

Now we can add another couple of lines to the rhyme:

SET	TERM	CYCLE 1				CYCLE 2				CYCLE 3			
I	Sequence	8	5	7	1	4	2	8	5	7	1	4	2
	Mode	E	E	E	E	E	E	E	R	R	R	R	R
II	Sequence	7	1	4	2	8	5	7	1	4	2	8	5
	Mode	R	R	R	R	E	E	E	E	E	E	E	R
III	Sequence	4	2	8	5	7	1	4	2	8	5	7	1
	Mode	E	E	E	R	R	R	R	R	E	E	E	E

33

Particular sets reflect in four steps
that repeat with three flips of the mirror.

The three polarities that reflect within each cycle are the referents to the music of a company. They are the rungs in the ladder that spell out a genetic language that is common to all companies. As with the DNA molecule, it is a three-word language. It is a common pattern to all mentation and behavior reflected through an animated spirit. But how are the referents read? To answer this question, we must look toward the universal centers, to how they integrate the particular terms of the six-pointed sequence. We must also take a brief look at how four centers divided into five sets define the meaning implicit in each of the nine terms. We will return to this task shortly.

The tent flap is opened to step outside and check the weather. The rain has almost stopped, diminishing to a fine sprinkle that peppers the surface of the lake with a barely audible high-pitched tingle. There is no noticeable wind. The lake is smooth. The ground squishes with each step. Leaves and twigs collect the drizzle into larger drops, then oscillate slightly as they let them tumble onto twigs below. Nervous trees with twitching fingers are fumbling as they try to catch the rain.

The clouds are winnowed into heavy furrows, slung in dark gray rows that strive to hug together to exclude the sky. The sky is brighter in the north; the furrows are coming with wider spaces in between. One fold betrays a small patch of blue. The signs are reasonably reliable. The sun should be shining in two or three hours.

Time to fetch some water from the lake. On the way back comes an unwelcome surprise. Damn! A black bear. He is coming up the path from behind the tent. We see each other at about the same time, and stop about fifty feet apart. Our eyes meet for a moment, then he turns tail and runs. He bolts back down the path, up through an area of hardwoods to the south. He is agile and fast. Powerful limbs propel his bulk in fluid strides. His body bunches and stretches like water sloshing in a big fur bag. Since he is already on the run, it won't hurt to encourage him a little. The water pail is dropped to give chase with lots of shouting. Already fifty yards ahead, he soon increases the distance and disappears. There is no point in pushing one's luck. The chase is abandoned. We will have to share the island for a while.

Bears have a relentless preoccupation with their stomachs. They will eat almost anything, but apart from fish and insects, they rarely kill. If no one had been in camp, this one would likely have destroyed everything, looking for a change of menu. With luck, he won't come back. There are lots of berries this time of year to satisfy his appetite. Nonetheless, bears are full of mischief—it will be wise to stay close to camp for a day or so.

Some dry kindling and birch bark are collected from the bottom of the cupboard, and a fire is started. The tea pail is used to heat some soup. The warmth of the fire feels mighty good, and with some hot soup in the belly, things start to look a little better. Thoughts return again to the system.

The four centers that relate in various ways to delineate nine terms are most easily identified through Term 9. This is the discretionary-hierarchy term, which has already been discussed to some extent earlier. Also the expressive mode of the "O" set of universal centers, it can be illustrated as shown in Figure 34.

In earlier discussions, a company hierarchy was described as follows:

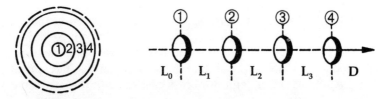

Term 9: Renewed Perception of Field   Discretion-Means

34

1   Managerial work gives form to idea and direction to knowledge.
2   Administrative work gives form to knowledge and direction to routine activity.
3   Supervisory work gives form to routine and direction to resources of labor, equipment, and materials.
4   Functional work gives form to resources and direction to a final product.

Note that each kind of work is defined as an identity between a level of form and a communicative direction. This implicates a primary activity in the identification of each center, direction being implicit in the successive tiers of the hierarchy. The form that idea takes lends direction to the formulation of knowledge, which lends direction to the organization of routine, which lends direction to the formation of a product.

The four centers of the discretion term are not confined to a business organization. They can be seen running as a common thread throughout the organization of the universe, though they manifest themselves in different ways and on vastly different scales. For the sake of simplicity they will be referred to as idea, knowledge, routine, and formation, respectively. But keep in mind that each center is an active interface of patterned energies. In the discretion term, the four centers are open and unbounded.

To exemplify the universal character of the hierarchy, it is worth reviewing how it applies in three cases already discussed and in one additional case. This can best be done in the form of a chart that outlines the tiers in the cosmic hierarchy that spans the organization of the biosphere, the planet, the solar system, and the galaxy. (See Figure 35.) Once the discretion term is known, the nature of the remaining terms in any creative process can be determined, because the pattern is always the same.

In order to introduce the terms of System 4 simply, yet in such a way as to glimpse a further insight into their universality, let us suppose that we are businessmen of a special sort, engaged in a very special business. Let us pretend that we are in the business of making daisies—not artificial daisies, but real daisies that sprout from seeds to bloom in legions across vast areas of the earth. We are in fact not human beings at all, but rather plant devas of the daisy genus—unseen spiritual beings refluxing vital energies through a product line of white and yellow posies. From this vantage point, the terms of System 4 can then be examined by contrasting how a business works to how a daisy grows.

Hierarchies in the Cosmic Energy Refinery

		Description	Type
IDEA SPIRITUAL ENERGIES	**BIOSPHERE**	Form is given to idea in the organization of man's nervous system associated with language and creativity. Creative energies are of cosmic origin.	IDEA Creative
		Form is given to knowledge through conscious reflection associated with the organization of the nervous system throughout the vertebrate series.	KNOWLEDGE* Conscious
		Form is given to routines of physical activity through animated responses to sensitive experience in the invertebrates.	ROUTINE Sensitive
		Organic form is given to inorganic material through the vital energies synthesized with light in the organic cell.	FORMATION Vital
KNOWLEDGE REFLECTIVE ENERGIES	**PLANET**	Ideas have taken forms of organic life in the evolution of the biosphere. This has been closely associated with an atmospheric consolidation.	IDEA Organic
		Distortions of magnetosphere, ionosphere, magnetic crustal memory, and internal convection all reflect behavior known in electromagnetic consolidation.	KNOWLEDGE Electromagnetic
		Internal convection routines are linked to geothermal consolidation to guide plate tectonics and shape the planet's face.	ROUTINE Geothermal
		Layered structure is linked to gravitational consolidation that still works with plate movements, tides, and weather to form the planet's surface.	FORMATION Gravity
ROUTINE DYNAMIC ENERGIES	**SOLAR SYSTEM**	The solar system consolidated within the sun's atmosphere after it began to convert mass to energy. Radiated energies still influence the lives of planets.	IDEA Planetary
		The sun's electromagnetic consolidation reflects differential rotation, torsional waves, sunspots, and extends to include planetary behavior.	KNOWLEDGE Electromagnetic
		Thermonuclear routines in the sun involve complex activity. Cyclic routines of planets and sun are interrelated.	ROUTINE Thermonuclear
		Gravitational form occurred in steps that preceded consolidations higher in the heirarchy. Delegations occur first at the functional level.	FORMATION Gravity
FORMATION MATERIAL ENERGIES	**GALAXY**	The galaxy idea is mirrored in regulation of its mass. This concerns the creation and regeneration of matter to sustain its stellar population.	IDEA Stellar
		Our galaxy has an enormous general magnetic field that reflects and monitors stellar events through distortions of its pattern.	KNOWLEDGE Electromagnetic
		The many possible routines may be linked to black holes in galactic centers, with ejections of matter related to creative reflux.	ROUTINE Matter Reflux
		Formation is associated with material content from gas and dust to stellar associations. It is continuously consolidated by gravity.	FORMATION Gravity

*Knowledge is taken to be a reflected pattern of ordered energies.

An underlying reason for taking this approach is to bring old superstitions to the fore again. At first there may be an inclination to protest, for daisies are invested not only with a spirit, but also with an archetypal-organs ghost and cell phantoms as well. The high priests of science have long implored us all to reject these things as superstitious nonsense—to believe instead in a vaguely conceived molecular mysticism. They would have us believe that the boundless complexity of a daisy is the result of a long series of mysterious molecular accidents. They have done their preaching well and not without some justification, but carried to extremes, we might all begin to ask why shouldn't much simpler things like cars and trains one day also begin to happen by themselves. Despite the sermons of sience, there is solid evidence to the contrary that should not be put aside. Kirlian photography and phantom-limb pain both substantiate the view that follows; it is presented to illustrate that spirits and ghosts are not just hallucinatory spooks resurrected by frazzled minds. They are an essential and integral part of the creative process, committed to the order that this implies. To understand this is to dispel what is meant by superstition in a way that molecular mysticism never can.

First let's look again to Term 9, the discretionary-hierarchy term that is also called the "renewed perception of the field" term. The four centers can be identified and described for a daisy company as follows:

1   Idea: As a deva of the daisy genus we are a universal Center 1, the embodiment of the idea of a daisy, just as any managing director is the embodiment of the idea of the company's product. The idea, however, must be translated through the universal discretionary hierarchy of knowledge, routine, and formation, to bring into form the product line of individual daisies.

2   Knowledge: The knowledge interface, Center 2, consists of patterned electromagnetic energies that reflect the accumulated techniques of the growth cycle. This is manifest as an archetypal pattern for all daisies, a ghostly electromagnetic essence that prescribes the design and function of the daisy's organs—its roots, stem, leaves, and blossom. The knowledge of every company is represented in the facilities it relies upon and how they are organized for use.

3   Routine: Whereas the knowledge interface is concerned with the administration of the whole organism, the routine interface is con-

cerned with the function of individual cells. Cells are like items of equipment that are arranged according to the company's overall facilities. Cells function at the supervisory level of delegation, committing resources in a specific way.

4 Formation: The formation interface concerns the chemical reactions that produce the molecular constituents of cells and their chemical by-products. This is the functional level of work that makes the physical daisy product. A daisy, however, is a sophisticated commodity, requiring continuous maintenance and servicing throughout its life. The company is never divorced from its product line.

As plant devas, then, we are managing directors of the daisy company, central to the universal hierarchy of idea, knowledge, routine, and formation. There is only one such universal "O" set of centers, which works together with the universal "X" set like man and wife in a family. Together, they regulate the family of all daisies by the relationship of each to all. It is the three particular sets, assigned in the six-pointed sequence to the growth and maintenance of each daisy, that are overseen by the universal parents. In the particular sets energies are quantized so that we devas host many lesser spirits with special duties assigned in each of the six regions of the company.

From the standpoint of the discretion term, it is not enough for us to be forever indulging in the dissemination of idea through the hierarchy to give organic form to the product line of petaled faces. All of this expends energy. It is exhausting work; we soon begin to wonder what is the use of endless work if no one is to appreciate it and respond to sustain our efforts.

When wonder brings us to reflect on the need for our discretionary efforts, a perceptual transposition occurs—our concern shifts from the *making* of a product to its *sale*. The universal "O" set transforms into the regenerative mode of a universal sales term, as shown in Figure 36.

The sales term entails a subjective-to-objective balance that is a subject of concern to devas. This balance is represented by the countercurrent identities R_1 and R_2, subjective to Center 1. The molecular formation of all daisies finds mutual identity with archetypal design as reflected through cell routines.* Both identities are mirrored in

*Recall here the shadow dance seen from two directions on the canvas of the tent. A good insight into each term requires patient study of the diagrams. The written text is only a brief introduction to convey the general idea of how the system works.

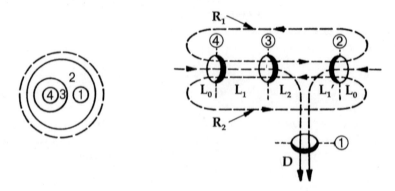

Term 8: Feedback from Creation   Sales

36

the routines of cells, where the commitment of resources takes place, thus providing a knowledge of resources expended for product formation. This occurs within the context of the product idea, Center 1, as we devas commit the idea peripherally out to the market. The sales term as a whole thus concerns the expenditure of resources associated with production, in the course of committing the product for sale. It reflects the cost of the product.

This universal regenerative mode of the term always coincides with a particular expressive mode of the term in Stage 3 of each cycle. In the expressive mode of the term, Centers 1 and 2 exchange places. Now, it's all well and good for a universal deva to have a reflective concern for costs in conducting the affairs of the company, but each particular daisy also has an idea, Center 1, of its own. It also has a personal ghost pattern, Center 2, complex routines unique to its own specific cell structure, Center 3, and a unique molecular form, Center 4. Furthermore, it doesn't much care about the cost. It wants to live. It wants to contribute to the market, to express itself.

In this expressive term, the countercurrent identities R_1 and R_2 reflect a mutual identity between the idea of a particular daisy and the molecular form of the daisy, both mirrored in its cell routines. It is each daisy's ghost pattern that subjectively reflects on this balance as it commits its knowledge to the market. Every salesman reflects his knowledge of his product through his person—through his accumulated experience. The value in the product is projected ghostlike with the essence of his person. When we appreciate the essence of a daisy gesturing in the breeze, we sense its character or personality—the simplicity and purity of a daisy's presence. It is in this way that a level of quality or value is recognized in the product as the basis for its sale.

When the regenerative and expressive modes of the term occur together, a basis of comparison is provided between product cost and product quality. This permits a price to be determined that is sufficient to sustain regenerative needs and that is also appropriate to the value of the product in the market.*

How then, as devas, do we assess the cost of daisies? This involves the facilities and spiritual organization of the daisy—the limits to which the daisy archetype may be strained. It concerns the ability of the daisy ghost to extend itself in mirroring a balance with molecular formation in the work of cells.

And how about the value of the daisy in the market? It must compete with the dandelion and thistle for the attention of the pollinating bee, but in addition it attracts appreciation from other neighbors and passers-by. There is a spiritual exchange. Of course, each plant must find a niche where daily rations are available, but resources must be shared. This sharing depends upon a balance effected through spiritual reflux and exchange in nature's marketplace of life. It is ultimately determined by biospheric resonance.

The fire is stirred up a bit and more wood added. Another cup of soup adds some fuel for further thought.

The "O" set of universal centers keeps going through double-steps back and forth between the discretion term and the regenerative sales term. The "X" set of universal centers is at the same time of vital concern to deva management. It goes through a three-term sequence which we shall turn to next.

Surely devas cannot be so different from human beings that they can undertake a discretionary search without, at the same time, some sort of goal in mind. A goal is provided at the beginning of each cycle by the transference-of-idea term as shown in Figure 37.

Two of the four centers are aligned facing the other two in mirror symmetry. The centers play peek-a-boo with one another in opposite directions at the same time. The routines of cells, Center 3, partially coalesce with archetypal daisy knowledge, Center 2, within the constraints of the daisy idea, Center 1, and formation, Center

*Because the sales term is concerned with a balance between price and value in the market, it provides feedback that sustains creative activity. It is therefore also called the "feedback from creation" term.

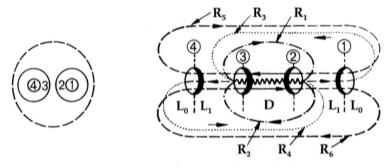

Term 3   Transference of Idea   Goal

37

4. Without elaborating on all details of the term, its main significance
lies in the two relational wholes R_3 and R_4, which portray two peek-
a-boo identities. In R_3, the routines of cells peek through the daisy
ghost to the daisy idea. In R_4, the daisy ghost peeks through the
routines of cells to the daisy's molecular formation. Together, these
two identities represent a transference of idea into a physical form
through the partial coalescence of knowledge with routine. This
is the overall goal of any creative process. As devas we must entertain it while conducting our discretionary search.

   We devas, then, have the two universal aspects by which we
undertake a discretionary search with a goal in mind at the beginning of every cycle. First thing we know, our search bears fruit, and
the communicative goal transforms into an independent-creation
term as shown in Figure 38. In this universal term, we find that
underlying the molecular formation of all daisies is a triadic relationship of idea, knowledge, and routine. As the embodiment of idea,
we daisy devas join hands with daisy ghosts and daisy cells, like
three musketeers in a pledge of one for all and all for one, even
while we sustain a discretionary search. The pledge is to enact a
balance between each and all through double identities in the triad.
Our deva idea is given explicit form in a company of spirits that
we employ to enliven the ghost of knowledge and animate cell routines, just as the departments of every factory are administered by
people, with people operating the machines. The people, facilities,
and machinery must be mutually appropriate to enact an action
sequence in the creation of the product. Energies must be organized
and balanced in an explicit way. This organization is itself a creation
independent from the molecular formation of all daisies, though it
underlies each daisy. The corporate body of the company, it shall be

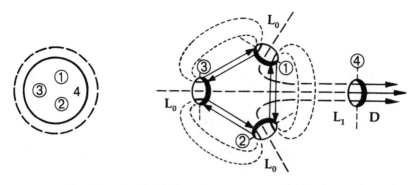

Term 6   Independent Creation   Consequence

38

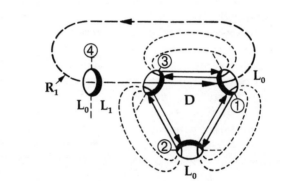

Term 2   Creation of Idea   Product Development

39

referred to as a mastermind triad. In Stage 2 of each cycle, the mastermind triad is committed to discretionary production, but in Stage 3 it is constrained by the cost concerns of the universal sales term. This change in emphasis occurs with the reflective flipping over of the master mirror associated with the "O" set of universal centers.

That there is an idea, organs, cells, mastermind triad underlying every daisy, just as there are creative people, factories, and equipment behind every car produced, says something about the processing of a product, but not much about the nature of the product itself. For this, it is necessary to invert the relationship into the creation-of-idea term, as shown in Figure 39. This inversion is occasioned through reflective concerns with product cost and value. It occurs across the master mirror to usher in Stage 4 of each cycle.

In this universal expressive mode of the term, the molecular formation of daisies is not the context for an underlying mastermind, but vice versa. The relational whole, R_1, is superimposed as a creative idea on the mastermind triad. The molecular formation of a daisy finds an identity with idea from within the context of cell routines. Thus, while we devas remain steadfast to our musketeer pledge, we also give genetic consideration to the molecular formulation that is undertaken by the equipment of cells. The design and operation of this equipment are carefully specified and encoded in the DNA molecule. In ordinary companies, the product-development function evolves product and equipment specifications—in a daisy company, these specifications are spelled out in genetic language. This is influenced as well by the other universal "O" set of centers, where we devas continue to sustain a reflective concern with costs.

The universal "X" set of centers always occurs in the expressive mode of the idea term in Stage 4 of each cycle. It also always coincides with a corresponding regenerative term in one of the particular sets of centers associated with each daisy. In the regenerative mode, Centers 1 and 2 are reversed, so that the superimposed identity R_1 is with archetypal knowledge, rather than idea. Ongoing product and equipment specifications are expected to meet known standards, a task delegated as an administrative function to each daisy ghost as part of a musketeer pledge of its own.

The two idea terms convene in a musketeer reunion to compare the expressive needs of all daisies with the regenerative needs of each daisy. In this way, the expressive idea is conditioned by the known capabilities of daisies, while some helpful hints of things to come lend overall direction to the regenerative process. Through long tradition, we devas have acquired the wisdom to reflect the conditioning we receive, as we move on to a new transference-of-idea term at the beginning of the next cycle.

This completes the transform sequence of the "X" set of centers, but let's go through it again briefly in point form:

1   In Stage 1, the transference-of-idea term mirrors a creative idea in created form through a coalescence of knowledge and routine. This is the goal of a company.

2   In Stages 2 and 3, the independent-creation term exhibits a mastermind triad of idea, knowledge, and routine underlying all product

formation. This corporate body evolves as a consequence of realizing the company goal through successive cycles.

3   In Stage 4, an overall expressive mode of the creative idea coincides with each regenerative mode. Mutual influence between these two idea terms directs the regeneration of resources in a manner appropriate to the needs of idea transference in a succeeding cycle.

The transform sequences of the "O" and "X" universal sets of centers indicate the significance of the mediating triangle and the flip-flops of the master mirror. The triangle, of course, has no geometric significance. It is only a way of illustrating transformations between a subjective and objective aspect across a master interface between them.

In the first two stages of each cycle the universal terms give direction to the discretionary transference of idea as it is realized through a corporate body. In the last two stages of each cycle, the universal terms interact directly with particular terms to regulate regeneration.

A couple of more lines can now be added to the rhyme:

> *Particular sets take alternate steps*
> *to see themselves in the mirror.*
> *Universal sets take double steps*
> *to flip themselves round with the mirror.*
> *Particular sets reflect in four steps*
> *that repeat with three trips of the mirror.*
> *Ideas are made and prices are paid*
> *to sustain reflections through trade.*

There are still four terms in the six-pointed sequence that haven't been introduced, but we will leave them for later. The general pattern should be reasonably clear, and the main points can be summarized again as follows:

1   There is an invariant character to a hierarchy of four centers that is involved in any creative process. Their mutual relationship in a term invests it with meaning.

2   The creative matrix is generated from five sets of centers—two of them universal, three of them particular. The particular sets follow

one another through the six-pointed sequence. The universal sets each have independent yet related transform sequences in the mediating triangle.

3   The particular sets recur in two alternating symmetrical positions in the six-pointed figure. Each set occurs in the mirror-image position after four transform stages.

4   The universal sets also both complete a transform sequence in four stages, but as they do there is a shift and inversion of the perceptual axis or master mirror, which normalizes again at the end of each cycle.

5   The six-pointed-sequence terms exhibit both expressive and regenerative modes, so that twelve stages, or three cycles, are required to complete a sequence of expression and regeneration.

6   The alternating emphasis on expression and regeneration is regulated by the inversion of the mirror and the alignment of a universal set with a particular set in each of Stages 3 and 4. Sales and product development are the two key terms in this regard.

Because we are most familiar with the workings of organization in business, the language of business is used to exemplify the terms in a daisy company. With adaptations of language, all of the terms apply equally well to the organization of the biosphere, the planet, the solar system, the galaxy, or whatever. Strange as it may seem at first, there are analogues to functions such as sales and product development associated with organizations of every kind; all organizations effect a transference of idea into form through a coalescence of knowledge and routine. The natural elements themselves dance to a different harmonic with a more universal beat, but the melody of the music is the same. It all jives to a master orchestration in which the idea center is never fully delegated to the world of form.

Enough of the system for now. The rain has stopped completely, and the sky is clearing: there are frequent patches of blue between the furrows overhead. The best news is in the north. The trailing edge of the storm center can be seen approaching as an ashen gray arch over the horizon. Beyond the arch is clear blue sky. A glorious remission is coming after five dreadful days of penance.

A spruce partridge is feeding near the tent. The same hen has stayed in the area most of the summer. She is plucking leaves from blueberry bushes, much as a housewife plucks canned goods from a supermarket shelf. She looks first to one side, then the other. She even has the supermarket walk, but without the buggy. Like most shoppers, she uses slow deliberate steps as she looks here, then there, cocking her head to read the labels. Each leaf is carefully selected. Gradually she works her way back into the thicket and disappears.

The shadow phantoms have returned to bring glad tidings. The sun is streaming down between the furrows, marching from the north in blessed beaming ranks of light. A liberating army has arrived to usher out the crippled captives of a former occupying force. Beaten, warmongering oppressors are on their way. A feeling of renewal fills the clear bright air, washed clean of heavy moods. Rations of warmth are issued out in waves to vitally rejoicing masses in a victory parade. The air is moved by radiating spirits to murmur sweet nothings softly through the trees. Gentle boughs respond by reaching out to hug the breeze, while little waves crop up to kiss the rocky shore.

The last limping stragglers of defeated troops mope off in broken file into a sullen southern sky. Their energies are spent, their surrender is unconditional. The sky has clothed itself in a spotless uniform of blue. The job of mopping up is already under way.

The tent flaps are tied open to air it out. The sleeping bag is tossed across a clothesline behind the tent, along with articles of damp clothing. Other clothes are taken to the lake to wash. The rest of the afternoon is spent cleaning up and cutting wood.

The fish are biting in the little cove again. During supper the whiskey jacks pay a brief visit. They vary their timetable from day to day, coming even on rainy days, if it isn't pouring down too hard. Two of them have become very tame, but pushy Number One is still quite timid. Although he will snatch food quickly from the fingers at arm's length, he won't venture to perch on the knee or hand.

As the evening wears on, the mood consolidates into a breathless quiet. Though warmer, the air is still quite chill and crystal clear—purged of vague uncertainty. Each leaf, each needle, each stone and pebble stands out distinct. Distant trees and rocks are striking in detail. The vision probes with telescopic depth. Minor sounds ring sharp in tinny detonations. Unnoticed birds chirp short soprano solos in fleeting fragments of disjointed song.

The lanterns are filled and lit as darkness begins to bleed the colors from the sky. The fireplace stones are spread to make room for a large green chunk of wood that will burn for two or three hours. The bear has not returned, but may still be waiting on the island to see what he can steal at night. Two lanterns and a fire should be enough to dissuade the hairy thief from venturing into camp, permitting some time for stargazing from the nearby point.

The benchlike rock on the point is shaped like a reclining seat in a planetarium—an ideal spot to watch the stars come out. The last vestiges of light are fading fast. There is a single, long, slim cloud stretched in black silhouette across the west, like a rip in the vault of the heavens. Gradually it blends into the darkness. A trace of northern lights appears over the horizon in the north. For a while they grope like distant searchlights from beyond the hills, then they disappear.

Watson's interest has also turned toward the stars, but unfortunately the island weather there has been less accommodating than on the island here. He has dragged Holmes off to a special church, a planetarium, where the mock night sky is always clear. The master sleuth is proceeding now to expound on the evidence in the mystery of the stars. He remains convinced that the stars are just a multitude of kitchens in a big bakeshop, believing that central to the case is the cooking of the natural elements in thermonuclear ovens. He is busy explaining about our own galaxy, the Milky Way, and about the different kinds of stars, about how they are born from interstellar gas and dust, how they mature, grow old, and die. He is careful, however, to avoid the implication that these are real life cycles, that the stars are living beings. He takes pains to describe how the laws of physics can be invoked to explain events, pointing out the special importance of the laws of thermodynamics, essential to his belief that everything is a bakeshop. These laws are his commandments.

"It is all very elementary, my dear Watson. Everything has happened in a most natural way. Our galaxy has condensed from a gigantic swirling eddy of gas and dust, just as all the galaxies have done. It all most probably began with a big bang about ten to fifteen billion years ago, from which the universe expanded, cooling into independent galaxies clustered into groups that continue to expand away from one another under the impetus of the initial explosion. There are some possible variations to the theme, but the big bang was the primal act of cooking in the bakeshop."

Watson is skeptical of Holmes' big-bang ideas; however, he is interested in the evidence. "I understand there are various kinds of galaxies and that ours is of the spiral type. Is that correct, Holmes?"

"Yes, our galaxy is a very large member of the spiral type, about 100,000 light-years across. Our sun is situated in one of the spiral arms about 30,000 light-years from the center, where the main disc of stars is about 3,000 light-years thick. The center of the galaxy is about six times thicker. Surrounding this swirling spiral disc is a vast, spherical-shaped halo of globular clusters of stars, each containing thousands of stars which may be in elliptical orbits about the galactic center. The majority of stars in the clusters and near the center are of an older type than in the spiral arms. There is also an intermediate flattened halo of stars surrounding the disc, which are mostly of moderate age."

"I see," says Watson. "There seem to be different regions of organization to the galaxy: the galactic center with older stars, the spiral arms with newer stars, a spherical halo with older stars, and an intermediate halo with stars of moderate age. It is amazing that you are able to judge the age of stars. How are you able to surmise such a thing?"

"It has been accomplished through a long process of classifying stars in various ways and observing their nature and behavior. All this is possible because stars emit electromagnetic fingerprints."

"Fingerprints!" exclaims Watson. "That does sound like a classic bit of detective work. Can you tell me more?"

"Of course, my dear fellow. Electromagnetic fingerprints are patterns of lines in the light spectra of stars, like tiny fragments of the rainbow. They reveal the surface temperatures of stars, their chemical constituents, and their radial velocity directly toward us or directly away from us. Clusters of stars that move together as a group also permit determination of their directional space velocity because they appear to converge toward a point. If we know their space velocity and radial velocity, it is possible to compute their distance from us. Now, as you know, the brightness of stars is an indication of their size. Knowing a star's brightness and distance, we are able to estimate its actual size, according to its fingerprint type."

"Let me see if I've got it straight," says Watson, a little confused. "You are able to compute the distance of stars from a knowledge of their radial and space velocities. Knowing their distance and their brightness, you are then able to estimate their actual size. Are you then able to determine their age from their size?"

"Not quite that simply, Watson. Fingerprint type indicates their temperature. When stars are plotted on a chart according to their size and temperature, an interesting pattern emerges. Most stars fall within a path diagonally across the diagram—these are called main-sequence stars. Stars above the main-sequence path have low temperatures, yet are very luminous because they are so large. These are called the giants and supergiants. Stars below the main-sequence path have high temperatures, yet are rather dim because they are small. These are called white dwarfs. The chart is called an HR diagram." (See Figure 40.)

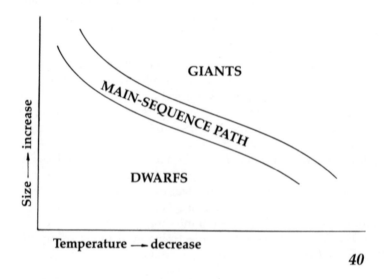

40

"Interesting, indeed! Above the main-sequence path is the land of the giants, and below the path is the land of the dwarfs. You have certainly been able to piece together a lot from a few fingerprints," commends Watson. "I guess that all of our knowledge of the stars depends on electromagnetic energy, but how are you able to translate this information into age?"

"It is a straightforward matter of elementary deduction," replies the sleuth proudly, getting set for a lengthy dissertation. "As a cloud of interstellar gas and dust tries to condense into a protostar, the gravitational forces of contraction are resisted by thermal pressure. If conditions are right, gravity wins the struggle, the cloud contracting until very high temperatures and pressures in its core bring about nuclear ignition. A star is born in the land of the giants. This can occur dramatically: a number of protostars are known to have appeared in the skies in the course of just a few years. Following ignition, the star continues to consolidate, contracting in size while increasing in temperature. It moves out of the land of the giants onto the main-sequence path, where it stabilizes for more than 90 percent of its life.

"Eventually its primary fuel supply of hydrogen begins to wane. Hydrogen is transformed through nuclear fusion into the next-heavier element, helium, which collects in the core of the star. As hydrogen supplies are used up, the star cools, weakening the internal support of thermal and radiation pressure. The core undergoes further gravitational contraction, releasing more energy as heat, which in turn restimulates hydrogen burning to more vigorous levels than before. The increased energy expands the outer layers of the star, increasing its total brightness even though surface temperatures are reduced. The star thus moves off the main-sequence path back into the land of the giants. Now a red giant, its core temperature continues to increase owing to further internal contraction. At 100 million degrees Kelvin, helium burning can begin to cook heavier elements such as beryllium, carbon, and oxygen."

"An admirable piece of detective work!" compliments Watson. "A young star begins as a giant that moves onto the main-sequence path for most if its life. Later it expands again, to spend its old age as a red giant while it produces heavier elements in its core. Does it keep doing this until it burns out?"

"Nothing so simple as that, Watson. It depends on the mass of the star. The most massive go through a series of contractions in the core which ignite a series of nuclear reactions that eventually cook the elements up to iron. Elements heavier than iron cannot be fused, because the reactions required do not yield energy. Continued uncontrolled core collapse produces uncontrolled heating that eventually results in a gigantic explosion called a supernova. The supernova event can outshine an entire galaxy, supplying the energy needed to cook the heavier elements all the way up to uranium. This material disperses as interstellar gas and dust, to eventually form again into new stars. This accounts for the difference in chemical composition between younger stars in the spiral arms and older stars in the center of the galaxy."

Holmes pauses for a moment to point out the location of the Crab nebula in the constellation of the Bull. Then he continues.

"The Crab nebula is the remains of a supernova explosion that was recorded by Chinese astronomers in the year 1054. It was visible in daylight for three weeks. Not all stars experience a supernova in their old age, however. Stars like our sun appear destined to have a nonviolent demise. Their cores continue to be heated as they shrink in size to the limit that atomic structure will allow. Our sun should one day shrink to the size of the earth—a spoonful of its material will weigh many tons. These white-hot stars shed their red-giant cloaks to become white dwarfs, crossing over the main-sequence path into the land of the dwarfs, where they continue to cool. At the end of its life, our sun will become a dark, cold cinder called a black dwarf. Another HR diagram can be used to illustrate the life cycle of a star." (See Figure 41.)

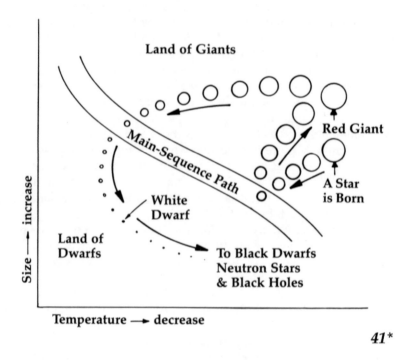

41*

"Very fascinating!" responds Watson as he studies the diagram. "It all seems to fit together beautifully, and you can estimate the age of a star from its position on the diagram. Can you show me some examples?"

"Yes, indeed," says Holmes, pointing out several red giants and white dwarfs. He then goes on to explain about neutron stars. "Some stars more massive than our sun may undergo even further

*Adapted from a drawing by Robert T. Nixon, *Dynamic Astronomy*, 3d ed. (Englewood Cliffs, N.J.: Prentice Hall, 1980).

contraction beyond the white-dwarf stage, to as little as twenty or thirty kilometers in diameter. Under intense gravitational forces, the electrons and protons within the atom may be forced to combine into neutrons to make such a supershrink possible. Rapidly pulsating radio sources are thought to be such superdense stars. There appears to be one in the center of the Crab nebula, the remnant of a supernova."

"I can't imagine how heavy a spoonful of *that* material must be." Watson is a little incredulous, adding "I guess that's the end of the line as far as shrinking goes?"

"Perhaps not," replies the detective masterfully, as if he has private access to a piece of earthshaking truth. "If a star is sufficiently massive, the neutron forces may not be enough to halt core contraction. Gravitational collapse may continue into a condition of infinite density and zero volume, which is commonly called a black hole. This condition is known in theory as a singularity."

Watson, a little shaken, stammers to get his question out. "Whwhat on earth is a singularity?"

"No need to get excited, Watson. It is all perfectly natural. Relativity theory merely indicates that there is a certain radius, called the Schwarzschild radius, associated with any given mass, which defines a sphere of critical density. If any mass contracts sufficiently to become enclosed within the Schwarzschild sphere, then contraction must continue until the mass vanishes in a pinpoint. The laws of science no longer have any meaning. A particle entering the sphere, as seen from within the sphere, can only fall toward extinction in the singularity. To an outside observer, however, this can never be seen to happen—particles can be seen only to approach the sphere without ever quite reaching it. This suggests that a particle entering the sphere splits in two, one part passing into extinction, the other part ejecting again.

Watson makes a valiant effort to be objective, but his anxiety shows a little. "Then you expect me to believe that an entire star several times larger than our sun can be squeezed to extinction in a pinprick under the force of its own gravity? Okay, I'll try! Is this Schwarzschild density the same for every mass?"

"Oh, no! It depends on the total mass involved: the smaller the mass, the greater the Schwarzschild density. For instance, if our sun shrank to its Schwarzschild sphere, its density would become 10 billion tons per cubic centimeter, and its diameter would be less than six kilometers. On the other hand, the Schwarzschild radius of the entire universe is about ten billion light-years, and the corresponding density is about 10^{-29} grams per cubic centimeter. This is within the possible range of the actual density for the universe. The universe may one day again contract into the singularity from which the big bang gave it birth."

This last example shatters Watson's efforts to restrain himself. "If I understand you correctly, Holmes, you are asking me to believe in the existence of black holes, which by your own admission do not exist. Seen from inside the Schwarzschild sphere, there is only extinction of mass and energy in a singularity, and seen from outside the sphere, nothing within it can be seen. If you will excuse me for saying so, Holmes, I have less trouble believing in the bogeyman."

Holmes, unamused, goes on. "I admit that the detection of black holes presents a problem. They have a closed horizon. Even light cannot escape the massive pull of infinite gravity. Nevertheless, evidence is mounting that such black holes exist. As particles approach black holes they should become accelerated and heated to extremes that result in X-ray radiation. The X-ray emissions associated with the star Cygnus X–1, for example, seem to indicate a black hole. This star behaves as if it is one member of a binary pair that orbit around one another. The unseen partner could very well be a black hole that is drawing material from Cygnus X–1 into a singularity. There are other candidates as well."

"I suppose that if there is one black hole, there are sure to be many scattered through the heavens like the pox, stealing the material substance of the universe from under our very noses. They sound like thieves in the night, black bandits robbing from the heavens to stash their booty who knows where."

Though Watson jokes about black holes, he is also perplexed. He senses an unreconciled dilemma in the two perspectives of a singularity, one from inside the Schwarzschild sphere, one from outside the sphere. This dilemma, concerning the relationship of center to periphery, is implicated in theories of the origin of the universe as well. It is ironic that Holmes's laws cease to have meaning under these conditions. Holmes himself is stuck with this dilemma.

Watson doesn't pursue the question further. He has no answer for it, either. Instead he turns to other questions about the great variety of stars, about interstellar gas and dust, and about the galaxy's magnetic field. Holmes describes how studies of polarized starlight have permitted the mapping of magnetic lines of force, which confirms a general pattern to an overall magnetic field.

Watson becomes perplexed again by news of the strange events going on in the center of the galaxy. A very compact radio source, perhaps as massive as five million suns, borders on being a huge black hole. Huge amounts of matter are being expelled away from it. What could it mean, an enormous black hole in the nucleus of the galaxy? The creative dilemma at the root of creative idea is in evidence at the galaxy's very core. Is the universal hierarchy working through the galaxy to sustain the lives of stars?

Holmes continues to respond as best he can to Watson's questions, candidly admitting the poverty of his evidence and ideas in the face of this vast mystery. The case is just beginning.

The night sky has become very dark and deep. The Milky Way is strewn across the heavens like a great celestial cocoon breeding suns from mysterious silken folds. It has turned directly overhead to view its own reflection in the water. The Big Dipper is sitting flat, as if a huge hand has set it on a table.

Memories of the experience come back again. A galaxy of stars was re-created in the void by the Cosmic Being. They appeared behind a dark interface of energy that swept in a sheet quickly through the void. It radiated from the center of the Cosmic Being as if he had waved a magic wand, and the galaxy was seen from outer space, recalled to form at his discretion.

This wasn't just a show without a message. It was followed by the two horrendous hemispheres of energy sustained in balance by a single fragile strand of light. It became vividly apparent that all order in the universe depends on this most intricate possible balance. The hemispheres were like reservoirs of energy straining for release, yet held in balance by a universal mind. They then reached a point of saturation, trembling on the verge of unthinkable instability, with the fate of the entire universe suspended in the balance. The Cosmic Being intervened. He began to gather the energies of the void. They were drawn from throughout the void, with the whole of experience being brought to a polar consummation in his being. There was no mind but his mind, no being apart from his being. Spanning all space and time, he was gathering himself unto himself. Eternal energies ordered through the ages were flying to their doom. He became an absolute polarity of center and periphery transcending all creation. His active center became an absolute singularity in a black expanse beyond the void. This realization wrenched the mind asunder with an inability to accept such total annihilation. But the being didn't complete the awesome spectacle. Turning from him was like a perceptual transposition; he recommitted his energies in the series of experiences that followed. The transcendent nature of his being was clearly shown, yet he is imminent as well.

The enigma of the singularity is not a mathematical problem confined to black holes in astrophysics or the cosmological origins of the universe. It is an expression of the creative dilemma at the root of mind. It is not an annihilation through a contraction into a final point of being. It is a basic recognition that sustains the creative process through a need to reconcile center and periphery.

A mood of sleep is cast across the deep. Only crickets resist the paralyzing quiet to sustain the rhythm for a psalm of slumber. Eventually their muted squeaks inspire the musicians of the lake to croon a lullaby. A solitary loon begins, a mile or two to the north. Its call is smooth and mellow as it utters a single note, prolonged and clear, without vibrato. The note begins with a single soft yodel, then it rises only slightly before it falls in harmony with its own resounding echo. The crystalline acoustics of the night replicate the solo into the distant fading chorus of a crowd. As it trails away, another loon captures the mood and melody to perfection. Another round of replicating sound is picked up by another loon. Links of replicating tune are passed from loon to loon. Each link is in exquisite taste, each concordant with the others. A fluid chain of sound is woven round and round. The euphony of echoes rings through the hills, but softly, rising only slightly, then trailing off, bidding peace and rest to all creatures of the wild. The water comes alive with the mellow hum of gentle song as the loons croon on and on their lullaby on the lake. It is a rendering reserved for very special nights.

The fire will be burning low; it is time to check the camp. There is only starlight to show the way, but the eyes have become accustomed. The gas lantern on the table, low on air, is pumped up. Some more wood is added to the fire. The bear hasn't returned— perhaps he has left the island. Another hour passes watching the fire and listening to the wood worms munching in the log. The black bandit won't be back. It is time for bed. However, just in case, a couple more large chunks are added to the fire, and the coal-oil lantern is left alight.

15

Ghosts and Ghouls

There is loud splashing in the small cove right beside the tent. It is very early morning; nothing but fog can be seen out the window. What is it?

The tent flap is opened to have a look outside. It is getting light, but the sun is not up yet. The mainland shore is completely concealed by fog. The small cove is full of mergansers feeding on a school of minnows. There must be thirty of them or more. They are swimming rapidly back and forth, diving all over the little bay. With the school of minnows corralled, they make throaty sounds of glee as they feast like greedy monsters.

It is earlier than usual to be up. Might as well catch a fish for breakfast. It will pass some time while the sun dispels the fog. In late summer and early fall it is common for fog to settle on the lakes at night.

The canoe is paddled slowly around the point toward the west side of the island. The thick fog makes for poor visibility. The world seems to end a few yards from the canoe. There is only a short distance to go, yet it feels like a journey in a time machine through the twilight zone. The mirror surface of the lake vanishes into a misty void as sleek ripples drift out into oblivion. Lost in time, the craft sifts through the vacant vapor, seeking out a destiny suspended as a memory in the past. Gaunt forms begin to loom ahead like apparitions in a crystal ball. Uncertain branches reach out for recognition and guide the intuition. Pale rock creeps down to join with its reflection in a point that gestures into nowhere. The time machine has found its mark: the point beyond the little bay which indicates the fishing hole. Casting begins into the blank white sea of emptiness.

A recall relationship between form and emptiness is a characteristic of all the systems higher than System 3. In System 3 the alternations between form and emptiness are enacted by the set of particular centers under the direction of the universal set. In System 4, the group of three particular terms alternate between form and emptiness, while the two universal sets direct the action. We have already had a look at the universal terms of System 4, which implicated two of the particular terms—the sales and product-development regions of a daisy company. This leaves four terms yet to discuss in the six-pointed sequence. Let's return to the daisy company to consider them two at a time, first the two in the "emptiness" grouping, then the two in the "form" grouping.

The emptiness grouping includes Terms 8, 7, 4, which correspond to the sales, treasury, and organization regions, respectively. Occurring in Stages 1 and 3 of each cycle, it brings with it certain anxieties. Even daisies are not free of worldly tensions, for they must express themselves in nature's marketplace by making commitments through their organizational structure, which places a drain on the spiritual reserves of their treasury. In Stage 1, we universal devas are somewhat aloof from these provincial concerns, but we nevertheless moderate them through a discretionary search with the transference of idea in mind. Then in Stage 3 we switch to a regenerative concern with costs, in the hope that it is not too late. All of this has nothing to say about the actual molecular formation of a daisy. The whole concern here is with the potential to produce the daisy idea. This potential idea is an identity in emptiness.

Let us turn now to the organization-and-manning term, which has also been called the mental-work term, Term 4, illustrated in Figure 42. Keep in mind that Centers 1, 2, 3, and 4 represent idea, knowledge, routine, and formation, respectively, and that these are particular centers associated with each daisy.

It's true that we devas are privileged minor gods exempt from mundane chores like mental work. After all, we have wider interests to attend to. Why should we do this kind of work when each daisy is like a self-reliant factory with ideas of its own?

In this term, each daisy's idea spirit, Center 1, is intimately familiar with its own archetypal facilities through coalescence with its ghost, Center 2. From this coalesced wedlock of idea and knowledge, each daisy's spirit-ghost finds an additional identity out through its cell routines, Center 3, with molecular formation, Center 4. There are two relational lobes, R_1 and R_2, to this identity of spirit-

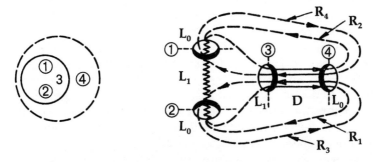

Term 4   Mental Work   Organization & Manning   **42**

ghost routines with molecular formation, but the two lobes are united in the coalescence. This is an eternal pattern of structure without any active timelike quality. In every ordinary company there is this same background pattern of people's ideas coalesced with the knowledgeable administration of facilities, which together underlie the equipment routines that form the product. The pattern represents the organizational structure as an eternal quantization of company technique.

Countercurrent to this background pattern are the two relational wholes R_3 and R_4, which can exist only alternately if they are not to sever the unity of the coalescence. In other words, R_3 and R_4 must be considered separately. As we all shall see, they represent alternative regenerative and expressive modes, respectively, to the term. This comparison of alternatives against a common countercurrent background is an all-pervasive pattern to mental work.

It can be seen, then, that the idea spirit of the daisy is locked in an eternal marriage with knowledge, such that it must live up to a regimen of routine. Through coalescence, it has an insight into archetypal knowledge—through that insight, it sees out through cell routines to molecular formation. Countercurrent to marriage vows, the daisy spirit then quite inadvertently gets involved in a very discreet and innocent relationship on the side. Quite independent of its coalesced knowledge of existing facilities, it receives an idea, R_4, which is feedback about the daisy's growth. This R_4 idea comes from molecular formation via the cells directly. This indicates a need for the idea spirit, which employs a host of vital spirits, to adjust itself accordingly. The structure of its spirit must be appropriate for expression through its cells. Similarly, for every company the organization must be structured and manned to meet the needs of production routines.

In the regenerative mode of the term, R_3 indicates that the daisy ghost now has *its* turn to get involved in a discreet relationship on the side. News about the daisy's growth is fed back not to the idea spirit, but to the ghost's archetypal knowledge of facilities. In any company this may indicate a need for expanded areas of expertise, manning changes in the organizational structure, or training to ensure an adequate level of competence.*

Since the organizational structure is funded by the resources of the treasury, let's next delve into the wonders of a daisy's treasury. The treasury term, which has also been called the transmission-of-product term, is illustrated in Figure 43.

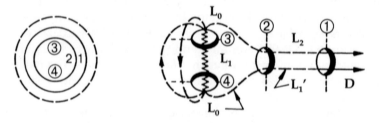

Term 7   Transmission of Product   Treasury

43

Here we discover another eternal marriage. But this time, the wedlock is between the molecular formation of daisies and their cell routines. This is really a marital documentation of previous growth experience carefully recorded by coalesced energies** within the daisy's ghost. This cell-formation knowledge is then transmitted out through the daisy's idea interface. It is a quantized mirroring of applied technique that underlies the daisy's spirit in the void. Furthermore, it is an accounting in knowledge of spiritual resources committed to growth.

---

*It is worth pointing out that the mental-work term transforms into the creation-of-idea term, Term 2, through the perceptual transposition of Center 3. This may be done to incorporate either one or the other of the alternatives of mental work as the superimposed idea on the mastermind triad.

**In this case, Centers 3 and 4 are themselves quantized, so that the term is a higher order of quantization.

In any company, a knowledge of resources committed to production routine as it relates to the transmission of the product idea amounts to an accounting of expenditures made. This is more than a tally of money spent, for money is exchanged between people for the application of technique toward a product idea. In this respect money is a tally of spiritual energies expended.

In the regenerative mode of the term, Centers 1 and 2 exchange places. Here the eternal marriage of cell formation is accounted for within the daisy's idea, which now precedes the knowledge interface. This precedence of idea over knowledge indicates an estimate of expenditures in advance of knowing them—a budget. Just as managers in every company must predict and budget for the needs of their departments, daisy spirits are required to predict the needs of daisies. This is done on the basis of previous experience.

When the treasury and organization terms are examined together, an interesting symmetry is apparent. (See Figure 44.) The coalescence in the organization term is between idea and knowledge, within the context of routine. This represents an eternal quantization of technique that is committed to the formation of a product. The coalescence in the treasury term is between formation and routine within the context of knowledge and idea. This coalescence mirrors quantizations of technique as either an eternal accounting or a budgeting of expenditures. The two terms are reciprocals of one another, both being involved in the recall process.* The recall of technique is perpetually linked to the resources required: when one is in the expressive mode, the other is always in the regenerative mode.

TREASURY   **ORGANIZATION & MANNING**

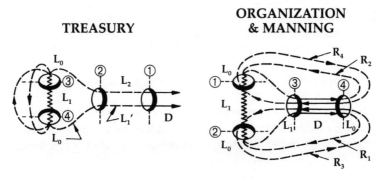

44

---

*The organization term is primary to recall because it responds to a formative stimulus through routine.

The third member of the grouping, the sales term, always occurs in the expressive mode. The three terms occur together in Stages 1 and 3 of each cycle. In Stage 1, the mediating emphasis is on the transference of idea, and the organization term is in the expressive mode. In Stage 3, the emphasis shifts to the regenerative needs of the company; the organization term is in the regenerative mode. This completes a description of the emptiness grouping. We will return to have a look at the form grouping shortly.

The fish are biting. Four or five nice ones have been caught. One has been kept and cleaned for breakfast. Although the fog is still heavy, the sun is now penetrating through. The canoe is floating on a dish of fluid satin that fades into a blazing limbo of forgotten forms. Sunlight has exploded in a brilliant sheen. The mist is all aglitter. Light is playing through a fairyland of mirrored dewdrops suspended everywhere. The few vague features that rise as shades to haunt the tinsel sphere become forestalled hallucinations in a vision. The resplendence of the specter conveys a message far too meaningful for words. Everything has been transformed into a world of light, with knowledge only of unending life. The features of the mystery have been curtailed. The puppets in the play have lost their place in the charade of life.

The canoe is paddled in a scintillating bubble through the luminescent spell. The tip of the island soon pokes through to show the turn to camp. Around the point, the light, dancing on the vagrant forms, has charmed them into enchanting beings. Trees and bushes glisten in a spangled luster as light plays host to surrogates of light.

The canoe is pulled up and tied. The fish is taken up to camp. A fire is started, and breakfast is prepared. Diffusing rays are playing now in streamers through the branches of the nearby trees. The channel has become an effulgent globe of light that slowly yields into translucence. Creations of the shoreline are merging out of mist. Forms are taking form from out of emptiness.

In System 4, the "form" grouping consists of Terms 1, 2, and 5. These correspond to the marketing, product-development, and product-processing regions of a company, respectively. They occur in Stages 2 and 4 of each cycle.

The anxieties that were introduced with the emptiness grouping change their complexion to a different set of tensions. Of concern is the processing of each daisy product incorporating the history of product development with a view to market acceptance. In Stage 2, we universal devas again moderate these concerns through a discretionary search, but within the context of the mastermind triad. Our universal spirit focuses corporate resources on production. In Stage 4, we turn to reflect on a sales concern with costs, while developing new ideas relating also to facilities, which influence the regeneration of equipment. This grouping, then, is concerned with translating the potential capabilities assimilated through the emptiness grouping into the actual making of a product as an identity in form.

Since the product-development term has already been described, let's have a look at Term 5, the product-processing term. Also called the physical-work term, it is illustrated in Figure 45.

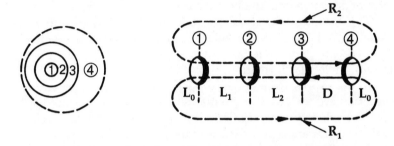

Term 5   Physical Work   Product Processing

45

Although we devas don't get directly involved in physical work, we are there in spirit, lending discretionary support to each daisy. In this term, R_2 portrays each daisy spirit busy disseminating its daisy idea, Center 1, down through the hierarchy first to be administered by archetypal knowledge, Center 2, and then to be supervised by cell routines, Center 3, which in turn find an identity with molecular formation, Center 4. As in any company, the central product idea filters down through the successive tiers in the organizational structure to find an identity in the physical formation of the product.

The effectiveness of the discretionary hierarchy is monitored by the countercurrent identity R_1, where knowledge and routine are eclipsed between daisy formation and the daisy idea. Each manager can directly assess the formation of the product by vital feedback through the hierarchy.

In the regenerative mode of the term, Centers 1 and 2 exchange places as usual. In R_2, archetypal knowledge now assumes preeminence in the hierarchy, preconditioning the daisy idea as it disseminates direction through cell routines to daisy formation. In this way, each daisy's spirit manager relies on accumulated knowledge to implement a regenerative concern with cell routines, just as every company manager must rely on administrative knowledge and advice to upgrade equipment routines. In the countercurrent identity R_1, product formation feedback now relates to archetypal knowledge, so that the effectiveness of changes in routine are monitored directly.

The last term remaining to be discussed is Term 1, the marketing term, as shown in Figure 46. Also called the "perception of the field" term, it displays a perceptual axis between a subjective company perspective and an objective market perspective.

This term exhibits simultaneously performed double marriages within each daisy. In both modes of the term, each daisy's idea spirit is joined with its knowledge ghost, while cell routines are married up with molecular formation.

In the expressive mode of the term, the daisy's spirit and its formation are reviewed in the marketplace—like wives on display— from the subjective standpoint of knowledge and routine, respectively. It is not enough for them to be spiritually and physically attractive; they are assessed from the perspective of the knowledge and disciplines of routine that they employ respectively. This mode

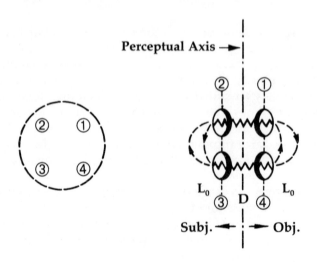

Term 1   Perception of the Field   Marketing

46

of the term reflects actual performance. In any company, the product idea must be well thought-out, and its form effectively produced. Since this mode reflects actual performance, it acts as a perceptual referent for the regenerative process, so that expected standards can continue to be met.

In the regenerative mode of the term, the daisy's ghost-idea marriage does a pirouette about the perceptual axis. Centers 1 and 2 exchange places so that archetypal knowledge is objectively perceived in the market, alongside the daisy's formation. The daisy's facilities thus come into objective assessment from the standpoint of idea, alongside the review of formation from the standpoint of cell routines. When a company's facilities are reviewed in the market in this way, its regenerative needs become apparent. This provides a perceptual referent for the expressive process, such that the company can perform without risk of overextending itself.

In Stage 2, the expressive modes of product development and product processing always coincide with the regenerative mode of the marketing term. In Stage 4, the regenerative modes of product development and product processing always coincide with the expressive mode of the marketing term.

This completes a brief description of all of the terms in the creative matrix. We will return later for another overall look at how they work together.

The sun has broken through the sleeping cloud; the trees across the channel have emerged above their fleecy bed. The mist has shriveled to a pit of vapors, confined within the serpentine contortions of the shore. They steam up into a multitude of tufts, endowing weird misshapen faces to a mass of ghostly forms gliding on the water. Their glossy heads are wreathing slowly to a funeral dirge, while the pristine oracle rises to exorcise their clammy spell. They weave in tortuous orbs, legions of them, wailing in remorse, seeking expiation from their imposed demise. Their futile pleas unheeded, they gradually expire, as throngs wander aimlessly through throngs hovering in a chasm.

The whisky jacks soar into camp and land in the dead tree. They jostle for position as usual and settle on the same pecking order, as usual. A stale pancake is taken out, and Number Three immediately flits down and lands on the knee, chirping softly. It hops up on the finger of one hand to take a piece from the other hand, then flies away. Number Two follows suit, while Number One lands on the ground a few feet away and watches. Not willing to be coaxed any closer, it waits to be thrown a piece, then flies off to hide it. A bevy of small ground sparrows ventures from seclusion in the bushes, but they are shy and stay together in a clique about ten feet away. Some pancake is crumbled up and tossed to them. They all rush to pick at crumbs, then the whiskey jacks return and steal the larger pieces. More pieces are doled out as two red squirrels begin to fight over dominion of the cupboard. One of them approaches, taking a piece of pancake from the fingers.

Meanwhile the ghosts have withered to an assemblage of trolls and gnomes. Wizened figures stir in a malaise, unable to escape the scourge of light. Streams of shimmering lances pike and shred their forms. They become dismembered, frayed, diffused—then lost. As their numbers slowly dwindle, the pace quickens with enlivened spirits in a cavalcade of little people that come dancing on the scene. Leprechauns and elves begin to twirl around their dying cousins, unconcerned at the fate that they themselves await. They glide— unaided by a breeze—in currents, swirls, and eddies, directing movements with a sorcery of their own. New swirls keep forming, changing, twining, mingling in graceful waltzing swarms. Fairies come, then the pixies, some marching time, then joining into streams that swirl behind a marching band. They keep calling smaller cousins with quicker tempos; then, as they tire, each does a final twist before popping up as it jumps out of sight.

A lone loon is swimming through some transparent wisps of remaining mist in the shadows across the channel. It begins to sing a note, loud and clear, but then its voice breaks into a rasping squawk. It is a bachelor loon that comes back to the same bay every year. It never tries to sing with the other loons. Perhaps it lost its mate long ago and since has lost its will to sing. Whatever the tragic circumstances, this bird is an outcast, required to live out its time in solitude. It makes a circle in the channel, returning to the south, without trying to sing again.

The system isn't always kind; sometimes it is hard to find much justice in the world. The ledger keeping is eternal. The budget and the balance sheet are worked out on a scope we haven't yet begun to comprehend. All we see is the screening of a movie. We don't appreciate the creative effort that goes into the script, the design of sets and costumes, the specialized development of techniques, the endless planning, and the learning and rehearsing of the roles.

System 4 illustrates how the energies of experience are drawn upon to structure the plot and evolve creative themes for screening in a marketplace of movies. The nine terms that delineate the primary creative process in System 4 are illustrated together in Figure 47.

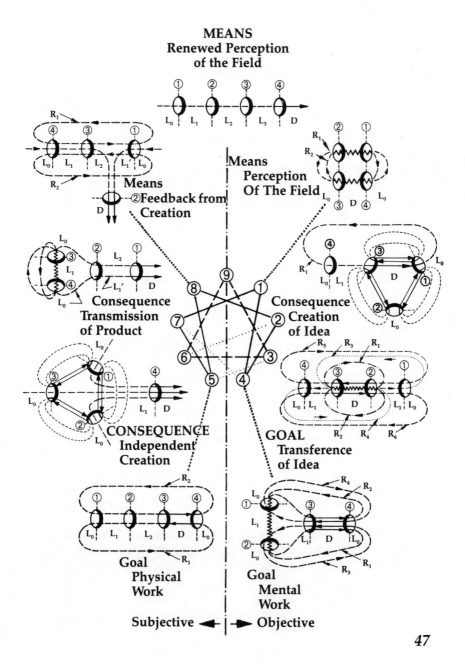

47

The terms are all shown in the expressive mode. In the regenerative mode of the six-term sequence, Centers 1 and 2 exchange places. Terms 9, 3 and 6 have no independent regenerative mode. Keep in mind that Centers 1 to 4 represent idea, knowledge, routine, and formation, respectively.

The two reciprocal activities of the six-pointed figure, one on each side of the medial axis, are integrated by the mediating activity. The form of the enneagram is thus an elaboration of the primary-activity triad, but System 3 also subsumes System 4 in a transcendent way. The alternate groupings of the six-pointed figure display a recurrent identity between form and emptiness, just as the particular centers of the primary activity do. The overall goal of System 4 is the simultaneous realization of idea in form, just as the goal of the primary activity is a simultaneous realization of inside and outside. The overall consequence is an independent creation, an identity in form, just as the consequence of the primary activity is an identity in form. The mediating means term is discretion, alternating with a regenerative feedback term that sustains the creative process, just as the means term of the primary activity alternates between discretion and a double identity that regenerates the activity. The terms are different but they mean the same thing. The primary creative process is an elaboration of the primary activity subsumed within the same pattern of meaning.

This completes a general description of System 4. The account has been kept to the bare essentials in an effort to communicate the essence of the system as a whole. Once the essence is grasped, one can explore the endless intricacies of the system for oneself. (See Appendix 1.)

After the fog vanished, the day warmed up quickly. Yet there is a taste of autumn in the air—quiet and mild, but not like a summer's day. It is more like a woman refined by the benefit of long experience, having acquired the grace to move into the autumn of her years with quiet dignity. There is a hint of color in the trees, like wisps of gray betraying the advancing season.

After some chores and a swim, the afternoon is spent casting in a bay across the lake. Along with some gathered greens and roots, a pickerel from jam-bag rock completes the menu for the evening meal. After supper the canoe is paddled west of the island, a good place to watch the sun go down.

Each day has a character of its own: today has been very calm, with just enough haze to subdue the glare of the sun. It has been warm but not hot, with a certain tranquility of moderation. Now, the messages of the day are digested into subtle evening residues, slowly subsiding into stillness. Many are the moods of the wilderness—never do they speak so clear as when they are most quiet.

The blue sky above is blended into a golden glare across the west. A single thin band of cloud, curling overhead, has transmuted into a floral necklace flung round a neck of sky. The evening colors promenade through the rainbow into violet, then pale into a lingering glow. The cloud of carnations finally wilts into a smudge of gray, cast off in a bunch toward the east.

All day the haze has muted shades of color, softened edges, and blended highlights into shadows. With the advancing night, the haze has concentrated near the water and in the bays, to hide the shorelines in the distance. Horizons have merged into the sky. The stars are twinkling in the water. The canoe has been transported into boundless space, floating in a sphere of stars. A point across the lake, and another to the north, intrude boldly through the haze in two big blobs, hovering like a pair of oblong asteroids growing trees from top and bottom.

Holmes has worked hard devising sophisticated instruments and theories in his effort to crack the ultimate mystery of the cosmos. Now his faithful companion, Watson, has dragged him back to the planetarium with many questions. Holmes is explaining how powerful telescopes reveal that there are as many distant galaxies as there are stars in our own Milky Way. Dispersed in clusters in all directions, they seem even to exhibit a pattern of superclusters, like a great skein woven through the firmament. Galaxies, however, are the focus of attention.

"As you know, Watson, galaxies come in a wide range of sizes, and types. When the first large telescopes began to reveal great numbers of galaxies beyond our own, they were classified very simply into three main categories: elliptical, spiral, and irregular. Elliptical galaxies are further subdivided according to the eccentricity of their shape, from spherical to elongated. They are generally dust-free and dominated by red giants. Spirals are subdivided according to whether their nucleus or spiral arms are their predominant feature. Some have a very bright, large nucleus with tightly wrapped spiral arms. Some, such as our own Milky Way, have a more even distribution of brightness between the nucleus and spiral arms.

Others have a much smaller nucleus and open predominant arms. These three broad subdivisions also apply to the bar-type spirals, which have an elongated, bar-shaped nucleus."

"Strange that galaxies should be so highly organized and yet differ so widely in shape. What are the irregulars like?" asks Watson, with his usual curiosity.

"Irregular galaxies seem to have no distinctive shape," replies the sleuth, with professional detachment. "Some are cloudlike, with young, hot stars and evidence of interstellar gas and dust. Others are composed of dim stars, yet they have gas and dust as well. Some eject material at high speed. A variety of galaxies exhibit violent, jetlike emissions far into space. Galaxies in general cover a wide range of size, from dwarfs a few thousand light-years across, to giants like our own, and larger."

"It is hard to even imagine the immensity of the universe," exclaims Watson. "More than a hundred billion galaxies, each with many billions of stars. The numbers are too immense to mean any-thing. There must be more stars in the sky than there are grains of sand on all the beaches of the planet earth."

"Yes, indeed," agrees Holmes. "More than if all the continents on earth were completely ringed with beach."

"Do galaxies differ other than in their optical appearance?"

"Very much so, Watson. Some galaxies are strong sources of radio emission, although the source is not understood. In some cases the emissions come not from the center, but from two regions thousands of light-years on either side of the optical galaxy. There is also a class known as Seyfert galaxies that can be reasonably strong radio emitters; their light output can also vary greatly in a period of only a few months. Among the strangest of objects are the qua-sars, which are sometimes also radio emitters. Considered to be the most distant objects from us, they have recessional velocities up to ninety percent of the speed of light. If this is correct, the most distant known quasar must be over ten billion light-years away. We are seeing it from the distant past, near what may be the origin of the universe."

"You mean, we are seeing the distant quasar as it was ten billion years ago!" gasps Watson. "All objects in the heavens are like ghosts appearing from the past, but to see one resurrected from ten billion years ago seems fantastic. Such an object must be very large to be visible from so far."

"That is the strangest part of all, Watson. Quasars appear to be much smaller than the smallest galaxy, yet they emit more energy than a giant galaxy, if they are in reality at the distances indicated. Their energy output can change drastically over periods of months, weeks—even days. There is yet another class of object called BL Lacterae objects—BL Lacs for short—whose distances rank with that of quasars. Their energy emissions are even more violent and variable. The first one to be observed, initially thought to be a variable star in the constellation of Lacterae, has recently been identified as the nucleus of a normal galaxy that is very faint. This finding confirms the great distance from us, yet energy emissions come from a nucleus as small as a light-day in diameter, overpowering the entire galaxy. The source of such enormous energies is a complete mystery."

"Amazing!" exclaims Watson. "From what you say, thermonuclear processes are not nearly sufficient to account for the energies of quasars and BL Lacs. Have you no ideas on the possible origins of such incredible energies?"

"Unfortunately, none that are very satisfying, Watson. Energies of the magnitude emitted by quasars could be produced if a body the size of a hundred million suns were to undergo gravitational collapse within its Schwarzschild sphere. Such an enormous black hole could theoretically release one-half the total mass as energy, but there is no way of knowing if such a phenomenon is possible or, if it is, what mechanism accounts for the form in which the energy is observed. If for some reason quasars are in reality much closer than they appear, then their energies would be much less, and easier to explain. The discovery of a faint galaxy associated with a BL Lac seems to confirm, however, that such huge energy sources really are great distances away."

"It is remarkable that you are able to assess the distances to other galaxies at all. How are you able to do this with any confidence?"

Holmes is a little uncomfortable, and he shifts in his seat. Since he is not allowed to smoke in the planetarium, he is toying with his unlit pipe. "There are two or three methods that can sometimes be employed, Watson, although the only method that lends itself to quasars depends on Hubble's red-shift law. This law states that the distance to any galaxy is directly proportional to its velocity of recession. In other words, the faster a galaxy is moving away from us, the farther away it is. The ratio between the recessional velocity and distance is known as Hubble's constant. As you know, galaxies have fingerprints or distinctive lines in their light spectra. The faster a galaxy is moving away from us, the more these lines are shifted toward the red end of the spectrum. You have no doubt noticed how the pitch or frequency in the sound of an approaching vehicle changes as it passes on the highway. This is known as the Doppler shift, and the spectral fingerprints of light are similarly affected. Their frequency decreases toward the red end of the spectrum, the faster the object is moving away from us.

"I see," says Watson thoughtfully. "This is why you are so confident that the universe is expanding. Knowing the rates of recession and distances of the galaxies, can you then calculate the origin of the big bang?"

"It is not quite that straightforward, Watson. Hubble's constant is not really constant but may change over long periods of time depending on the nature of the universe. As you know, Einstein's general theory of relativity greatly revised Newton's concept of space and time. Newton believed that space and time are independent from one another and from the material content of the universe. Within this framework, he recognized that force is related to the acceleration of mass—not to velocity, as was thought previously. The measure of acceleration in any moving frame of reference is the same; observers in different moving frames of reference will agree on the magnitude of a force acting on a body, but will not agree on its velocity. When it was discovered then that the velocity of light is the same for all observers regardless of their moving frames of reference, a serious conflict arose."

Watson interrupts. "Sometimes I get the feeling that I actually understand all your talk about relativity. If the measure of acceleration is the same in any moving frame of reference, and if the velocity of light is also observed to be the same, then something must change in the different reference frames themselves. The measurement of mass, space, and time must change."

"That's the general idea, Watson. In his special theory of relativity, Einstein recognized that inertial mass is not constant, but varies with velocity, and velocity is a measure of space and time. In other words, Einstein recognized that space and time are not independent from one another, nor are they independent from the material content of the universe, as Newton thought. Space, time, and mass are intimately related. In order to extend this idea into a general theory of relativity, Einstein had to make the additional assumption that gravity and acceleration are equivalent. For instance, if a person is accelerating upward in an elevator, he feels heavier, just as if there were an increase in the pull of gravity. The resulting generalized theory defines the universe as a space-time continuum with a curvature conditioned by the distribution of its mass. The universe may conform to one of three or four possibilities; in each case, Hubble's constant will change in a different way."

"It all sounds very complicated," complains Watson. "The assumption that gravity and acceleration are equivalent seems to me to be a troublesome point. It is like saying that a bucket of water and a bucket of wine are the same because they may look and weigh the same. Nevertheless, I gather from what you say that the general theory of relativity favors the idea that the universe originated in a singular state, from which it has expanded since the big bang. This appears to fit in with Hubble's law. If you can determine the curvature of the space-time continuum from observations, then you can divine the historical origin of the big bang that gave birth to the universe. You should then also be able to divine the ultimate destiny of the universe. Is that the idea, Holmes?"

Holmes is very casual about the whole affair, as if he is talking about last week's cricket match. "Yes, that's the general idea, Watson. For instance, if the universe is of sufficient density, the rate of expansion will not exceed the velocity of mutual escape between galaxies. Gravitational attraction will win a tug-of-war with expansion, slowing it down until it stops and reverses into the singularity from which it began. In this case the curvature of the space-time continuum is closed or spherical, resulting in an oscillating universe that goes through an endless series of big bangs. If the universe is closed, the last big bang likely occurred about ten billion years ago. It should collapse into a singular state again in about seventy billion years."

"I think I am beginning to see what you're getting at," says Watson a little skeptically. "If I throw a cricket ball straight up in the air, it will slow to a stop as it rises to its maximum height, then fall back to the earth again. This is because I am not strong enough to accelerate the ball beyond the reach of the gravitational pull between the earth and the ball. In a similar way, if the density of the universe is great enough, the big bang may not have been strong enough to accelerate the expanding galaxies beyond the reach of their mutual gravitational pull. The curvature of the entire space-time continuum will be closed because of the density of mass involved. If the mass of the universe is not great enough, then one big bang is all there can ever be, and the universe will keep expanding indefinitely, I presume. It is like throwing the cricket ball up so fast that it never comes down."

"Yes, you're getting the drift of it, Watson. You really are quite a clever chap to catch on so quickly. If the expansive thrust is just sufficient to overcome gravity, then the big bang occurred about thirteen billion years ago. If the expansive thrust is more than sufficient to overcome gravity, then the big bang occurred about fifteen billion years ago. In these cases, the curvature of the space-time continuum will be open, and the universe will continue to expand. The galaxies will fade from view as mutual recessional velocities eventually approach the speed of light in about twenty billion years. Moreover, the stars in our own Milky Way will gradually expend their energies, marching through their life cycles to a heat-death doom. One by one the fires will be snuffed out for a final time, leaving a frigid wasteland of discarded cinders."

Watson undoes the top button of his shirt and loosens his tie. "You certainly don't offer much hope," he pants. "Either the universe is going to be crushed again into an unthinkable singularity, or it is headed for a frigid oblivion of eternal night. Either possibility, however distant, leaves me wrenched of a sense of humanity."

"Nonsense, Watson! There is no room for anthropomorphic feelings in science. It is all a big bakeshop, I tell you, and the evidence strongly favors a big-bang beginning. The bakeshop started as infinite temperature and density, cooling very rapidly as it expanded. After the first one-hundredth of a second, the temperature had cooled to 100 billion degrees Kelvin; after the first second, to ten billion degrees; and after three minutes, to one billion degrees, though it was still seventy times hotter than the center of the sun."*

Beads of sweat are standing out on Watson's forehead. He feels entrapped by the web of evidence. Holmes seems to take a morbid delight in his friend's discomfort. It is the old triumphant feeling that comes with closing in to wrap up a case. He continues.

"Before thirty-five minutes had passed, a neutron-proton balance was reached that determined the primary proportions of hydrogen and helium that predominate in the universe. The nuclei of heavier atoms could not form at this time, and the universe was still much too hot for neutral atoms of any kind to form. Radiation predominated over matter for about the first million years. As the temperature dropped to about 4,000 K, free electrons were used up in the formation of stable atoms, the universe becoming transparent to radiation. With this decoupling of matter and radiation, gravitational influences began to hold sway. Turbulence and magnetohydrodyn-

---

*An interesting account is given by Steven Weinberg, *The First Three Minutes* (New York: Bantam Books, 1979).

amics also had roles to play as matter condensed and fragmented into the clusters of galaxies that we observe expanding away from one another today. This all took about one hundred million years, a short time, when you consider the universe is presently ten to fifteen billion years old."

"I see," says Watson slowly, trying hard to maintain his composure. "Everything exploded from a pinprick, condensing into the galaxies a hundred million years later. Let me take a moment to recapitulate. The universe had a heat birth. Unless it contracts into a singularity again, it is headed for a heat death. The bakeshop's energies will all be dissipated into darkness, never more to cook a cake. The first fruit of cooking was the nuclei of hydrogen and helium, the predominant constituents of stars and interstellar gas, which still constitute about 98 percent of the universe. It is within the stars, however, that the heavier elements are cooked, then distributed to the planets by large old stars that go through their life cycles more quickly, ending in a supernova. The gas and dust thus dispersed collect again into a second generation of stars. Five to ten billion years after the initial creation of the universe, our earth was born with a second generation star, along with the good fortune to have conditions amenable to the evolution of biological life. This process itself took nearly four billion years, until we humans accidentally emerged on the scene, puzzled by the whole affair. After a few thousand years of wars and wondering, we gradually begin to gather evidence, then upon devising some laws to explain the evidence, we conclude it is all an accidental bakeshop. Is it not possible that there has been some misinterpretation of the evidence? Surely there are other possible alternatives."*

Holmes, who has begun to chew rather nervously on his pipe stem, is obliged to confess some weaknesses in his theories. 'Other alternatives have been considered, Watson, and, to be sure, there are a few embarrassing bits of evidence to detract from the big-bang options. For instance, the helium levels that would theoretically be produced in the big bang are uncomfortably high, compared with actual levels. Also, some galaxies appear to be much older than big-bang theories allow. Steady-state models of the universe have been considered, but because the universe is expanding, these must postulate the continuous creation of matter from nothing to compensate for the expansion. Otherwise, the receding galaxies would all long

*A review of various theories is given by Jagjit Singh, *Great Ideas and Theories of Modern Cosmology* (New York: Dover Publications, 1970).

ago have disappeared from view. Also, there is no known process that turns heavy elements back into hydrogen—the nuclear transformations going on in stars should have run their course eons ago. On the other hand, steady-state theories offer the advantage of avoiding the singular state in the big bang, in which all the physical laws that are invoked to explain the universe must be suspended. A steady-state universe has no beginning or end."

"Surely the continuous creation of matter is no less objectionable than the big bang," protests Watson. "Why aren't steady-state theories favored?"

"Because the evidence still favors the big-bang alternatives, especially since the discovery of a background radiation that permeates the universe. It is thought to have expanded and cooled with the universe from a time early in its creation, when the decoupling between matter and radiation occurred, corresponding now to a very low temperature of about three degrees Kelvin. Steady-state models have difficulty in offering a convincing explanation. Other models and ideas have been investigated as well, some of them having recourse to dimensionless numbers that stand out like landmarks in the field of evidence."

"What is a dimensionless number?" queries Watson, who has become quite baffled by so many aspects to the case.

"No need to become confused, Watson. Dimensionless numbers are perfectly straightforward. They are pure numbers, independent of units of measurement. For instance, consider two trees, one of which is twice as high as the other. The ratio of the height of the tall tree to that of the short tree is 2—a dimensionless number, independent of the units we use to measure the trees, whether feet, meters, inches, or broom handles. Such numbers crop up from time to time, sometimes bearing special relationships to one another that seem to reflect an underlying cosmic structure."

"That sounds very mysterious. Can you explain a little more?"

"It is all quite elementary, Watson. For instance, a dimensionless force constant can be derived for an electron and a proton. If the force of their mutual electrical attraction is divided by the force of their mutual gravitational attraction, the ratio is a very large number, about 10^{39}. It is also possible to construct a dimensionless time constant for the universe, by dividing its approximate age by the time that it takes light to cross an atomic nucleus—again a very large number, about 10^{39}. Another dimensionless number called the cosmical number can be derived by dividing the mass of the universe by the mass of a hydrogen atom—a much larger number, about

10^{78}, roughly the square of the force constant or the time constant. It is a curious fact that the force constant and the time constant are approximately equal, and that the cosmical number is their square. Various attempts have been made to incorporate these and other dimensionless numbers into cosmological theories, without great success."*

Inspired again, Watson sees in dimensionless numbers a relationship between each and all. Unable to restrain himself, he proceeds to expound. "The three dimensionless numbers that you selected all exemplify a certain relationship between the universal and the particular. In the force constant, gravity is a universal phenomenon, implicitly associated with all matter in the universe, although very weak between particles so tiny as an electron and a proton. On the other hand, electrical attraction is a particulate phenomenon associated with particles of opposite polarity—very strong, compared with gravity. The force constant is thus a ratio between a universal and particulate property. So is the cosmical number."

Holmes senses that Watson may be getting wound up again, and he interrupts. "Get to the point, Watson!"

"The point is that certain aspects of the evidence may have been misinterpreted. The relationship of the particular to the universal may show itself in various ways. For instance, maybe red shifts can occur for a variety of reasons; Hubble's red-shift law, though it may indicate great distances, may not indicate recessional velocities. Velocity is a measure of space and time, and when light spans the great distances from far-flung galaxies, it also spans great periods of time. Light, then, is also a measure of space and time. Velocity is a particular measure, whereas light is a universal measure. If a particular measure of space and time, determined as velocity over a short interval, can indicate a red shift, is it not then reasonable to suspect that a universal measure over a long interval may also indicate a red shift? The red shift may indicate only great distances and time. Maybe the universe is not expanding at all."

Holmes, annoyed at Watson's impertinence, fires a question back. "What then is to keep the universe from collapsing under its own gravity? Magic? Before it was known that the universe is expanding, Einstein accepted a kind of magic in his equations in the form of a cosmological constant that balanced gravity, permitting a

*For one such attempt see Sir Arthur Eddington, *The Expanding Universe* (London: Cambridge University Press, 1933).

static universe. He later rejected the idea as the biggest blunder of his life."

"I'm not suggesting magic, and I'm not suggesting that the universe is static," protests Watson. "I *am* suggesting that there is an organization associated with the very being of the universe that sustains its form. There is no question that the universe is highly organized. It is reasonable to think that, like any organism, it has a capacity to respond and change according to its needs in a manner that is not predictable by physical laws. Specific relationships of the particular to the universal are indications of an organic system of order where parts have a place in relation to the whole. It is also reasonable to suspect that there are processes that can transmute heavy elements back into hydrogen and helium. If elements heavier than iron can be cooked, why can't lighter elements be recycled? Prodigious energies verging on those of enormous black holes are a common feature of the centers of galaxies. Perhaps these are instrumental in sustaining a balance in the distribution of the natural elements. Is it not reasonable to suspect a link here with the two perspectives to a singularity?

Holmes ignores the implication in Watson's remarks that the universe is intelligent and alive. Instead he resigns himself to what he considers to be a magnanimous, yet humble, philosophical overview. "Of course, many things may be possible, Watson, and many questions of this sort have been explored. The problem is that there is little evidence to support these possibilities, nor are there coherent theories to suggest them. We are left with the big-bang options as the most credible alternative, despite the shortcomings. If there is an underlying cosmic organization to the universe, it is probably forever beyond our grasp. Perhaps the cosmic mystery is too vast a case to be solved by the minds of men."

Watson is not satisfied. He is unable to accept deficient answers to quench his sense of wonder. He can't help but feel that there are obvious clues that have been overlooked. He sees that the examination of the evidence has been preconditioned by assumptions restricting the scope of thought. The compulsion to seek an origin and an end to things is shackled to ideas of space and time.

The galaxies don't exhibit the distinctive life cycles that have been devined for stars. As huge communities of stars, there is no direct evidence that they ever had an origin or will ever face an end. More than mere collections of their member stars, galaxies may evolve and change just as any community may. Whatever the case, the center-periphery dilemma is the prime culprit in the mystery of creation. It is implicit also in the mystery of the singularity, hovering in the hearts of galaxies.

Holmes and Watson sit quietly gazing at the simulated stars. Watson doesn't pursue his feelings with his trusted friend. He can't formulate them properly into words, and he feels that Holmes is in a similar fix. Despite Holmes's commitment to his theories, Watson is aware that in silence they share a common sense of wonder. They share the social mystery of each and all through wonder. It is in words that they become divided. Even in a man-made theater of stars, words tend to pale to insignificance.*

In nature's theater, the projectors are within the stars and galaxies themselves. The stars and distant galaxies encode the stories of their lives in telltale fingerprints, then beam them out in all directions. The whole of space and time is bubbling full of history. Ghost images are streaking through the cosmos at the speed of light, metering out the scenes in the celestial drama with memories of the way things were. Events of yesterday are shaping up the scenery for today.

A ghostly mist is settling in the bays again. Dank, wan spirits, converging for a seance, are reticent at first, then progressively encouraged by their swelling numbers. The sphere of stars has been severed by a ring of spooks with forebodings of some sorcery to come. Their spell infiltrates slowly into the haze to dim and daze the asteroids. A caterpillar of ghoulish green light begins to creep across the northern sky. Vertical shafts of the aurora shunt in undulating bunches through a phosphorescent crest that wavers unsteadily above one of the asteroids. A trough reflected underneath provides the mate to a pair of terribly trembling hands that fear to fully clasp the spiny boulder stranded in the firmament. Suddenly the hands jump away, then spread in forks like crooked scissors clipping at the sky. The ghosts that gird the ragged heavens absorb and then exude the fiendish flickering neon glow of green.

Gradually the shears exchange their shape for sabers, that slice the night in irridescent slivers, rising almost to the zenith. The slivers fade to greenish yellow, as complex shifting patterns begin to wind in switchbacks, like mountain trails weaving up a trelliswork. Caravans of angels are ascending and descending a zigzag Jacob's ladder into paradise. Their mission of forewarning has cast a horo-

---

*The author of Sherlock Homes, the late Sir Arthur Conan Doyle, was a physician, spiritualist, lay preacher, and an outspoken critic of the scientific method.

scope across the sky with mesmerizing omens of redress. Slowly the trails begin to slip and slide as colors deepen into a nest of squirming serpents. Greens and yellows change to hues of red, as fire-spewing dragons wage incendiary war. The northern sky has ignited into flame. Ghoulish ghosts, encircling the waters of a fiery pit, transform to vampire shades, injected full with bursts of blood. The canoe is suspended in a holocaust. Purgation comes as hell fires fade to greens and yellows, rising into another trelliswork. Processions of angels have revived to bridge the heavens with redeeming grace.

The stars have been relegated a backseat to the display, but some peer on from overhead and from the south, with reassuring twinkles that the galaxy goes on eternally. The experience indicated that the galaxy is eternally sustained, through the polar balance of energies. All order in the universe is dependent on such a balance. The experience demonstrated a responsible human relationship both to the galaxy and to the dilemma of a cosmic mind. The creative dilemma, demonstrated in the singularity of the Cosmic Being, is the focus of galaxies and men alike.

The Cosmic Being went on to show how memories work, how energies are refluxed through the nervous system into the creation of ideas. Memories went streaming out through the eyes into ideas. Visibly organized with active interfaces of energy, they transformed rapidly through a sequence before they vanished in the void. They were animated with images of light in rich colors. Their pattern of organization was projected in three dimensions, similar in essence to the diagrams that have been used to depict the system.

As the ideas began streaming from the eyes into the city of light, each time there was an inversion of emotional energy through the autonomic nervous system, like a master shift transformation regulating the event. The significance of the city became more apparent as ideas began streaming into it from other "places" in the void. There is a gathering of experience going on. We are building an eternal home through the creative reflux of energies from the void. What's more, the gathering is not confined to strictly human experience. The landscape vividly illustrated that the same process relates to hills and forests, rivers, ravines, and desert shrubs. The whole biosphere is involved. This series of experiences, involving the recall, creation, and gathering of ideas, all concerned a dynamic routine to creative activity resulting in the explicit formation of images of light. The bottom two tiers in the universal hierarchy were explicitly involved.

Following this came the series of bursts of light in which everything was known. Questions and thoughts kept coming to mind, which brought a discretionary gathering of refined energies from the void in an extended area surrounding the body. Personal discretion was involved as these refined energies infused the body. As they did, each burst of white light was experienced. There was both an objective and a subjective component to each burst, yet the components were not separate or distinct from one another. Each time, there was a coalescence that involved both the autonomic and central nervous systems, yet the bursts were not confined to the nervous system or to the body. Everything about each question or thought was spontaneously and completely known as each burst occurred. There were inferences of images and patterns within each burst of light, but there were no specific shapes or forms or movements. The knowing was in the experience of the light itself, with the implication that complete knowledge is possible for every meaningful question or subject of wonder that can be formulated by the human mind. This knowledge is a personal experience, possible for human individuals. It is not a knowledge that can be reduced to formalized information. This series of experiences was also orchestrated by the Cosmic Being, though he was no longer visible, and although personal discretion was also involved. Knowledge, the third level in the universal hierarchy, was thus represented as a higher level of delegation.

The fourth level in the universal hierarchy, idea, was manifest in the Cosmic Being, in the singularity of his nature and in the need to reconcile the center-periphery dilemma through creative activity. The communication of the system was the idea.

The orchestration of the experience was performed within the subsuming context of the primary activity through the identity between form and emptiness. The Cosmic Being demonstrated that he transcends and subsumes the void, and with it all of space and time. He suspended the entire universe of form. He recalled to form, and created form, within the void as he wished. He consumed the void, gathering energies from throughout, recommitting them as he wished. He also showed how human creative activity works in a similar way to gather energies from the void, then reflux and recommit them. The process works the same with every human being, though not on the same scope or scale as with the Cosmic Being. We also transcend the void, spanning space and time to the extent we are concerned. The experience ended with the realization that absolutely everything is included by the system. All possibilities, however endless, are prescribed by the manner in which the system works, yet the system itself rigidly predetermines nothing.

The attempts of science to reduce the universe to a physical and mathematical synthesis must inevitably face dual problems. They must take into account both universal and particular centers that change from open orientations to closed ones, and from quantized energies to particular forms. Pursuing the problem in the particulate direction leads to the wave-particle dilemma. Pursuing the problem in the universal direction leads to curvatures in a fabricated space-time continuum and to the enigma of the singularity. These problems are both expressions of the creative dilemma. They can find no objective resolution frozen into mathematical equations, because space and time are not determining conditions of the primary creative process. We cannot relegate the responsibility for living to man-made laws. Science is a social tool, not a god.

The hell fires have returned. An inferno is devouring the northern sky, searing into the depths of the abysmal pit beneath. The ghoulish spirits are closing in from all directions. Having already eaten through the asteroids along the waterline, they will not be satisfied until they consume the interface between two hells. A loon attempts a lullaby to soothe the apprehension at the conflagration in the skies. The lonely call is answered only by a distant wolf. It is not a night for music.

The inferno makes no offering of warmth. The night is cold. It is time to paddle back to the refuge of the tent.

Graveyard Chess

It is late September; the weather has been damp and cold for a couple of weeks. Sometimes September is a warm and pleasant month, but this year there have already been several frosts. One day it snowed hard for a while. Fish have been difficult to catch; the daily swim has become a shivering ordeal. It is time to break camp and head for home.

Adam and Agnes stopped in for a visit the other day and offered a place to sleep at their camp tonight. It will make the trip back much easier. Things can be loaded in the boat and canoe today, so that it will be possible to get an early start from their camp tomorrow morning.

The small tents have been taken down and packed, and many things have already been loaded in the boat. After lunch the remaining food supplies are packed, along with the stove, the pots and pans, and dishes. The big tent is thoroughly cleaned out, then taken down and folded. Fortunately the weather is clear and dry today, although there is a cold north wind.

The whiskey jacks fly into camp and can't seem to understand what is going on. They flit from tree to tree, chirping and watching as things are carried down to the boat. They wait patiently until the loading is completed to get their ration of pancakes. An extra batch was made this morning to give them a special treat. They eat some, then cram their bills as full as they can to fly away and hide the rest. Some is tossed in the bushes for the ground sparrows, and the whiskey jacks soon dispense with the remainder. Their curiosity appeased, they leave.

The campsite is cleaned up. The garbage and refuse are burned along with the bough bed that was under the tent floor. A few tin cans are buried, then the embers in the campfire are thoroughly doused. A last check is made to make sure nothing has been forgotten.

The canoe is pushed out, then tied on a length of rope behind the boat. As the boat is paddled out and turned, the whiskey jacks come back. They fly anxiously from tree to tree, chirping as before, then they start to whistle. They have been good company for nearly three months. Now their friend and food supply is leaving. All of us will miss the daily visits. I whistle back a few times, start the motor, and head up the lake. The birds fly from tree to tree around the point as I take a last look at the island that has come to feel like home.

The load is not as heavy as during the trip in, but with a strong head wind it takes nearly an hour to reach Adam and Agnes's camp. After supper, we sit out on the chairs looking up the lake and talking.

Agnes has just finished showing me pictures of her children and grandchildren, also telling a few stories about the small Indian village she lived in as a child. One winter when she was still quite young, her father fell through the thin river ice, and the current carried him away. There must have been some difficult times afterward, but she doesn't dwell on this.

The conversation changes to the fishing. Adam also has been having trouble catching enough to eat. Live bait is often better when the fishing is poor—Adam uses minnows a lot. There is a pond nearby where he can trap them easily.

"I should shoot a moose before the season starts," he says, explaining, "Indians don't have to wait till hunting season."

"I've seen one a couple of times in the small bays near the island," I suggest.

"Maybe it's the same one I've had my eye on in the next long bay to the north. Sometimes they go back and forth between the marshes there. The next day or two I'll go down and try and get him. We won't have to depend on the fishing then."

"Biologists are concerned about the future of the fishing," I interject.

"What do you mean?" queries Adam. "Not near enough people come way in here to fish the lakes out."

"It has to do with acid rain." I go on to explain, "If the lakes become slightly more acid than they are at present, nothing can live in them. Have you ever been down to Sudbury?"

"Not for a long time," Adams answers with a long face. "There's no reason to go back. Pollution from the nickel smelters has killed everything for miles around. There's no trees, no grass, no birds. Even the bare rock has turned black."

"Have you seen the big superstack?"

"Yeah, I've seen it," says Adam dryly.

"The twelve-hundred-foot superstack at Sudbury belches two thousand tons of sulphur compounds into the atmosphere every day. Although this is the worst case, the total for North America is more than eighty times as high. It falls back to earth in the form of acid rain. Hundreds of lakes in the south have already died, and many thousands more are threatened. The forests and agriculture are affected as well."

Adam looks off in the distance. He doesn't say anything for a while and gets very serious. Then he mumbles, "The Lord is going to turn the world over someday."

"What did you say?" I am uncertain that I heard him right.

He makes a flipping motion with his hands and repeats, "The Lord is going to turn the world over someday."

It is a strange thing to say—even he is not sure what he means by it. He is anything but a religious fanatic, and he doesn't try to explain. He seems to sense that somehow, someday, a balance must be restored. A little sorry that I brought the subject up, I return to the moose hunt.

"I wish I could stay and help you get the moose."

"Why don't you? It shouldn't take long."

"Everything is packed now, and I can't depend on the weather. Besides, if I want to hunt I have to buy a license and hunt in season. I'm not lucky enough to be an Indian. If I were, I might build a camp like yours and stay here."

"I'll help you find a good Indian wife," offers Agnes cheerfully.

"When are you coming back?" asks Adam.

"I don't know. I must go away to work. White man need too much money."

"I have a steady job," says Adam. "I'm the caretaker of the lake. The money is not very good, but I like the work."

"The weather is already getting cold. How much longer will you stay?"

"Until just before freeze-up. Sometime in November. We'll trap a few beaver before we go, and maybe I'll come back alone for a short stay during winter."

"Winter too cold for me now," explains Agnes. "I'm getting old. Can't go on snowshoes anymore."

Before we know it, we have talked away the evening. Adam

shows me to one of the sleeping cabins and leaves me with a lantern. The next morning, after an early breakfast, we say our good-byes.

"Come back and stay," urges Agnes, waving from the dock as I paddle the boat out.

"We'll look for you on the island in the spring," says Adam.

"I'll be back. I'm just not sure when. Good luck. Take care." Waving back, I start the motor and maneuver the canoe into tow. Waving again, they walk back to camp as I begin the long trip home.

It has been a good summer, with time to absorb many things never fully appreciated before. Even growing up close to the wilderness is not the same as living alone with it for an extended period of time. So much of our experience is preconditioned by thoughts constrained by language that focuses on transient social situations. We depend most heavily on our senses of sight and hearing, integrating the information we receive according to predetermined social feelings. These feelings are like social spirits we have come to accept, often without any special notice. Alone in the wilderness, feelings become integrated in a different way. The spirit of the wilderness is also a social community that has been working out a social harmony for much longer than humanity's faltering efforts. Prolonged exposure brings direct absorption, not just through the eyes, the ears, and thought, but also through the skin and visceral organs. The spirit of the biosphere is absorbed directly into feeling. Our natural heritage is our heart. Immersed in wilderness, the inadequacies of social feelings constrained by language become much more apparent.

We keep trying to use words far beyond their usefulness. Language is a social instrument, yet we try to extend it beyond the social sphere into a means of deciding ultimate solutions to the human dilemma. The human dilemma, however, concerns a creative process that can neither be constrained nor brushed aside by words, although language is an essential feature. A brief look at the place of language in the creative matrix can illustrate this further.

The formulation of language corresponds to the product-processing region of a company, Term 5. Perceived in polar relevance to social organization, Term 4, it is tensionally coupled with the creation of idea, Term 2. The creation of idea in turn is perceived in polar relevance to resource capacity, Term 4, which can be considered as a treasury of memory. Memories, quantized through experience, are tensionally coupled with structures of social organization. In this way, recall is stimulated through ongoing social relevance. The two tensional pairs alternate. The social-organization/memory pair is in the emptiness grouping, and the language/idea pair is in the form grouping.

The alternating tensional pairs are assessed from the perspective of sales and marketing, respectively. Language formulation is sold through speech, gesture, the written word, or even silence, and the process is sustained through the reception received in the social marketplace. Certain energies are projected and received. Although this creative process uses emotional energy, the energy must be tailored to sights and sounds of current relevance. The creative process deals in thoughts, formulated through mentation in the central nervous system of the head. Yet market acceptance is the domain of the autonomic nervous system, often referred to as the heart. The autonomic nervous system is mute; it deals in feeling. The linguistic formulation of ideas cannot dispense with this trial in feeling, any more than feelings can escape tailoring through mentation.

Although this sounds straightforward enough, many complications are introduced through conflicting frameworks of understanding. In addition, the social marketplace is not confined to strictly human concerns. Through the autonomic nervous system we are socially linked to our biospheric heritage, by a reciprocal creative process that fuels and regulates the biological energies required to animate our bodies. The mirroring between feeling and mentation across the limbic polarity seeks a mutually reciprocating balance.*

The first few days of the experience exemplified such a balance. There was a complete feeling of harmony with the biosphere and a visual perception of the energy processes involved in living things. Everything was bathed in living light. The whole of creation was a living dance of light. This ended when the ghostlike face of all humanity appeared. The deficiencies of human understanding were written in the suffering of the face, in the incredible forbearance of its being. The dilemma that it faces is far beyond the power of language to express. It concerns the collective burden of humanity's social failures and the karmic result that lies in store. The eternal ledger keeping must exact its dues to produce a balance sheet.

The trip back to the cottage takes most of the day. Although everything looks the same, it feels very strange to be back in civilization. Lunch in a roadside restaurant seems almost weird. Obvious things

---

*The various dimensions to feeling are associated with the mirroring of polar relationships. These are anchored to, but not limited to, the autonomic nervous system. See Figure 16.

usually taken for granted—an electric light, a paper napkin, curtains, chrome, plastics, manufactured textures, pleasant service, and a menu with a wide selection—are appreciated in a different way. No fish today!

At the cottage, things are unloaded onto the porch. There will be time to unpack and put them away later. The canoe is turned over in the shade, the boat returned to the lake and tied up at the dock. It is a treat to look across the old familiar lake again.

There is much more deciduous foliage here than farther north, and it has exploded into flaming colors in its usual spectacular fashion. The autumn air is reeking with special fragrances. Many of the leaves have already fallen. The wooded hills are doing their annual striptease, exposing naked limbs to public view. Patches of pine and spruce punctuate the hillside, all in green, as if some governing authority has declared their nudity taboo. The white birch and poplar along the shore are always late to don their costume for the show. There is no variance to their color, only the purity of a yellow-gold garland held in place for dramatic effect until the end.

Soon everything will be covered with a soft blanket of snow. The ducks and geese have already begun their migrations south. Some nights the geese can be heard honking their way across the sky, performing their miracle of navigation in the dark. A marvel of avian intuition guides them with unerring accuracy on their journey through the biosphere.

The journey to an understanding of the system is a long and sometimes arduous one. Those who have made the trip thus far may see that it is only just beginning. It is a multifaceted evolving expedition of growing to appreciate the social mystery of each and all.

As the system unfolds from phase to phase, the universal hierarchy keeps recurring in different disguises.* There is a transcendent subsumption of pattern associated with meaning that occurs from one system to the next. This has been compared to a movie, where the primary technique of movie projection exhibited in System 3 is elaborated upon with an evolving plot as exhibited in System 4. This elaboration of the movie continues in distinct phases with each higher system. For instance, there is a meaning implicit in System 5 that is subsumed within the pattern of System 4. The same goes

---

*The meaning of each of the terms can also be seen in pure abstraction, without reference to the universal hierarchy, but it is more difficult.

for the relationship between System 6 and System 5, and so on, from system to system up the line.

There is another interesting feature to this elaboration from each higher system to the next. There is a pattern to the pattern of elaboration that recurs every third system. System 1, for instance, consists of one center, whereas System 4 consists of one enneagram, which is an elaboration of a center. System 2 consists of alternating expressive and regenerative modes defined by two centers, whereas System 5 is made up of two enneagrams, one open in an expressive mode, one closed in a regenerative mode. System 3 defines a primary form to activity through its terms, whereas System 6 is a primary activity made up of enneagrams. The pattern appears to continue in this way, as shown in Figure 48.

There is no apparent orderly series to the increasing number of terms from system to system, and the number increases quite rapidly. System 4 has 9 terms, System 5 has 20, System 6 has 48, System 7 has 115, and System 8 has 296. Within each system, all the terms concerned are ordered into a single, integrated pattern of transformations, so that there is a high degree of complexity to the higher systems. They also exhibit a high degree of integrative power. Some terms of the lower systems persist within the core of certain terms of the higher systems, acquiring a discretionary capacity. Some terms are related, sharing the same term positions in different sequences of transformations. Other terms display more than one mode of organization with different sequences. Perceptual images within terms begin to come into play with System 5 and higher systems.

From this brief survey of the higher systems, it can be seen that there are hierarchies of a more elaborate sort involved than that simplistically displayed by a succession of centers in discretion terms. There are enneagrams subsumed within enneagrams. In other words, there are creative processes taking place within creative processes. Each enneagram has universal and particular sets of centers; the degree of universality is constrained by the subsuming context.

This is exemplified throughout the natural order of things. For instance, within the biospheric hierarchy, each higher tier of biological life refluxes energies from the lower tiers, from plants to invertebrates to vertebrates and man. Although each tier represents a level of independent creative activity, each higher tier is dependent upon and biologically subsumed by all the lower tiers. We know that plants support all higher forms of life. In a similar way, patterns of

Description	Symbolic Designation

SYSTEM 1
   Center, whole, or the
   active interface between
   light and darkness.

SYSTEM 2
   Complementary positive
   and negative identities.

SYSTEM 3
   The primary activity.

SYSTEM 4
   The primary creative
   process in the form
   of the enneagram.

SYSTEM 5
   Complementary enneagrams,
   one enclosed and one open.

SYSTEM 6
   A primary activity
   of enneagrams.

SYSTEM 7
   An enneagram
   of enneagrams.

SYSTEM 8
   Complementary enneagrams
   with each term an
   enneagram.

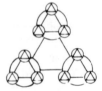

SYSTEM 9
   A primary activity with
   each term an enneagram
   of enneagrams.

SYSTEM 10
   An enneagram with each
   term an enneagram of
   enneagrams.

48

sensitive response worked out by invertebrates are essential to all of the vertebrates and man. Likewise, the patterns of conscious reflection explored by the vertebrates are essential to man's mentation.

The tiers in the biospheric hierarchy have evolved in dramatic jumps, with abrupt adjustments in the hierarchy, just as one might expect in the delegation of new levels in the hierarchy of a company. For example, the rapid extinction of the dinosaurs was accompanied by the rapid appearance of many mammalian species. There are other similar examples, such as the extinction of the giant club mosses and seed ferns, after they had existed for millions of years, giving us the coal beds of the world. There have been analogous, though less dramatic, periods, when giant insects and mammals have vanished with the appearance of more refined species in higher tiers of the hierarchy. It is a pervading evolutionary pattern.

The delegation of successive tiers in nature's hierarchy introduces a pattern of discretionary subsumption reciprocal to that of biological behavior outlined above. The vital energies of plants are subsumed by the sensitive responses of invertebrates, which in turn are subsumed by the conscious reflection of the vertebrates, which in turn is subsumed by the creative capacity of man.

These two patterns of subsumption are mutually complementary—they seek an appropriate balance. Creative mentation and biological behavior are mutually reflected in the resonating spirit of the biosphere.

Man has been invested with great creative potential through language and the related bilateral polarization of his brain. We have the capacity not only to comprehend a biospheric balance, but to experience it through the reciprocal mirroring across the limbic polarity. However, language alone does more to inhibit than to help. Every language embodies certain structural principles that are implicitly accepted as the basis for integrating meaning. In this way, there is a limited degree of isomorphy between language and the system, the nature of which varies from one language to the next. Different languages emphasize different structural aspects of the system, although they share other structural aspects in common. A Chinese person, for instance, thinks quite differently than a Spaniard, largely because of differences in language. Every language has its strengths and weaknesses; all are deficient, harboring deficiencies of thought.

Quite apart from the shortcomings of languages themselves—including languages of science and mathematics—they don't embrace the whole of experience. Tools of social expression, they are predominantly confined to one hemisphere of the brain. The intuitive hemisphere is much better at assessing and conceptualizing structural relationships, but it is mute, hampered by the shortcomings of the language hemisphere. The limbic polarity, the third member of the triad, can only voice its displeasure at the imbalance between its two partners through animated grunts and grimaces.

All of this serves to indicate the importance of delineating the system in a way that is not dependent on language. The diagrams that have been used to show how the system works facilitate a direct insight into the structural dynamics of experience. They are not confined by implicit linguistic assumptions regarding structure. They function as a kind of science for the intuitive hemisphere of the brain, so that better guidance can be provided to the language hemisphere. In this way languages can be liberated from some of their deficiencies as social tools.

On the surface, this may sound like a cure-all, but it is far from it. The two hemispheres of the brain do not work in isolation from the limbic polarity. They must deal with energies refluxed from experience through the autonomic nervous system. All three members to the triad of mind are involved in working out a balance. The suitability of a balance with our natural heritage is perceived through the limbic polarity as well, and our natural heritage also includes a cultural component. An insight into the system cannot avoid recalling cultural frameworks into question to various degrees; such reassessment introduces change, with all of its attendant problems.

Although the method of illustrating the system is not dependent on language, an understanding of the system is not divorced from language either. Neither can it be divorced from the evidence of experience—*all* experience, not just an objective component that suits the linguistic assumptions of science. Mentation necessarily implicates the language hemisphere of the brain, but through an insight into the system, it loses its dominant status. The other two polarities, the intuitive hemisphere and the limbic polarity, can be taken into account and accorded proper recognition.

Thus, it is necessary to pursue three disciplines, one discipline for each polarity. Though intimately related, they must be independently practiced. There is a physical discipline (including also the intellectual sphere), a spiritual discipline, and a moral discipline.*

---

*The brief description of the three disciplines to follow is intended only to show their relationship to the system and to the three polarities of the human nervous system. For an excellent description of what they entail read J.G. Bennett, *Long Pilgrimage* (London: Hodder and Stoughton, 1965).

The physical discipline concerns our bodily needs, our social obligations, and our need to earn a living. It includes all forms of behavior and social expression, all intellectual interests, and all techniques of overt performance—from the arts and sciences, to mundane chores and recreation. There is a process of reflection and intellection involved that selects and tailors a course of action to the needs of circumstance. This is true whether we are practicing our golf swing, shopping at the supermarket, or operating on a patient in the course of fulfilling our role as surgeon in a hospital. We work out the physical details of our lives, fitting them together according to frameworks of understanding that we accept. We are not always conscious of the process because we succumb to the anesthetizing effect of words, but this only amplifies the need for a discipline. We must study and learn from experience to intelligently apply ourselves toward making a contribution of worth and providing for our needs. Our discipline must measure up to our commitments.

The spiritual discipline, although complementary to the physical discipline, is not directly concerned with the specifics of behavior. It does not address questions of good or bad, right or wrong, judgment or salvation. Rather, it seeks after intuitive and spiritual insight into the nature of truth. It is a pursuit undertaken with wonder, from the standpoint of not knowing, a spiritual quest into the universal aspects of experience. The quest is not formulated or conditioned by thought, nor can it be resolved in thought. Insight is experiential—it comes when thought is exhausted, suspended, or balanced in a special way. An appreciation of the wonders of nature is helpful; various ritual practices, devotional exercises, and prayers may also serve to tune the mind. The mind, however, must be honed and sharpened, cleansed and concentrated through intensive meditation. We must fish in earnest.

While the physical discipline is concerned with socially directed specifics, the spiritual discipline is concerned with privately realized universals. Spiritual experience is personal and direct, sometimes requiring great adjustments in the physical discipline.

The third discipline, the moral discipline, is much more than simple conformance to a set of moral rules or standards. It concerns a struggle between conflicting spiritual influences that are emotionally experienced and consciously observed. Conscious self-observation is a prime requirement, as the moral discipline concerns not just *what* is done, but also *how* it is done, in what spirit. It concerns the spiritual energies that we reflux through the autonomic system, refine through mentation, then bring to balance and project through a commitment to behavior. These patterned energies are selected and emotionally entertained to animate us in a manner consistent with our karmic history, yet they are subject to tailoring according to our understanding. An effort of self-observation is essential to select between the evolutionary and involuntary forms to activity. The moral discipline is a tug-of-war between these conflicting spiritual influences that are opposing variants of the creative matrix. The evolutionary variant leads to an appreciation of the social mystery of each and all. The involutionary variant degenerates into fragmented perspectives, where each is opposed to all. This inversion of values hinges upon the perceptual referent term of System 4, Term 1. (See Appendix 1.)

Although the three disciplines must be independently pursued, they are mutually complementary, converging toward a balance between insight and behavior reflected through the spirit. They have been widely recognized by various religions, despite the deficiencies of their language.* Unfortunately the practice is too often subordinated to a dogma. Practice cannot be reduced to a belief in language. The three disciplines must be practiced as a way of life.**

After a hot bath and some supper, the evening is spent unpacking a few things. It feels a sumptuous luxury to have a warm cottage, hot water, an electric stove, and lights.

A desk lamp on a small table near a window has attracted a large variety of insects on the outside surface of the glass. They are milling around endlessly in search of a hole, that they might reach the light. Each one is itself like a tiny center of light searching through the darkness for identity. The activity of the moths is especially interesting. They move with a rapid vibratory rhythm in time with a similar vibratory tremor through their wings and bodies. Their construction is exceedingly intricate, with two large eyes glowing brilliantly, themselves like windows flooding light into the darkness.

---

*The three disciplines have been most clearly expressed by a remarkable Hindu known as the Shivapuri Baba. He died in 1963 at the age of 137. He spent forty years of his life on a pilgrimage by foot around the world, hence the title of Bennett's book, *Long Pilgrimage*. They are also expressed in the central writings of Buddhism, known as the Tripitaka, or three baskets, one group of writings roughly corresponding to each discipline. The Christian Trinity and the related triad of mind (insight), body (behavior), and spirit (morality) also reflect the three disciplines.

**The *Tao Te Ching* expresses them through poetry.

In the corner of the window, a spider, who has capitalized on the situation with a web, has found a regular bonanza. Nearby a daddy long-legs crawls into view over the windowsill. One small fly has a narrow escape as it buzzes frantically through the spider's legs before it can close the gaps between them. The next one is not so lucky. With stealthy, quick movements the spider cages the fly within its legs, then with two shorter legs in front it scoops the fly into its mandibles and crawls back out of view. In all, it is a regular mixed society of insects, complete with predators, the only ones that show indifference to the light except to use it to their own carnivorous advantage.

There is a certain analogue between the human social situation and that of insects. Insects live in an invertebrate jungle, the second major tier in the biospheric hierarchy. On a treadmill of activity determined by their species, they lack a capacity to individually reflect, as minnows do. The third-tier vertebrates are able to integrate patterns of activity in a socially more meaningful way. Humans are the fourth tier in the hierarchy, but there are four tiers within the human tier that are associated with the development and use of language. This delegation in tiers includes also the evolution of ideas, the manner in which thought is organized.

The first human tier has been worked out at a functional level of understanding through a diversity of languages and cultures. It is with the second-tier development of ideas, those that exert control over resources, that man's jungle instincts have come to the fore in grand fashion. Over the past few centuries this has blossomed to global proportions as man has explored all manner of organized ideas in technology, applying them to more and more sophisticated machines. The development has in fact been characterized by a competition for survival in a jungle of ideas. Behind every idea stand people with a social commitment that is often less than sociable, often hostile to the point of oppression, insurrection, revolution, genocide, or war. There are no doubt some who would throw their full support behind a nuclear holocaust. Human beings are not the masters of ideas but their slaves, chained to a treadmill of activity without a capacity to individually reflect, as minnows do.

We are like insects searching through the darkness for identity in the light of objective circumstance. We look for it in ideas—or reactions to them—of every kind. The list is very long: a capitalist ideal, a communist cause, a nationalist dream, a liberation front, an Islamic revolution, a Christian or a Zionist extreme, a cult, a movement, a far-out lifestyle, a work ethic, a cop-out, a self-indulgent pursuit, an ascetic discipline, whatever. The point is that we commit ourselves *to* organizations, not just *through* organizations, and this includes organizations of all sorts, even systems of ideas organized into sciences. We work for them, believe in them, strive for them, sacrifice for them, sometimes even kill or die for them.

There is no escape from the need to organize our thoughts and activities. We are biologically structured to reflux, refine, and project energies according to how we think and behave. What we have not yet begun to recognize is the need to reflect on the nature of organization itself. We have not yet begun to reflect on the system, and the relationship of each to all. Our organizations are structured in such a way that we commit ourselves to each as *opposed* to all. In order to refine and project energies at the administrative level of delegation, we must perform a metamorphosis from insects into minnows. This entails the reflux and restructuring of ideas in such a way that we can apprehend the nature of the social mystery.

The three disciplines are implicitly involved. In particular, this requires attention to our sciences, to the physical and intellectual discipline, from the perspective of the other two, the moral and spiritual disciplines. We are morally responsible for our behavior through technology, and the dangers of denying a place to spiritual insight are already far too apparent. The two hemispheres of the new brain must learn to work in concert if we are to contribute to the music of the biosphere.

The plight of the insects on the window is brought to a halt by turning out the light. Although late, it is a beautiful, clear night that suggests a walk before bedtime. The moon is almost full. The air is chill—frost may come before morning. The trees look lifeless, withdrawn to mere cardboard cutouts glued to a make-believe landscape. They stand with nearly leafless, outstretched limbs, poor relatives to scrawny scarecrows silhouetted in the moonlight.

From the top of the hill behind the cottage, a mist has settled on the lake like a cloud captured in a pocket of the land. The moonlight glistening on the mist gives it an eerie, incandescent glow. Transcendent vapors are rising from a wizard's giant cauldron. It is a brew of life, teeming full of varied forms and sublimating essences according to a mysterious eternal plan. There's the wizard's helper up above. He doesn't provide ingredients, but he has seen them all go in, mixing them with the same unending rhythm. His face is slyly turned a little to one side as he casts an old familiar grin into

the pot. The forlorn howl of a hound echoes in the distance. It
sounds more like muffled incantations to the brew.

The top of the hill slopes gently in the direction of the graveyard. There is a place to get through the graveyard fence where it is
partly down. It is particularly peaceful here. A pause by Father's
grave, then a walk on amongst the tombstones, which stand up like
stolid chessmen in a partly finished game. The participants have
left to await another move. The rules by which we are taught to play
are very often misleading, because the real rules are nearly all implicit, to be discovered as we play. The game is a great social mystery
that offers each of us a chance to find a communicative relationship
to all. It doesn't end with death. The stakes are eternal life, though
we may incur an eternal debt instead.

A circle is taken around the graveyard, past the big spruce tree
in the center, then down the hill and through the rail fence into
the cedars. It is a short distance through the dark shadows to the
shore, where the mist is moving slowly in a semitransparent mass
across the surface of the water. The damp, cold air sends a shudder
through the body.

The experience transcended death. It demonstrated how energies are refluxed from the void through the nervous system and
restructured for an eternal gathering. There was no gratuitous
pledge of a holy city, a promised land, or happy hunting ground,
although they were clearly shown. It was the manner through which
energies become refluxed and restructured that the Cosmic Being
stressed. There is a personal involvement and responsibility. Each of
us quantizes particular elements of technique through how we
make commitments. Those of value to the whole are gathered and
sustained by a universal discretion that transcends human individuals. There is a relationship of each to all involved in an eternal creative work. It is much the same as making tables.

So much was shown in a short time with such intensity. As the
experience ended, uncontrollable energies began coursing through
the body with extreme tension in the mind. A firm hold on sanity
and life depended on the ability to endure the tension, yet it reached
infinite extremes, breaking again and again, with everything lost in
a vortex. Why would the Cosmic Being reveal himself to someone as
omnipotent creator transcending all creation, then demonstrate
how the whole creative process works, only to abandon them? Why?
Traditional concepts of God usually fall into one of two extremes: he
is considered either as the fulfillment of man's yearning for a justice

wrought through vengeance, or as the fulfillment of man's narcissis-
tic yearnings, a sort of benevolent tranquilizer as compensation for
the injustices we suffer. The Cosmic Being measured up to neither
standard.* There was nothing in any way malevolent in his nature,
and the experience was anything but tranquilizing. Still, he just
cut me loose, or seemed to. It was suddenly as if there were no God;
there was instead an infinite chaos to make sense of. How does one
give social expression to such a spiritual insight? It was impossible.

The creative dilemma *is* impossible. There cannot be an absolute
polarization of center and periphery apart from the creative process.
The Cosmic Being demonstrated that to witness such an absolute
polarization is to witness the end of all creation. The whole of space
and time was spanned in the absolute polarization of his being into
center and periphery as he consumed the void. All creativity seeks
to reconcile center and periphery—we are all participants in the
creative process. We are each abandoned to the creative dilemma.
Each of us relates to all through the creative dilemma. We are not
simply presented with a social mystery. We are the social mystery of
each and all. The social mystery is personal.

Misty spooks have begun to stray away from the lake into the cedars.
Lonely souls are searching through the woods, pursuing doubts
and dreams and crowding against the landscape of experience.
Their quest is for a balance with eternal rest. The game of graveyard
chess goes on beyond the grave.

---

*This is not intended to mean that we do not reap according to how we sow. Neither
does it mean that God does not extend comfort on occasion. The point here is that
God has a personal identity; it is a mistake to attempt to stereotype his nature in
this way.

17 Harmony of Completion

Imagine, if you can, the stupendous stellar conflagration
Through which the universe is born.
To the puny mind of man,
Its vastness is a mystery that seeks to be explored.
To the mastermind that made it,
No speck has been ignored.
In what may seem to us a primal burst of being,
Another kind of seeing sustains a stream of worlds.
Countless suns, each in its turn,
Are given space in which to burn,
To cast their light upon the plight
Of planets orbiting in flight.
Moons and meteors have their place,
While comets try to win a race,
As rhythmic movements set a pace,
To harmony.
Energy—cascading through the cosmos—
Works its wonders in the night,
To bring to light a life that's right,
In harmony.
A theater has been constructed
Without a place for view obstructed,
That all participants might know the show
To which they come,
In harmony.

Our earth is there among the rest.
It's not the worst; it's not the best.
Its birth is bleak—its pulse is weak.
Within a shroud of cloud

It starts to taste the breath of wind.
Companion moon is there as well,
And starts to tell
The tempo for a tune.
Unshaded from the sun,
It knows the story's just begun.
It beats its restless, wreathing rhythm
Deep in a dank and dreary sea
Of dreadful mighty mystery.
Great oceans in convulsion,
Revolving in revulsion,
Have only wind to make it worse,
Compounding this horrendous curse.
What is this beating in the depths
That seems to tell of other steps?
Then just when things are at their worst
The tremors start, it's going to burst!
Eruption spawns eruption
With uncontrollable seduction
Till all seems ended in corruption
To quench a primal thirst.
But something's new!
These were not here before!
The oceans have been parted,
Whole continents have started
To show their face in place of misery.
Mountains grown like fountains
Spread their red hot running rock
In shock proportions.
Now ash spews into wind.
Now rain is known.
The ocean's roar is thwarted by a shore.
That marvels such as these
Should lie beneath the seas
To tease a tested memory,
That's harmony.
But still the moon
Beats out the tempo for a tune.

The continents are born in scorn.
They shout bald faces to an acrid sky
To question, why?

They shift and tilt to find a place
Without the guilt of being there.
Stark shape stuck in gloom.
Frightening lightning
Ripping through a wretched rage of rain.
Ceaseless driving drench,
Eroding, eating, etching out
The element of life.
Wind and torrent winning over rock
To prepare a stock of soil
Flooding onward into valleys,
While at the shore there's more
From the pounding of the surf.
But the continents are restless
And they squirm to get more firm
As if to cry,
"Is there a place for me to be?"
Then one first fine day
A ray of sun is seen to penetrate the sky.
It glistens in a puddle
To play its part in now another
Start to life.
A cell is born.
A microscopic cell!
But what is that amidst the hell?
What kind of answer to a yell?
Be still and listen to the moon.
It beats the tempo for a tune.

Alone in anonymity
With only mud in its proximity,
What can it do?
In a muddle, in a puddle,
It cannot know the shore in store.
But divide it can and does—
So do its parts—
To make from one, a multitude of starts
In mud.
Lifted on the rising tide,
It moves to ride the ocean's glide,
Just to divide and thus provide
Some company.

Other versions, just begun.
Join in the fun
To catch the fleeting glimpses
Of the sun across the surf.
They move and jostle near the surface,
Then they toss upon the earth as
If a wave has bid them
Stay there on the shore.
The ones that dive there
Cannot thrive there
So they die
To lie in muted memory.
From this selection, time's collection
Gathers for a new election
On the land.
They will have a resurrection.
So the past that didn't last
Is started new, with just a few
Developments.
These clutch on shores
To mock the rock
And spew their spores
Upon the wind.
The oceans now are teeming full,
The land is covered with a wool
That mildly mitigates the scene
And wildly instigates an atmosphere of life.
A tiny note was sounded—
An endless chord resounded—
To the tempo of a tune
That's beat out by the moon.

The starkness of the stage has been subdued.
The darkness of the stage has been imbued
With filtered hues of light.
The gloom is still receding,
While life is now proceeding
In a regular succeeding
Leading pleadingly for more.
Plants have grown in classes,
While weeds have grown to masses
That multiply to magnify the plight.

Once food has been provided,
A cell that once divided
Is given to another kind of life.
Now its division makes provision
For a kind of vast revision
That proceeds from an incision
At its core.
It grows a skin to be within,
One it can wiggle like a fin,
To move about
And so to scout
For food along the shore.
Thus cells that once divided
Are given to a life provided
With new miracles of mystic form
And novel modes of motion.
Microbes are turned to monsters
That feed like fiends on former fellow friends!
What new sudden shock is this?
Have things been snatched from one abyss
To turn and once more go amiss?
Be still and listen to the moon.
It beats the tempo for the tune.

An atmosphere has been transformed.
The acrid murk has been reformed
To furrowed clouds on wings of wind.
Exposed and shy within their folds,
There often holds
The truest bluest hues of sky,
And through them fly
Some streaming beaming bands of light
That march in flight across the lands.
Crawling creatures now are many,
Though you'd hardly notice any.
Some have shells and suck on sand;
Some have wings yet crawl on land.
Some have left their humble croft
To look up and leap aloft
In ethereal celebration
Of an aerial liberation.
Exceedingly incited by exhilarated insects,

Certain seedlings strain to shed
Their shackles with the ground.
Plants take their ponderous plunge
But can't even turn around.
They soar to heights of dizzy sights
But cannot get unbound.
In consummate grandiloquence,
With magniloquent magnificence,
Luxuriant splendiference abounds.
Some critters crawl and cuddle,
While other sneak and snuggle,
In great forests as all struggle
Goes unwound.
The strife of life has been subdued
In huge and horrid magnitude,
And given to the work
Of many mannered minds to manage.
Let's rest awhile
And watch their style.
Tiny partners pertly prance,
Shifting shadows suavely dance—
Flowing movements to enhance
Melodious magnificence.
Hush, and listen to the moon.
It beats the tempo for the tune.

Just when things were settling into place,
A new disgrace has been concocted in the sea.
Gigantic apparitions
Without externalized partitions
Have a bony structure housed within a hulk.
The first configurations
Of such a floppy form were few,
But new ones grew
Of even greater size,
Complete with flippers, fins, and eyes.
It wasn't long before a breed
Had found a need
To nudge their noses at the shore.
Then, as before,
A miracle of intervention
Transformed a watery convention

To the land.
Horrifying creatures now have terrifying features
That they use to bring abuse
To others of their kind.
Gnashing teeth and slashing tails,
They tear at flesh with screeching wails,
To gorge their full on slivered meat,
Lap the blood for added treat,
Then leave the carcass in retreat,
For grubs that find the sinews sweet.
Even bugs have turned carniverous,
Why has life turned so vociferous?
What was a garden of revival
Has turned into a trial of torture for survival.
Disrupted by the rummages
Of bungling trundling tonnages,
The earth is trembling,
Life's reassembling
To maintain some sane resembling.
How could all of this be caused
In answer to the bliss that was?
May we expect things to get worse?
Will there be some bigger curse?
Are things reverting now to ruin?
Is an answer coming soon?
Be still and listen to the moon.
It beats the tempo for the tune.

In the face of this insane affliction
New conviction
Flouts ferocious fangs with fragrances of flowers.
These smaller shoots have turned to beauty
With a bloom for double duty.
They show a place to trade sweet fare
For pollen brought on insect hair;
Then they bob upon the breeze
To give their thanks in special silent prayer.
They stretch their stalks toward the sky,
To turn the purity of their eye
Toward the sun—then linger some—
Before they bow their tired heads
To once more fertilize their beds.

Brilliant colors unforeseen,
Caress the meadow's former green,
And infatuate the air
With rare aromas for a queen.
Very flattering indeed,
As they spread from sprinkled seed,
But can such fragrant fragile friends
Make those monsters make amends?
Hush and listen to the moon—
It beats the tempo for the tune.

The dinosaurs are dying off
As if their bulk was prying off
A lid to life of lesser size
But great diversity.
Was their massive size and suffering
To provide a psychic buffering,
To break the ground
For newly found
Forms of phantasy?
Is there through it all a plan,
That's going to culminate in man,
And guide him to some final destiny?
It seems a door has been flung open
To a flood of forms in legions,
Marching through remotest regions
In research of mystery.
With new scales and skins and feathers,
They fight and flock together,
To measure every movement
In their history.
Into every nook and cranny
Through every kind of weather,
They suffer every spectacle of change.
For each one the scene is different
As they hunger, thirst, bleed, or burst,
Burn or sneeze, or wheeze and freeze.
They adjust and make some changes,
Modify their ranges,
And learn to bring some harmony to strife.
But when finally all these things have been explored,
Will there then be something more?

Will there be another door?
Is something better now in store?
Be still, and listen to the moon—
It beats the tempo for the tune.

The universe is ready,
The pulse is strong and steady,
The stage is set,
A sigh is let
Then quietly,
The first crude forms of man appear.
His life was earned through what was learned
By multitudes in suffering.
This struggle has been won,
But another's just begun
To shape itself from apely origin.
The first great shore, to reexplore
The limits to experience,
Proceeds with bulges in the brain,
But little other variance.
This spans a vast expanse of time,
To spare man's mind the rasp of time,
To form a firm and finished base
On which to build with quicker pace.
He learns to cultivate the soil,
To use the animals for toil,
Then as his tools unlock his mind,
He starts to find another kind of world.
It's a world of his construction,
Which often brings destruction,
Through wars or insurrections,
With periodical corrections in spasmodical erections
Requiring collections of society.
By this alternation of creation,
With hostile confrontation,
The range of man expanded
Till finally he landed round the globe.
He's now begun to probe
Into some superficial secrets,
With a science of compliance
To special rules of sorcery.
He's making motorized contraptions

With industrial adaptions.
His taste has turned to waste
In willful ways and wanton wars.
He's utilizing brutalizing bombs,
While stocking more,
In case some need should intercede
To eliminate it all.
Overpopulating cannibals are killing off the animals,
Destroying all the greenery, mutilating scenery,
And poisoning the skin of soil and sea.
Is this the purpose of the plight
From out the darkest night
Into the dawning of the light of life
In myriads of form?
Has all the sacrifice and care
Been there throughout the ages,
To end now in the rages
Of a maniacal tear?
Be still, and listen to the moon.
It beats the tempo for the tune.

Long shadows reach toward the darkness,
Blending streaks of cool relief on blushing cheeks,
Beckoning the earth bride to her lover's bed.
Her negligee of sky, transparent to the eye,
Transforms its fluffy trim to crimson red.
Her husband in the heaven
Sinks his hallowed head into her bosom,
Joyful at her answer to his light.
Soft whispered breezes settle into slumber
Under pandemonium of color,
As a silent hand draws the shade of night.
Sweet songs of day
Have left a last lament
To a symphony of stars
Swarming far into the firmament.
Tired limbs are soothing in a pool of rest,
Assimilating chords from distant humming hoards,
Swirling in an unseen nest.
The profound procession passes,
A crowning halo, rousing in the east,
Repeats its offer of a feast

In harmony with heaven.
The air's infused with angels, singing in the dawn
To spawn anew the wonder of a world.
Will they help us tend the garden,
Learn its needs, distinguish weeds,
Give it room, watch it bloom?
Will we learn the answer soon?
If we listen to the moon.
It beats the tempo for the tune.

Appendix 1

Further Discussion of System 4

There are many further aspects to System 4 that could be elaborated upon. Although an exhaustive presentation is not possible here, a couple of further points deserve mention.

The creative matrix incurs an activating spirit that helps to effect an identity between mentation and behavior. Instigated through the universal centers, it works to impel the particular centers through their sequence of transformations. It also induces the tensional anxieties mentioned earlier. Let's take a brief look at how this works.

The manner in which the mediating triangle inverts at the middle of each cycle, then reverts back at the end of each cycle, does more than regulate the transitions from the expressive to the regenerative mode. It also induces alternating inverse activities in the operation of the six-pointed figure, as shown in Figure 1A.

Figure *a* shows the inverted alignment of the mediating triangle. This induces a complementary inverse activity, as shown in Figure

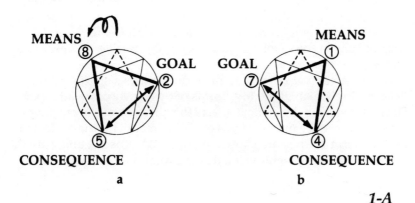

a

b

1-A

b. There are two curious things about these inverse activities. First of all, the goal-consequence relationships are the inverse of what they are in the sequence. Terms 2 and 7 are consequence terms, while 4 and 5 are goal terms in the sequence. Second, and most important, the goal and consequence terms of the inverse activities occur together, and they are out of step with their respective means terms. The consequence terms do not succeed the goal terms. They do not occur as a consequence of realizing a goal. This fundamental contradiction introduces tensional components in the matrix that impel the sequence of transformations onward. It becomes an intensional process. The tensional pairs are also emphasized. The idea/ physical-work pair alternates with the treasury/mental-work pair. They are perceived from the perspective of marketing and sales, respectively.

To this point, all discussions have referred to the evolutionary form of the creative matrix, through which all experience is integrated. There is also an involutionary form that leads to fragmentation. Outlined by exchanging the positions of Centers 3 and 4 in the terms of the matrix, it has an expressive and a regenerative mode as well. There will not be time to go into the involutionary form in detail except to mention that it can come into play through an inverted perspective in the perceptual-referent term, Term 1. Values become inverted. Ideas become translated into routines rather than into forms with communicative value. Things are done for their own sake, whether they make sense or not.

In addition, there are two more possible forms to System 4. They concern remembering, as distinct from recall that is directly committed to activity. Remembering in itself does not require overt activity. Since there is both an evolutionary and an involutionary remembering process, altogether there are a total of four possible forms to System 4, each with expressive and regenerative modes. The terms of the evolutionary remembering matrix involve an interchange in the positions of Centers 1 and 2 with Centers 4 and 3, respectively. In the involutionary matrix, Centers 1 and 2 exchange places.

The perceptual-referent term, Term 1, plays a special role in determining which of the four forms of System 4 comes into play. How we perceive the context affects the outcome of the creative process. There are only four possible alignments for the coalesced pairs of Term 1. They are shown in Figure 2A. Cases 1 and 2 are the expressive and regenerative modes of evolutionary activity. Cases

3 and 4 are the expressive and regenerative modes of involutionary activity. Cases 1 and 3 are the expressive and regenerative modes of evolutionary remembering. Cases 2 and 4 are the expressive and regenerative modes of involutionary remembering. It is thus apparent that activity and remembering share a common perceptual referent in Case 1, as the evolutionary form of expression, and in Case 4, as the involutionary form of regeneration.

In Cases 2 and 3, the perceptual referents are at cross-purposes. Case 2 is the regenerative mode of evolutionary activity and the expressive mode of involutionary remembering. This means that the same perceptual referent can both sustain a remembering of past mistakes, and also guide the active formation of a creative idea. Case 3 is the expressive mode of involutionary activity and the regenerative mode of evolutionary remembering. This means that the same perceptual referent can be used either to guide the regeneration of resources needed to perpetuate mistakes, or to guide a creative remembering of what should be done instead.

The remembering forms of the creative matrix permit a cross-linking of evolutionary and involutionary activity. There is a tug-of-war involved, a moral struggle, through which involuted energies can be redeemed.

Case

Subjective ◄—|—► Objective   *2-A*

A final word of caution is offered here to anyone who may pursue an understanding of the system in depth, with a view to its application. One can invite reactions and phenomena of many kinds. Please be careful. Know when to set the pursuit aside for a while.

Appendix 2

A Fresh Approach to Science

Introduction

System 3 is used to introduce new perspectives to number theory, to the nature of identity in simple equations, to atomic structure, the mechanics of motion, kinetic force, gravity, coulomb force, relativity, quantum mechanics, and cosmology. The intention is to demonstrate as simply as possible the everpresent underlying place of the system. Understanding that the system is always there, making experience what it is, can offer a fresh approach to our understanding of the natural order.

Numbers and Identity

The language of mathematics begins with the progression of natural numbers as in ordinary counting. Counting helps us to assimilate experience—there is an integrating idea involved. It is from this integrating *idea* that the mental routine of counting ensues. Through the successive *routine* of adding one more, we *formulate* each successive number by assigning it a name. We thus find that counting conforms to the idea-routine-formation hierarchy of the primary activity.

The currently accepted definition of number is given by Bertrand Russell in the opening pages of his book *Introduction to Mathematical Philosophy*.* After some discussion of "primitive" concepts and classes, he defines a number as follows:

The number of a class is the class of all those classes that are similar to it.

*Bertrand Russell, *Introduction to Mathematical Philosophy* (New York: Touchstone Books, 1971).

> *. . . In other words, a number (in general) is any collection which is the number of one of its members; or more simply still:*
> **A number is anything which is the number of some class.**
> *Such a definition has a verbal appearance of being circular, but in fact it is not. . . . This kind of procedure is very common and it is important to recognize that it is legitimate and even often necessary.*

The difficulty which Russell has in defining number stems from the recurrent character of the primary activity and from the universal and particular nature of the two sets of centers involved.

Numbers have two aspects in a mental activity. In one aspect, successive numbers correspond to the successive space frames in which we perceive an independent relatedness between the idea of counting, the routine of counting, and the name formulated for the number of separate things counted. We thus recognize a quantitative aspect of number. In another aspect, between each space frame, we recall each successive number as a quantized whole. We perceive the routine of adding one more coalesced with the formation of a new name, as an integrated idea. We thus also recognize a qualitative aspect of number. For example, before we recognize four independent things, we recall the quality of fourness.

To define a number is to recognize a simultaneous equivalence between these two aspects, as when we recognize a quality of fourness to a quantity of four apples. There is a catch, however, for the quantitative space frame and the qualitative quantum frame are not simultaneous. They are always one step apart, indicating increments of time in counting successive numbers. In the definition of a number there is thus a spanning of space and time involved.

This brings us to a deficiency in the so-called law of identity, often stated as A is A, or in algebraic terms, $A = A$. Is it sufficient to define the number four by saying $4 = 4$? The statement may be quantitatively correct, but it ignores the quality of fourness. Fourness is a whole just as oneness is a whole.

The deficiency in the law of identity can be demonstrated by the transposition of A in the simple algebraic equation $A = 1$. In order to transpose A from one side of the equal sign to the other, we divide both sides of the equation by A, thus maintaining the equality. The equation $A = 1$ becomes $1 = 1/A$. By all of the accepted rules of mathematics, we are then entitled to write $A = 1/A$. This obviously does not correspond to the law of identity.

Every number is considered to have both a numerator and a denominator, but when the denominator is 1, it is not usually written. If A/1 is taken to represent a number of apples, then one apple denominates a unit whole, and A numerates the number of whole apples. If we look at $1/A$ in the same way, we now find that A denominates or names a unit whole. If A is four apples as numerated in units of whole apples, then as a denominator A becomes a unit group of four apples. The expression $1/A$ then means that there is one unit group of four apples. It does not mean that there is only one-quarter of an apple. There is thus a very real sense in which the expression $A = 1/A$ is quantitatively correct, not only in the special case where $A = 1$, but for any value of A. Moreover it has something qualitative to say about the identity of A.

Normally, however, the denominator is interpreted not as a denominator, but rather as a quantitative devisor. An arithmetic routine is given importance over the formation of a name. There are thus two perspectives possible to simple operations regarding identity, and there are reasons to believe that the new perspective offered possesses a more fundamental significance.

The relation $A = 1/A$ corresponds to the form of the primary activity, the left-hand side representing a quantitative space frame, the right-hand side a qualitative quantum frame. This can be seen by examining Figure 4A (below), in which Centers 1, 2, and 3 represent idea, routine, and formation, respectively. Inside each of the three large, particular centers of the space frame is one common universal-idea center represented by the three small ellipses, Center 1. In the quantum frame the particular centers are coalesced as one inside the universal-idea center, represented this time by the large ellipse, Center 1. There is an inversion or transposition involved between the space and quantum frames, just as there is between the two sides of the equation. The particular centers on one side are objective to the idea, while on the other side they are subjective to it. One side is quantitative, the other qualitative.

Expressions of the form $A = 1/A$ will be called *primary relations* to distinguish them from equations of the usual sort. They differ in two outstanding features: there is a qualitative difference between the two sides of the equivalence, and the two sides are not simultaneous. *Definitions of all kinds give simultaneity to the recurrent properties of primary relations.* A quantitative aspect is equated to, or identified with, a qualitative aspect. This invariably involves a spanning of space and time.

The successive addition of one in counting is illustrated in Figure 3A as successive frames in a primary activity.

The arrows indicate transformations to each goal term, while the equals signs indicate transpositions back to the corresponding consequence term in each case. The successive addition of one is coalesced with forming a new number as a quantized whole on the right-hand side, then recalled as a spatially distinct number of wholes on the left-hand side.

We have seen that there is a quantitative equivalence across the equal sign in each case; however, if we grant simultaneity to the primary relation $4 = 1/4$, treating both sides in the same way as in a normal equation, then by transposing we get $16 = 1$. The right-hand side still qualitatively represents one whole, but it is a whole that is quantitatively defined by the square of 4. This can be shown to have a special significance.

Quantum frames in Figure 3A summate or integrate differentiated counting routines with a name. When the two sides of the primary relation are granted simultaneity to get $16 = 1$, the differentiated space and quantum frames in the counting process *itself* are quantitatively summated, up to and including the quantum frame that defines the quality of fourness. To follow through the sequence from top to bottom in Figure 3A:

$$0 + (0 + 1) + 1 + (1 + 1) + 2 + (2 + 1) + 3 + (3 + 1) = 16.$$

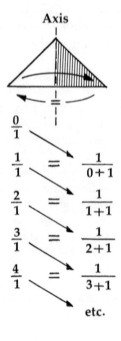

etc.   *3-A*

The number four is not a special case. The square of any whole number is equivalent to the quantitative sum of all the space and quantum frame sequences involved in counting up to and including the quantum frame of the number concerned. All of the differentiated frames in the creative activity of counting are thus integrated throughout the history involved in arriving at the number concerned. This can be written in algebraic fashion, where A and n are whole numbers, as follows:

$$A^2 = 2 \sum_{n=0}^{n=A} n - A \qquad \qquad \textit{Equation 1*}$$

This amounts to a method of natural integration. Since it is linked directly to the history of the creative process, it will be called historic integration to distinguish it from integral calculus. Although the result is quantitatively similar to integral calculus, it does not presume that creation is a continuum to be arbitrarily differentiated into infinitely small increments. The discretely differentiated frames in the creative process in fact prescribe a limit to the applicability of differential and integral calculus. We will return later to investigate the significance of historic integration to some fundamental laws of physics.

From the preceding discussion it can be seen that the primary activity can provide new insights into number theory from which new mathematical techniques can ensue. Many related insights follow. For instance, irrational numbers derived from square roots can have no rational place in the creative process of counting, since they do not themselves come from squares that integrate differentiated counting sequences. Numbers in themselves are not natural phenomena, but a man-made language exhibiting relationships that recur in every creative process.

Atomic Structure

The world of physical form that delineates space is a rapidly recurring series of independent frames that give a timelike continuity

*There are more complex relationships for higher powers.

to events in the projection of a cosmic movie. Molecular form that constitutes the bulk of physical bodies is discontinuous yet synchronous on a hierarchy of levels, alternately appearing in form, then disappearing into quantized energy, then reappearing, and so on. Myriads of particular centers, in sets as numerous as the atoms in the universe, are all regulated in this eternal jig between form and emptiness by a common universal set of centers. This general scheme can be most simply represented by System 3 as illustrated in Figure 4A. Centers 1, 2, and 3 respectively represent *idea* in a photonic interface, *routine* in an electronic interface, and *formation* in a protonic interface.* Although there is only one universal set, it is illustrated in the space frame as three small sets of centers working through and linking up the particular centers shown as larger ellipses. The universal set works through all particular sets at once. In the quantum frame, the larger ellipses are the universal centers, and one particular quantized set is illustrated by the small ellipses within Center 1.

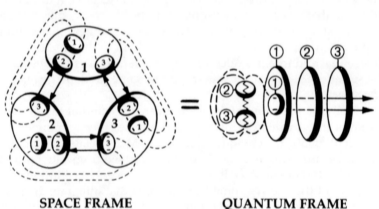

SPACE FRAME   **QUANTUM FRAME**

4-A

In the space frame, particular and universal centers have their corresponding interfaces with darkness mutually aligned only between Centers 2 and 3, the electron and proton. It is between these two centers that electronic charge is observed, suggesting that

---

*The energy levels associated with orbiting electron routines are a manifestation of light, and atomic form is centered in the nucleus.

charge is associated with the subjective-to-objective imbalance in the partitioning characteristics of light by the universal centers. This idea is reinforced by the mutual relationship of the electron and proton to the photon, Center 1, which indicates an equal and opposite character to the imbalance as it relates to the particular centers. (Examine Figure 4A carefully.)

In the quantum frame, electrons and protons become coalesced within photons and are subjective to the universal set. They become structured electromagnetic energy, both charge and mass losing spatial distinction.

It can be seen from the space frame that the universal centers can work through the particular centers in a clockwise rather than counterclockwise direction. Together with symmetries possible between different particular sets, these variants can account for such things as antimatter, spin, etc. Although these questions cannot be pursued here, it's also worth mention that meson and baryon symmetries correspond to those of Systems 4 and 5. Since the system embraces all possible relationships, it should not surprise us to find that it encompasses those of atomic structure.*

Relative Motion

Motion is observed between different molecular collections of particular sets that we see as physical bodies. Just as, in an ordinary movie, the action results from rapidly projecting a sequence of still pictures on the screen, so also, in the cosmic movie, each space frame can be regarded as a three-dimensional still projection. Activity within each space frame is restricted to the electromagnetic projection of atoms and associated phenomena. Changes in position between physical bodies are effected through the quantized mode when the cosmic screen is void. Motion thus manifests as change in position between two or more space frames, spanning one or more intervals of time.

Time as we are able to measure it, whether by the sun or by atomic clocks, is based on relative motions, and it therefore concerns the successive recurrence of space frames. A primary interval of time is prescribed by two successive space frames, which for the

---

*Through the relationship between universal and particular sets, the system also accommodates both Mach's principle and the paradox of Einstein, Rosen, and Podolsky.

atom is very short, perhaps the time for light to circumscribe an atom, in the order of 10^{-17} seconds. Normally, relative motion across a single interval of time is a very small fraction of an atomic radius.

Velocity is thus a series of quantum jumps in position. In order to measure it, relative positions must be compared between space frames, requiring an observer with a capacity for memory. A mental activity is therefore introduced that is distinct from, yet related to, the activity that determines the bodies themselves. The mental hierarchy concerns the *idea* of motion, a *routine* of change in position, and the *form* that the change takes, measured as a ratio in arbitrary units of distance (d) with respect to intervals of time (t). The quantitative ratio d/t is thus defined as equivalent to the quality of velocity (v).

Newton's first law of motion observes that bodies remain in a state of relative rest or uniform motion, unless some event introduces a change in the routine of change between successive space frames. This is a statement about momentum, a quality defined as the product of a body's mass (m) and its velocity (v). Momentum (mv) is considered to embody inertial force, changes in momentum being brought about through force.

Newton's second law of motion defines force (F) as proportional to the rate of change of momentum, that is to mass (m) times acceleration (a). Except for very high relative velocities, this is written as $F = (k)ma$.

A curious thing about this relationship is that the units of measurement are not consistent. Units denominate what is measured, yet the units of force are the same as those for mass, not the product of mass and acceleration. The device of introducing a constant (k) for dimensional consistency does not alter this intrinsic curiosity. Questions about the qualitative nature of force thus arise which concern the spanning of space and time as evidenced by the unit discrepancy d/t^2.

Force enacts a change in the routine of change of bodies between one space frame and the next. Forced changes result from interactions such as collisions between different sets of particular centers, whereby for every action in one body there is an equal and opposite reaction in another, as observed by Newton's third law of motion. Such exchanges of energy, effected through the quantized mode, are implicitly associated with the quantization of mass. We shall return to see that this is related to the inconsistency of units concerning force.

Special Relativity

The measure of velocity depends on the capacity to compare relative positions in successive space frames, and this is closely associated with the ability of light to span the distance involved in successive space frames. Over very great spans of time and distance, or when the relative velocity of a body approaches the speed of light, light is unable to bridge quantum jumps in position to a significant extent. For instance, in any given space frame, light can traverse only a small factor* in excess of a maximum diameter for an atom, so when the successive displacements in position of an atom approach this limiting distance, perceptual gaps tend to open up in the spatial field of observation. These gaps collect as a relative skipping of space frames and accumulation of quantum frames in observations between different inertial systems, with the effect of contracting distance and accumulating mass, together with increments of time.

Skipping in relative frames of reference occurs with a frequency determined by the ratio of the historic integration of the velocity of the moving body with respect to that of light. This ratio, given by the dimensionless number v^2/c^2, is a measure of the proportion of space and quantum frames skipped and accumulated, respectively, in any sequence of observations. The proportion of frames included is given by $(1 - v^2/c^2)$. This is consistent with the Lorentz-Fitzgerald contractions of special relativity. For instance, if D and D_0 are the diameters of an atom moving and at rest, respectively, then the contracted diameter in the direction of travel is determined by the proportion of space frames not skipped, as follows:

$$D^2 = D_0^2 \left(1 - \frac{v^2}{c^2}\right) \qquad \text{Equation 2}$$

It is electromagnetic energy acting through centers in space and quantum frames that constitutes the mass, character, and inherent energy of atoms. The requirement for closure of particular centers in each space frame makes a measure of mass, distance, and motion possible, while the universal centers require that the motion of light must be the same for all atoms. The distance that light can travel in the interval of each successive space frame represents an absolute velocity for light (c). That this velocity is associated with a "static"

---

*Perhaps π.

inertial momentum (mc) involved in the creation of all atomic mass can be demonstrated by writing the primary relation:

$$mc = \frac{1}{mc}$$ \hfill *Equation 3*

The expression $1/m$ on the quantum side of this relation defines a quantization of mass as energy (E). If it is written as E and both sides are granted simultaneity, the mass-energy relationship of special relativity ensues:

$$mc^2 = E$$ \hfill *Equation 4*

The contraction of mass for comparative observations of a mass at rest (m_o) and in motion (m) is given by:

$$m_0^2 = m^2(1 - v^2/c^2)$$ \hfill *Equation 5*

This can be rewritten in the following form:

$$(mc)^2 - (m_0c)^2 = (mv)^2$$ \hfill *Equation 6*

The above equation indicates that the difference in the historic integration of "static" inertial momentum between different inertial systems is the historically integrated kinetic momentum of the moving system. In other words, kinetic momentum is a quantitative measure of the proportion of skipped space frame sequences, accumulated as quantized energy associated with a moving mass. The force embodied by kinetic momentum is thus an expression of accumulated energy, which is the complement of historically missing mass. This offers an insight into the inconsistency of units concerning force. It further indicates that exchanges of momentum represent a reflux of past accumulated energies recommitted to a different future course. We shall see that this historic reflux has a place in relation to gravitational and electrostatic forces.

Gravitational and Electrostatic Forces

Newton's universal law of gravitation recognizes an inherent unity to all mass in the universe, which manifests itself as a force of mutual attraction between bodies separated by distance. In other words, physical bodies are both spatially distinct, and an indistinct unity, both particular and universal. In each space frame the universal set works through all particular sets, while in each quantum frame all particular sets are subjective to the universal set. This is given mathematical expression by Newton's law as follows:

$$k \frac{m_1 m_2}{d^2} = F \qquad\qquad \text{Equation 7}$$

The force (F) on the quantum side is an expression of unity defined by giving simultaneity to two primary relations, one directly proportional, and one inversely proportional. The unity of two masses (m_1) and (m_2) can be defined by equating the space frame of one to the quantum frame of the other, as in the primary relation $m_1 = 1/m_2$. The nonunity of the two masses can be defined by the inverse of the primary relation for their distance apart, $1/d = d$. Combining both primary relations, transposing, and adding a constant for dimensional consistency gives Equation 7.

Through the agency of the universal set, gravitational force acts at a distance on all particles of mass everywhere at once. It thus defines a universal present.

The force exerted between two electrical charges, Q_1 and Q_2, is expressed by Coulomb's law in a form similar to Newton's law of gravitation as follows:

$$k \frac{Q_1 Q_2}{d^2} = F \qquad\qquad \text{Equation 8}$$

We have seen that charge, like mass, is both distinct and indistinct, particular and universal, so that two primary relations are again involved in defining force, one relating to charge, the other to distance.

The system indicates that the universe is electrically neutral, the number of protons being balanced by exactly the same number of electrons, the two mutually neutralized in atomic form. Electrical charges and related electromagnetic phenomena arise when electrons become separated from protons by distances greater than light can span in a single space frame. Yet the span must be made by the electromagnetic energies of the universal set, since this determines the electronic character of electrons and protons. We thus have particular centers defining spatial distances greater than light can span, yet linked by universal centers that are not constrained by the spatial closure of the particular sets. A polar relationship is thus introduced between the propagation of light through space, and a universal manifestation of electromagnetic energy that transcends space. This polarity exhibits itself as a force field that spans the historic separation of charged particles to effect a reconciliation in the universal present of each space frame.

We thus find three complementary forces operative on the macroscopic scale. Kinetic force, as embodied in *routines* of space-time motion, incurs a continual reflux from the past deferred to a future of change. Gravitational force, while defining a universal present, provides gross *form* to celestial bodies. Coulomb force acknowledges a universal present yet spans the kinetic reflux of historic change. It reconciles the *idea* of reflux to a universal present. These three forces in this way prescribe a hierarchy in the primary activity of space-time events as explored in the main body of the book.

Quantum Mechanics

A central theme of quantum mechanics is the impossibility of knowing both the position and the momentum of a particle at the same time. As the probability of knowing the position increases, the probability of knowing the momentum decreases, and vice versa. In view of the very short periods of time and high velocities that quantum mechanics is concerned with, some of the reasons for this are apparent from previous discussions. Precise relative position is knowable only in a single space frame, whereas the determination of momentum, by its very nature, must span two or more space frames. Momentum cannot be instantaneous in the way that position is. Furthermore, the methods of differential calculus do not lend themselves to quantum events, because a minimum limit to the increment of the differential is prescribed by the primary interval of time. Add to these factors the relative discrepancies in frame sequences associated with high velocities, and the problems of quantum mechanics take on a new perspective.

The idea of the quantum of action originated with Planck. He related the energy of electromagnetic radiation (E), to the frequency (f) of its wave propagation in space-time, by introducing a universal quantum of action (h). Planck's law, believed to define the energy of a photon, is given by:

$$hf = E \qquad\qquad \text{Equation 9}$$

Planck was greatly puzzled by the fact that electromagnetic radiation does not come in just any amount across a continuous spectrum, but must be packaged into discrete amounts determined by a universal constant. This occurs because the frequency range of the electromagnetic spectrum is determined by System 2, whereas frequency is measurable only in units of time derived from relative spatial motions that are dependent upon System 3. There is a hierarchy involved that has never been recognized. Electromagnetic radiation is therefore a subsuming level of activity within each space frame that is interrupted at each primary interval of time by the successive recurrence of frames in the cosmic movie. The electromagnetic spectrum is thus sliced across its entire breadth with each frame sequence. The quantum of action (h) is then a measure of recurrence expressed in terms of the energy and frequency of electromagnetic radiation.

De Broglie glimpsed something of this in deriving his wave equation for a particle of mass. It is worth going through his derivation and some of his comments* step by step, making some points along the way.

I was led to define an internal rest frequency (f_o)** of the particle, connected with the energy $m_o c^2$ of the rest mass by the relation

$$hf = m_o c^2 \qquad\qquad \text{Equation 10}$$

De Broglie substitutes the rest energy of a particle ($m_o c^2$) for electromagnetic energy (E) in Planck's law, Equation 9. This specifies what is already intimated in Planck's law, that the rest frequency of a particle is a measure of the recurrence of space frames in terms of electromagnetic frequency, being the same for all particles in any inertial system.

This led me to think of the particle as being like a little clock in motion. I was then greatly smitten with the fact that the transformation formula of a wave according to Lorentz is

---

*Price; Chissick; Ravensdale, eds., *Wave Mechanics: The First Fifty Years* (London: Butterworths, 1974).

**Equation numbers and some of the symbols have been altered to make them consistent with the text.

$$f = \frac{f_0}{\sqrt{1 - \frac{v^2}{c^2}}} \qquad\qquad \textit{Equation 11}$$

and the transformation formula for the frequency of a clock, translating the famous "retardation" of clocks in motion, is

$$f = f_0\sqrt{1 - \frac{v^2}{c^2}} \qquad\qquad \textit{Equation 12}$$

The idea that a particle is like a clock in motion introduces two perspectives from the standpoint of an observer, one from the outside and one from the inside, corresponding to space and quantum frames, respectively.

Intrigued by this difference I asked myself how a particle similar to a little clock should be displaced in its wave in such a manner as to remain incorporated in the wave, that is to say, in such a manner that its internal phase remains constantly equal to that of the wave.

This idea is in accord with the transformations back and forth between space and quantum frames, a quantum jump in position being effected with each recurrence.

Applying this picture, albeit a little too schematically to the simple case of a plane monochromatic wave being propagated along the x-axis I was led to write for the variation dφ of the phase of this wave

$$d\phi = 2\pi\left(fdt - \frac{dx}{\lambda}\right) = 2\pi\left(\frac{f_0}{\sqrt{1 - \frac{v^2}{c^2}}} dt - \frac{dx}{\lambda}\right)$$

$$= \frac{2\pi}{h}\left(\frac{m_0 c^2}{\sqrt{1 - \frac{v^2}{c^2}}} dt - h\frac{dx}{\lambda}\right) \qquad\qquad \textit{Equation 13}$$

Motion along the x-axis is relative to a stationary observer implied by a coordinate system. From this external perspective the motion of the particle relative to the observer tends to open perceptual gaps in particle space frames because of the inability of light to span accumulated quantum jumps in position. By applying the transformation formula for a wave, Equation 11, the relative frequency of particle space frames is increased in order to close the perceptual gaps. Since particle and observer share a universal present, this indicates a *relative* omission of space frames in the inertial system of the *observer*. The observer's space frames are lost in the perceptual gaps of the particle. This can be seen by examining the terms of Equation 13. The *fdt* term gives the phase of waves for both particle and observer if the particle is at rest. The difference in phase introduced by the particle's motion is given by dx/λ, which is equivalent to vdt/λ. The only wavelength (λ) that can be ascribed to the moving particle is each quantum jump in position, but the derivative of time (dt) does not correspond to a primary interval, so the ratio dx/λ is a measure of the relative skipping of space frames. This is compensated for by applying the transformation formula to the *fdt* term, which closes the gap opened by the dx/λ term.

De Broglie continues:

and for the variation in the interval of time dt *of the internal phase of the particle being displaced along the* x-*axis with speed* v

$$d\phi_i = 2\pi f_0 \sqrt{1 - \frac{v^2}{c^2}}\, dt = \frac{2\pi}{h} m_0 c^2 \sqrt{1 - \frac{v^2}{c^2}}\, dt \qquad \text{Equation 14}$$

Since the internal phase of the waves corresponds to quantum frames, there can be no observations of relative motion, the dx/λ term being given no quantum counterpart.

This time it is the inverse transformation formula, Equation 12, that reconciles phase relations, indicating a *relative* skipping of *particle* quantum frames with respect to the observer. However, in this case the quantum sequences are deferred. They are able to accumulate in the void since particular sets are eternal in the quantized mode. The timelike character of the primary activity is regulated by the universal set which prescribes a universal present. The skipping of the observer's space frames is thus complemented by a relative accumulation of quantized energy associated with the particle and manifest as an increase in its relativistic mass.

De Broglie next performs a historic integration:

on combining dϕ = dϕ_i *with* dx = vdt

$$\frac{m_0 c^2}{\sqrt{1 - \frac{v^2}{c^2}}} - m_0 c^2 \sqrt{1 - \frac{v^2}{c^2}} = \frac{m_0 v^2}{\sqrt{1 - \frac{v^2}{c^2}}} = \frac{hv}{\lambda} \qquad \text{Equation 15}$$

is obtained, whence for the momentum p of the particle

$$p = \frac{m_0 v}{\sqrt{1 - \frac{v^2}{c^2}}} = \frac{h}{\lambda} \qquad\qquad \textit{Equation 16}$$

Thus two fundamental relations of Wave Mechanics have been found, E = hf, p = h/λ associating with them the image of a localized corpuscle which is displaced in the wave along one of its rays yet remaining constantly in phase with it. This was the concrete image I had when I had the first idea of Wave Mechanics. Perhaps I didn't explain this sufficiently thoroughly in my thesis but I emphasize that it was this which guided me.

By combining Equations 13 and 14, simultaneity is granted to the expression for the external and internal phase of a particle with respect to an observer, to perform a historic integration. The derivatives of time (*dt*) thus cancel out, and the expressions of rest energy ($m_0 c^2$) vanish. In the final form the equation states that the kinetic momentum of a particle is equal to the quantum of action divided by the distance it is displaced in a primary interval of time, λ.

A strange implication of De Broglie's wave equation is that the complementary skipping of observer space frames and accumulation of particle quantum frames is completely independent of the relative rest mass of both observer and particle. It is dependent on the *perspective of the observer*. This is not just an arbitrary affair where the vantage point of observation can be hypothetically switched to that of a moving particle. Atoms don't have eyes to scan the heavens as humans do. Can a human individual be the equal of the universe?

But look again. The universe is gone. It vanished when De Broglie performed a historic integration. The observer is left with accumulated patterns of momentum, a history of change deferred to an indefinite future in a void. This eternal reflux keeps going on and on, in quantized increments determined by the relationship of electromagnetic radiation to the frame sequences in the cosmic movie.

Cosmology

It is apparent from the view presented that the system is not consistent with the generalized theory of relativity. The mathematization of events into a fixed concept of a space-time continuum with curvatures dependent on concentrations of gravitational mass, over-looks the hierarchies implicit in the natural order. The essential character of the universe as an eternal reflux of experience is masked. Instead the general theory lends its support to a big-bang origin to creation, an origin that serves to refute the theories on which it is based.

In pursuing the implications of the system, one can be led only in quite a different direction. The pinwheel rotations of spiral galaxies,* in which they turn as a single mass about their centers, is knowable only relative to other galaxies, that is, to the peripheral universe at large. This center-periphery relationship involves the entire mass of the universe, conforming as it does to a single underlying creative pattern to atomic structure. Associated therewith is a universal present, through which the rotational motions of galaxies must introduce a skipping of space frames at their centers relative to an accumulation of quantum frames at their peripheries. On a cosmic scale, this center-periphery dilemma will tend to accumulate to infinite extremes unless the energies involved are alleviated through creative reflux of their material content. There is direct evidence of this reflux in the apparent black holes at galactic centers, in the material observed being ejected from galactic cores, and in the observed gravitational discrepancies associated with their peripheral rotations. This being the case, galaxies are creative cells of activity refluxing experience through their electromagnetic, kinetic, and gravitational organization.

The evidence for an expanding universe leans heavily on the red shift in the light spectra of distant galaxies, an effect that can be related to skipped frame sequences. Given the nature of galaxies as cells of creative reflux, the billions of years that light travels from the most far-flung, and the universal present that we share with their material content, one must suspect that red shifts are associated with more than recessional velocity. The spanning of space and time, of historic reflux, is involved on a grand scale, incurring major frame-sequence discrepancies between galactic centers and peripheries as observed between different galaxies. The magnitude of energy output from distant quasars with their rapid periods of variation is indicative of this relative skipping of space frames— a compounded observational effect—manifest as accelerated reflux associated with the rotations of galaxies themselves, and as observed from one galaxy to another.

*No doubt there are comparable patterns of motion within the elliptical and irregular galaxies.

Concluding Remarks

I appreciate that the viewpoint presented here represents a radical departure from current scientific thinking. Nevertheless a great number of otherwise disjointed pieces fall into place. Peculiarities of numbers, identity, kinetic force, the nature of gravitational and electromagnetic fields, the quantum of action, the wave-particle dilemma, relativity, galactic organization, and cosmology all come together into a common synthesis of meaning prescribed by the reconciliation of centers to periphery in the terms and transformations of the system. The list goes on into every area of experience from socioeconomic organization to evolutionary theory and the structure of the nervous system. Such all-embracing integrative power, even in these early stages of the system's development, cannot be a matter of coincidence or idle conjecture. Regardless of whatever shortcomings there may be in this sketchy introduction to the system, it is hoped that it will be given the most serious investigation, with a view to furthering its development and application. If we are ever to evolve mutually compatible understanding in the diverse areas of our experience, we must seek out the nature of the creative process.

Appendix 3

The Evolution of a Business Enterprise: A description of the principles involved in structuring an organization as it evolves from a one-man operation to a large four-level company.

Introduction

A consulting engineering company has been selected to exemplify the organizational principles involved in the growth of a company to four levels. From this example and the previous discussions on business organization, the essentials of structuring any company as it grows to four levels should be reasonably clear.

This is not intended as a formula for the instant correction of organizational flaws in existing companies. Structural faults tend to evolve a variety of compensations over long periods of time; it takes time to properly recognize them and to safely navigate a course to their correction. The destination of the course is indicated here, but the navigation of the route depends on the capabilities of the crew and the circumstances encountered in each particular case. Of more immediate value, an insight into these essentials of structure can aid in avoiding fundamental errors as a company grows, and in painlessly taking advantage of opportunities to correct errors when they present themselves.

The First Stage of Delegation

Functional Assistance

As a company takes root and begins to grow, delegtion nearly always occurs first in the area of product processing. An engineer beginning to freelance as a consultant will most likely first hire a draftsman, a surveyor, or a technician to assist him directly in processing the engineering product. Only after several such people are involved is he likely to hire full-time clerical assistance such as a bookkeeper. About this time he may also hire a junior engineer or two.

At this stage, the company remains a one-level affair. The direction that the engineer gives to his assistants is functional in nature.

His employees are given specific details to perform rather than overall objectives to achieve. Certain basic skills are assumed: these are more sophisticated in the case of the junior engineers than in the case of the bookkeeper, but the format within which all skills are performed is carefully specified by the engineer. The books must be kept in a certain way, the plans must be drawn in a certain way, and the technical ideas must be developed in a certain way.

Product Regions
The engineer may be a consultant, but he must also work at the most basic level, giving functional direction to others. The functional level of work always relates to the end product associated with the region concerned. In this case, there may be draftsmen concerned with final product processing. The junior engineers will be concerned with idea or product development, but only as it relates to a specific product, not as it relates to the evolution of the company as a whole. The bookkeeper will be concerned with the distribution of costs, income, and the keeping of records accordingly.

At the first level of organization, things are very flexible because the consultant is always involved. Since the delegated elements are simple, the consultant has no problem keeping things in proper perspective. This is the only level at which the consultant can safely delegate work in two separate regions to the same person in order to meet contingent circumstances.

The Limits to First-Stage Delegation
Although the number of people who can be involved in a one-level company of this sort can vary, depending on the complexities and levels of skill involved, in a consulting company it is not likely to exceed a dozen. The transition to a two-level company will probably coincide with an opportunity for substantial expansion. At this point, a chief draftsman will be formally appointed, along with the hiring of more draftsmen. A project engineer or two may be hired, or a junior engineer may be effectively promoted by giving him the assistance of a new junior engineer. At this point, the complexities of the business may also warrant a full-time accountant.

The Second Stage of Delegation

New Horizons
The second stage of delegation requires that the consultant withdraw to the position of supervisor in relation to the chief draftsman,

project engineers, and accountant. His direct communication with the others in the company becomes restricted. If his time permits, he may still undertake consulting projects himself. In this regard, he must be careful not to distinguish himself from the other project engineers.

As the general level of the organization's proficiency rises, more sophisticated projects may be undertaken, bringing new pressures to focus on the consultant. He must more carefully think out the evolution of his organization (organization-and-manning region). He must assess his resources and capacity for financing (treasury region), and must think of this as it relates to the company's overall direction (product-development region). All of this must be seen as fulfilling specific market needs (marketing region). He must also assess his ability to reach that market (sales region). The horizons have widened, and the pressures focus on the specifics of hiring the appropriate people, arranging the necessary finances, and acquiring the desired contracts.

Scheduling Assistance
Much of the consultant's time must be devoted to these areas, but at the same time, he must continue to specify objectives, monitor results, and maintain a proper balance in the ongoing activity of the existing organization. At this stage, he cannot properly delegate this responsibility to others. To assist in this area, he will need clerical monitoring assistance on the functional level. This will mean a clerk to collect specific informational feedback to enable him to identify bottlenecks and scheduling problems associated with the organization of specific projects. The consultant or consultant/supervisor, as he may be described in this context, must ensure that adequate resources of manpower, equipment, and materials are available and properly distributed to meet specific project demands. It's worth noting that clerical assistance in this area is a precursor to a full scheduling function. Such assistance is analogous to an organization-and-manning function, but does not relate to the evolution of the organization as a whole. It is restricted to the organization of specific projects within the overall organizational context.

The Limits to Second-Stage Delegation
As business prospers, the company will continue to grow, until at a certain point, pressures will dictate that another stage of delegation be considered. At this point, there may be lead draftsmen responsible to the chief draftsman for different disciplines. There will be

several project engineers with a complement of junior engineers and technicians. There will be a small accounting section, two or three secretaries, and one or more schedulers. The total number of people concerned may vary, but it is not likely to exceed sixty or seventy in a consulting company. In certain construction or manufacturing businesses that have a large number of repetitive task cycles, the total number may be much larger.

The Pattern of New Expansion

This time, at least one engineering supervisor will be formally appointed, and probably two or three, each responsible for different engineering disciplines. Delegation by geographic area is not desirable. Supervision is best when it relates to its own discipline.* Also, the consultant may decide to keep one or two of the project engineers reporting to him directly, thus retaining part of the company as a two-level organization until it develops some more. In any case, the organization should not be constrained by the unnecessary concept of having but a single engineering supervisor.

Another very important and distinguishing factor of this stage of growth will be the appointment of a sales engineer to bid for work and extend client contacts. This is likely to be followed shortly by the appointment of a personnel officer, and also another stage of delegation in the treasury region.

The Third Stage of Delegation

New Horizons

The third stage of delegation requires that the consultant further withdraw to the position of administrator in relation to employees on the supervisory level. This will mean that direct communication with project engineers and with accounting people becomes restricted. On the other hand, the consultant will have a new sales engineer to deal with, initially on the functional level. There will also be a new treasury supervisor, and a personnel recruiter to assist on the functional level with screening, processing, and indoctrinating new employees. Initially, at this stage of delegation, the consultant/administrator, as he may now be described, may still engage

---

*This is not necessarily true of an engineering group in companies not devoted exclusively to engineering.

himself in some areas as a part-time supervisor, but this will be phased out as the organization continues to grow.

The third stage of delegation can provide for much greater creative potential, but the transition and subsequent growth should be thought out clearly and executed carefully to avoid serious mistakes. Since organizational mistakes have a strong tendency to become self-perpetuating, relatively simple mistakes can have very damaging consequences.

The Sales Engineer
The appointment of a sales engineer is desirable not only from the standpoint of taking advantage of the newfound growth potential of the young three-level company. It is also an organizational necessity. Until now, the consultant has been able to maintain direct functional involvement in the bidding process, although other engineers have contributed input to various degrees. With a three-level organization, the need to keep a greater volume of work in circulation and to maintain a greater diversity of clientele requires that something be delegated. However, it is of basic importance that the consultant cannot delegate this sales function to an engineering supervisor without defaulting in the overall direction of the company. The sales-marketing polarity must be sustained in his own mind, and marketing is not yet a delegated region. The consultant must retain a direct and independent relationship to the sales function in order to do this. Otherwise, the sales-marketing polarity will be sustained by an engineering supervisor, coloring his performance to the detriment of the other regions of the company. Serious internal problems can rapidly develop.

Initially, the new sales engineer will be concerned with assembling bid packages and interfacing with engineering supervisors to get their input into the bidding process. He will also maintain customer contacts, providing for an independent feedback of engineering performance and customer satisfaction. He will ensure prompt invoicing to reduce cash-flow problems, and, as time permits, he will explore the market potential with new clients and try to expand the company's horizons in a compatible fashion. Although this job is initially on the functional level, it requires an intimate familiarity with the company's activities. Therefore it is a reasonably senior position.

The consulting business is low-profile in terms of sales technique, depending largely on an established reputation with a limited clientele. The sales engineer will soon find it necessary to think and work on more than one level and must have the capacity to do so.

The Personnel Officer

The personnel officer would not normally be necessary in a consulting company until into the third stage of delegation, but under special circumstances it may be a necessary appointment much sooner than that.The personnel officer will also work essentially on the functional level, but must be experienced. This is a reasonably senior position. The main priorities of the job will center on recruitment, and the screening, processing, and indoctrination that goes with it. There are also ongoing liaison problems with employees, especially where housing and travel are concerned. The main guidelines are nevertheless prescribed by the consultant/administrator. He retains all decision making about the organization structure until the company becomes much larger. Recruitment requirements should be carefully specified by the consultant, but the supervisor directly concerned will provide input and should also concur on the specific selection of his employees. By the time the company expands to the limit of third-stage delegation in product processing, there may be second-stage delegation in this personnel region. Normally, this is more likely to occur early in fourth-stage delegation. Along with the personnel-supervisory level will come such things as job analysis, formal job descriptions, and organizational analysis. This will ensure that people interface properly and wherever possible will have the opportunity to develop and apply their talents to maximum advantage. It will also prepare the company for the next major expansion—to the fourth stage of delegation in the product-processing region.

The Accounting Supervisor

Further delegation up to the supervisory level in the treasury region means a formalization of the budgeting and cost-accounting functions. These areas become rapidly more complex as the company grows and it becomes necessary to formalize the flow of information, the processing of data, and the circulation of reports. The consultant/administrator will outline the general guidelines as to the nature and extent of this activity, but the input will come predominantly from the treasury supervisor, with feedback and input from the other supervisors to the extent that they are involved.

The Engineering Specialist
As the degree of sophistication of the company grows, it is possible that delegation on the functional level of the product-development region can begin before the next major stage of expansion. This depends on circumstances and potential opportunities, and it will involve highly qualified engineering specialists working at developing engineering techniques. These techniques must find practical application and enhance the engineering capability of the company. At this stage of development, delegation in this region is not likely to make much impact in a broadly based consulting company.

The Limits to Third-Stage Delegation
Before the fourth stage of delegation becomes a serious consideration, the company will have grown substantially. There will be several engineering supervisors, a well-established scheduling group on the functional level, and one or two chief draftsmen. There will be a substantial treasury group probably under one supervisor. There will be a quite small personnel group, probably under one personnel officer, but in special circumstances this could grow to reach second-stage delegation. There will be at least one sales engineer—perhaps two—each with functional assistance. Finally, there may be some minor delegation in product development. The marketing region will remain undelegated until the company is well established in fourth-stage delegation. The total number of people concerned at this point is likely to be in the order of two hundred or more for a consulting company, but some types of companies can grow to four or five hundred with reasonable ease.*

The Pattern of New Expansion
The transition to a four-level company will be characterized by delegation on the administrative level in the product-processing region. At least one engineering administrator will be formally appointed, but the number should not be restricted to one as a matter of policy. At the supervisory level, it is desirable to delegate according to engineering discipline. This provides for the greatest flexibility and growth with the least number of senior people and interdisciplinary conflict. Conflict will also tend to arise within disciplines if things

---

*The limiting factor is span of control: there are no rules regarding it. It depends on the complexity of the work and the capacity of individuals to sustain a diversity of commitment.

are done differently in different areas. Delegation by area is premature at the supervisory level and will tend to fragment and constrict the growth of the company. The reverse is true at the administrative level: delegation by discipline here will lead to fragmentation through lack of cohesion. At this level, the company is best segregated into divisions associated with geographic areas, or with diverse areas of consulting that still fall under the general umbrella of engineering. The transition to a four-level company will be marked by further delegation in the other regions as well, but this will be less pronounced and keyed to developments in the product-processing region.

The Fourth Stage of Delegation

The Consultant as Manager
With the fourth stage of delegation, the consultant withdraws to the position of manager in relation to those on the administrative level. This will mean that direct communication with engineering supervisors, chief draftsmen, and schedulers becomes restricted.

The Sales Supervisor
The sales engineer will continue to interface with engineering supervisors in the preparation of bids, but bid packages will tend to be larger and more complex, and delegation on the supervisory level in the sales region will become necessary. The sales supervisor will interface with the engineering administrators in the final assembly of major bid packages, which will continue to get the blessing of the consultant/manager prior to submission. In a four-level consulting company, delegation may not proceed past the supervisory level in the sales region, but this will be a very senior position that will deal on a high level with major clients. Sales may become involved in major project liaison on a progress basis. Also, a costing function may emerge in the product-processing region to facilitate bidding, budgeting, and progress billing.

The Treasurer
The undertaking of more major projects requires more complex financing arrangements, resulting in delegation on the administrative level in the treasury region. This position may carry the title of treasurer. Long-term financing arrangements and more elaborate accounting and budgeting procedures will play an increasingly important role.

The Personnel Supervisor
There will be several personnel officers who will continue to interface with supervisors and others in all regions. There must be a quite senior personnel supervisor in the organization-and-manning region. There will be a growing emphasis on the development of the organization from detailed analysis and evaluation. Much greater attention must be given to such things as equitable pay rates, and employee performance must be scanned continuously with a view to developing a better organization. The luxury of a small organization, where everyone knows everyone, fades sharply in a four-level company.

The Product-Development Supervisor
With more sophisticated projects under way, more sophisticated engineering techniques are required, and this will require supervisory delegation in the product-development region. There may be one or more task groups developing computer programs for the solution of complex engineering problems. There may be considerable emphasis on simplifying approaches to other problems, or in developing and testing new engineering methods, techniques, equipment, and so on.

Delegation in Marketing
With such expanded horizons the consultant/manager can no longer depend on his personal intuitive perception of the marketing region without assistance. The functional level of delegation is largely concerned with market surveys to identify market needs or areas of moderate competition and risk. At the supervisory level, these areas are assessed in the light of the company's technical capabilities to determine if the techniques exist, or can be developed, to pursue potential opportunities. Of equal importance is the need to identify and assess market areas where demand may decrease and create an unhealthy, overly competitive situation. With sufficient advance warning, commitment to these areas can be reduced in time to avoid a potentially serious problem. For a four-level consulting company, delegation beyond the supervisory level is unlikely in this region. Close attention to this region is nevertheless essential to the continued success of the company, for it permits the organization to adjust and evolve to suit a changing market environment. This may not always mean growth.

The Limits to Fourth-Stage Delegation
By the time a consulting company evolves to the limit at the fourth stage of delegation there can be well over a thousand employees. Certain other types of companies can reach two or three times this size, perhaps more in special cases.

At this point there is a major discontinuity in the evolution of a company. There is an eclipse that takes place between the product-processing region and the company as a whole in such a way that the product-processing region assumes the characteristics of an independent company. The four stages of delegation recur again with a different emphasis. However, Systems 5 and higher are beyond the scope of the brief discussion here.

Also in New Science Library